The
MAGIC
of
TAROT

About the Author

KEYWORDS: Author, Adventurer, New Yorker

UPRIGHT: Sasha Graham teaches and lectures around the world. Her work has been translated into Chinese, Italian, Russian, French, Spanish, Polish, and Portuguese. She is the author of *Tarot Diva*, *365 Tarot Spreads*, *365 Tarot Spells*, and *Llewellyn's Complete Book of the Rider Waite Smith Tarot*. She is editor and author of Lo Scarabeo's *Tarot Fundamentals*, *Tarot Experience*, and *Tarot Compendium*. She has contributed to *Llewellyn's Magical Almanac*, *Witches' Datebook*, and *Llewellyn's Witches' Calendar*. Her tarot decks include *Tarot of Haunted House*, *Dark Wood Tarot,* and *Tarot of the Witch's Garden*.

REVERSED: On less productive days, Sasha can be found watching reruns of *Vampire Diaries*, staring into the sky for hours on end, and dreaming of faraway places and adventures yet to unfold.

SASHA GRAHAM

The
MAGIC
of
TAROT

Your Guide to Intuitive
Readings, Rituals, and Spells

Llewellyn Publications
WOODBURY, MINNESOTA

FIRST EDITION
Second Printing, 2022

Book design by Rebecca Zins
Cover artwork by Abigail Larson
Cover design by Kevin R. Brown
Rider-Waite-Smith cards are based on those contained in *The Pictorial Key to the Tarot* by Arthur Edward Waite, published by William Rider & Sons, Ltd., London, 1911

Llewellyn is a registered trademark of Llewellyn Worldwide Ltd.

Library of Congress Cataloging-in-Publication Data
Names: Graham, Sasha, author.
Title: The magic of tarot : your guide to intuitive readings, rituals, and spells / Sasha Graham.
Description: First edition. | Woodbury, Minnesota : Llewellyn Publications, 2021. | Summary: "*The Magic of Tarot* opens your eyes to a richer, more enlightened style of divination. Sasha encourages you to flex your intuitive muscles, confidently use tarot magic and spells, and perform readings for other people. She also walks you through all the card meanings, introduces you to dream and shadow work, helps you interpret colors, numbers, and patterns, and brings the tarot to life"—Provided by publisher.
Identifiers: LCCN 2021019244 (print) | LCCN 2021019245 (ebook) | ISBN 9780738763583 (paperback) | ISBN 9780738763644 (ebook)
Subjects: LCSH: Tarot. | Magic.
Classification: LCC BF1879.T2 G65675 2021 (print) | LCC BF1879.T2 (ebook) | DDC 133.3/2424—dc23
LC record available at https://lccn.loc.gov/2021019244
LC ebook record available at https://lccn.loc.gov/2021019245

Llewellyn Worldwide Ltd. does not participate in, endorse, or have any authority or responsibility concerning private business transactions between our authors and the public.

All mail addressed to the author is forwarded but the publisher cannot, unless specifically instructed by the author, give out an address or phone number.

Any internet references contained in this work are current at publication time, but the publisher cannot guarantee that a specific location will continue to be maintained. Please refer to the publisher's website for links to authors' websites and other sources.

Llewellyn Publications
A Division of Llewellyn Worldwide Ltd.
2143 Wooddale Drive
Woodbury, MN 55125-2989
www.llewellyn.com

Printed in the United States of America

To my daughter, Jack, who teaches me
every day that love is the greatest magic.

Contents

Chapter 6: Bringing Magic to Life 157

Chapter 7: Seven Sacred Cornerstones of Constant Tarot Magic 199

Chapter 8: Card Meanings **213**

Gratitudes

My sister and I share a gratitude practice. We exchange daily emails marked with a list of what we are thankful for. Gratitude is deep magic.

Thank you to Barbara Moore, who believes.

Thank you to Rebecca Zins, who collaborates.

Thank you to Susan Wands, who empowers.

Thank you to Autumn Walking Butterfly Marie and Ajay Kumar, who teach.

Thank you to Bill, who loves.

Thank you to Jack, who sparkles.

Thank you to my Tarot Space Tuesday crew—Lisa O'Neil, Tracey Culuko, Holly Buczek, Claudia Ferrari, Virlana Kardash, Kris Lopez, Marianela Mendoza, Lauri Panopoulos, Magdalena Olvera, Dené Linn, Jo Masters, Larry Gregg, Bonnie Grisandra, Maria Cotter, Teresa Shaffer, and Lucien St. Germain—who inspire.

Introduction

People sidle up close to me sometimes when they think no one's looking. They'll whisper in my ear, "How did a nice girl like you become a tarot reader?" I look into their eyes and smile coyly, as if I know something they don't—because I do. If they knew what I know, they wouldn't ask. I respond with a question: "I was born on Halloween—what else was I supposed to do?"

But it's just you and me right now. No one else is around to hear us, so I'll give you the real answer. I can tell you'll understand what I am about to say. The real reason I'm a tarot reader is because I am a storyteller. What most people fail to realize is that they are storytellers too; we all are. Tarot is storytelling. It's what we do when we read the cards. Telling stories imbues us with supernatural power—the power to change your story.

Lean in closer.

Let me tell you a story...

Tarot and I never "met." It was always inside me. Tarot was a seed waiting to sprout, a sweet tooth longing for a lollipop. Tarot was the softest of lips aching to be kissed.

Halloween babies enter the world like a hushed tone and whispered secret. We rarely cry, yell, or fuss but are content gazing at specters dancing circles above our velvet cribs. Scorpio children bear the blessing and

1

curse of seeing through the veil separating the visible and invisible worlds. We recall with vivid clarity the sweet embrace of that which made us. We carry it with us even when we are told by others to fear it.

Walking with a foot in each world is a gift that turns treacherous when the body becomes a prison. The material world has vicious teeth; it is a hungry thing. Sensitive souls are often tempted to take their ephemeral lives and cross back into the void too soon. We search, ever hungry, for glimmers of that sweet embrace in others: parents, friends, teachers, lovers. We think if we relinquish ourselves, if we burrow deeply inside the core of another, we might return to peace.

But if a Halloween baby holds out long enough, she realizes the sweet exhale, the soft embrace she longs for, is available in every waking moment. It is not through the absorption or abandonment of her body and self in another but through an ecstatic collaboration that the sweet nectar and tender tears of love are tasted once again.

She learns to balance her gifts like the Temperance card, even when those gifts terrify or abandon her. She gathers her fruits, moves further into the unknown, and, like skin diving into black water, she slices through uncertainty to discover something new. Naked and wet, she never breaks the surface empty handed. Deep diving into the mystery is why mystics roam the earth. It is why we bear the brunt of longing and desire. We are never given gifts we cannot shoulder.

I grew up in a drafty farmhouse crafted of inky black and orange crepe paper. I devoured jellybeans for breakfast, cinnamon donuts for lunch, and dark chocolate cupcakes for dinner. When my sister and I weren't flying around the house with cobwebs strewn in our hair, we were in the woods making mud pies full of stones, worms, and pine needles. We spoke with trees and buried ourselves in the vegetable patch. We listened to the carrots grow while dreaming of our future.

Tarot populated my world. The Page of Swords beat me at Scrabble because she's the cleverest card in the deck. The Page of Pentacles and I devoured books by the dozens. The Knight of Swords egged me on to ride my bike faster down gravel roads. He always left me in a cloud of dust digging wet, bloody pebbles from my skinned knees.

The Devil loomed large as the man of the house. He lit Marlboros and blew dry smoke in my face every night after dinner. My mother couldn't bear the weight of her Empress crown, so she handed the family jewels off to him. She'd hunch over the sink, scrubbing his dirty dishes, while he made faces at me. I saw through him as easily as the smoke rings he blew in the air. Children know the truth when they see it.

One day, during the hormonal quagmire of middle school, they asked for volunteers for a fundraising fair. I knew my role. I, proud Halloween baby, would read tarot under a tent like a gypsy fortuneteller. I ran to the local mall and bought a tarot deck. I tore at the crinkly cellophane, opened the box, and seventy-eight slippery, shiny cards fell into my hands. I gazed at them in horror. I hadn't a single clue how to read them.

I was saved that same night by a born-again Christian. Blond, feathered, and lip-glossed, born-again Debbie was my stepsister's best friend. Born-again Debbie thought preaching the Lord's name made up for all the drugs, sex, and smokes she enjoyed while Jesus looked the other way.

Debbie howled when she saw my cards. "These are the Devil's work!" she cried. I laughed and calmly explained that I was already on intimate terms with the Devil. Not once, never ever, did his hot breath whisper anything about tarot cards.

Born-again Debbie responded by wresting the cards from my hands and teetering from the house in her boots and skin-tight Jordache jeans. She threw them into the trashcan, soaked them with lighter fluid, and set them ablaze. They exploded like pyrotechnics at a Van Halen concert.

It was a dramatic moment. It got me off the hook from reading the cards at the school fair. It gave me my first lesson in how powerful tarot is. History has a habit of burning potent things like evidence, books, and witches.

It wasn't long before I learned to read the cards. Tarot continues to unfold, flip, and appear with a brilliance I wouldn't have dared allow myself to expect. Tarot taught me about magic—true magic. Real magic is always more mind bending and exciting than you could anticipate. Dreams and desires, devils and angels—they come and go, but true magic thrives inside you forever.

That's why I wrote this book. I want you to know what I know.

Lean in closer. I am going to tell you a secret I've never told anyone. But before I do, let's quick talk about the contents of this book. Tarot brings enchantment into your life. It fills you with power. Let's be clear: I'm not talking tricks or sleight-of-hand magic. I'm talking big magic, life-altering magic, game-changer magic. I'm talking sorceress power, goddess-rising magic, as in the textbook definition of magic: the power of influencing events by using mysterious and/or supernatural forces.

How? Because life IS mysterious, and you ARE a supernatural creature. You are made of pure magic and made of luminous energy. Tarot invites you to play inside the mystery surrounding you. A tarot practice opens wild doorways brimming with unlimited possibilities. This book is a gateway into your inner sorceress, your authentic self, and it's a direct line to unbridled manifestation.

You will begin by learning to read tarot right away. Do you read between the lines? Do you look for patterns and hidden codes? Are you obsessed with mystery and what someone might be hiding? Me too! We tarot readers dive deep; it's what we do.

This book will show you how to combine simple magical practice with the cards for extraordinary results. I've ridden my tarot like a magic carpet around the world. I've flipped cards at the Dead Sea in the heaving shadows of Masada while spirits of the dead whispered in my ear. Tarot and I sat inside China's teahouses and sipped coffee together in the Italian Alps. We sat in the pre-dawn pregnant darkness of Tibet to watch the sunrise from Mt. Everest's base camp. The cards and I warmed ourselves with yak butter candles in the world's highest meditation cave hidden deep in the Himalayas. Where will you bring your deck?

Here we will examine the esoteric theory I've learned through witchcraft, Qabalah, and Ashtanga yoga, and you'll discover how all of it can apply to the cards. A tarot practice teaches you three precious truths: first, everything in the world repeats, just like the cards in the deck. Second, people are all the same, regardless of who they are; they want love, security, and safety. Did I mention love? You'll see this soon enough when you read cards for others. Finally, change is always possible. Evolution is our natural state and is magic in action.

It sounds simple, doesn't it? But just because something is simple doesn't make it easy.

Simplicity's paradox is a tease. Why do we battle complicated emotions around simple issues? Why is the easiest, most obvious course of action often the hardest? Why do we bump up against the same issues repeatedly? Why is it so hard for us to change? Why does fear keep us safe while destroying us at the same time? Why does the past lock us in the prison of the smallest version of ourselves? Why do we fear what we desire and desire what we fear?

The Magic of Tarot contains journal-style writing prompts to help you answer these questions. Your responses to the writing prompts are where you will discover essential information about yourself. Take them seriously and answer them often.

You will learn the fine art of constructing the very best questions. Tarot is a simple system containing vast complexity and infinite depth, just like the world you inhabit. This book has been written as an experiential and personal process of uncovering the magic thriving inside of you. It is the perfect book for a beginner or someone who has been working with the cards for over twenty years.

This book teaches somatic tarot, which brings tarot into your physical body. You will enter cards through your sacred imagination. A somatic embodiment of the cards is a game changer. It takes you out of your head and into the intelligence of your muscles, bones, and blood.

The book is constructed so you can begin reading the cards right away. Don't wait; dive right in. The cards' meanings are found near the end of the book. Everything you need to cultivate your tarot and magical practice is found in between.

Once upon a time, tarot reading was about discovering what your future held. These days tarot helps you craft exactly the future you desire. What do you want? What do you dream of? Let's get you there, the faster, the better.

Are you ready for the secret I've never told anyone? Truth is, between you and me—and please, don't share this with too many people or my publishers will have my head—you don't even need a deck of tarot cards to do any of this work. All you need is you. All the answers you are looking for are inside you. The universe is constantly sending you hints, messages, and help. Tarot will help you learn how to recognize them.

Tarot is an incredible metaphysical device. It is your gateway to the supernatural and the mystery surrounding you. Tarot gives you a gorgeous, mystical framework through which to explore and play inside the mystery. Tarot allows us to tell stories, engage in art, dive into history, strengthen our psychic ability, and study symbols. It breeds intimacy. Tarot helps us sort out the most important relationship in our lives: the relationship between you and yourself. And when you heal yourself, you heal the world.

The secrets, the answers to everything you have ever opined and questioned, are inside of you. You are already the mystic, the sage, the seer. You are the High Priestess, the witch, and the shaman who knows where you belong, what is right, and how to get there. Your path is obscured by branches and brambles because you are here to figure yourself out and enjoy the journey. If it weren't challenging and scary sometimes, it wouldn't be a mystery.

Tarot teaches you to become the storyteller of your life. And it isn't enough to own our story. It is up to us to reimagine our stories. Doing so, we reimagine ourselves.

The love story of tarot unfolds like all epic and operatic romances. Real life dictates sometimes you'll be close with the cards and sometimes you'll drift apart. At the end of the day, you'll look at the cards and smile as you return together again.

So take my hand and let's walk into the darkness together. We'll flip some cards, light some candles, and figure you out. We'll empower your intuition, dive into your dreams, and get to the heart of the matter. Let's adventure like the Fool card. Let's bring tarot into your body and craft a divine, sparkling destiny. Do you see that glimmering, shimmering light up ahead? That glittering treasure is you. It is waiting for you to claim it.

Let's go!

Sasha Graham
CATSKILL MOUNTAINS, NY

Chapter One

Tarot, Magic, and You

Start Reading the Cards Right Now

Tarot reading is like wading in an icy swimming hole on a cool summer night. Diving in is easier than tiptoeing. You can read tarot right now. There's no need to be versed in occult secrets. You don't need to be the love child of a certified witch. You don't need to memorize card meanings.

The most important part of tarot reading is the intuitive space you create while gazing at the cards. Tarot's power springs from YOU. You hold the magic. You hold the power. You arrive at a message. The cards are simply a tool with which you can engage your intuition.

You are a walking symbolic dictionary. Your life is chock-full of symbols holding deep associations and profound meanings for you. It is exquisite that your experience of symbol, color, sound, and shape is unique to you. No one will ever read the cards or arrive at the answers just like you.

You already know what the cards mean because tarot is a reflection of the human psyche. Everything you have or will experience is reflected in the arcana. The cards are a reflection of life. Every day you grow richer with experience. Apply this knowledge to the cards.

Don't let preconceived notions of tarot throw you off your reading game. You may have suffered the prickly experience of walking into a metaphysical shop and asking a question only to have an employee blow you off or make you feel silly because you didn't know what something was. Maybe you've met a psychic or "tarot expert" who wore their esoteric knowledge like a tattooed arm sleeve. The saddest thing someone can do is make you feel like a dummy when you ask a question or overkill you with their presumed knowledge. Rest assured, if this has ever happened, it was all about them and never about you. Don't let a negative past experience affect your ability to read the cards.

This isn't to say you shouldn't have respect for schools of occult knowledge or someone with years of tarot experience. You should. Tarot knowledge is enriching and exciting. But trust me, I've seen ten-year-olds read cards brilliantly with no experience. Their tarot interpretations are amazing. Why? Simple: they respond to the card instead of fear. Children are not afraid to get it wrong.

Don't be afraid to get it wrong. Fear of being "wrong" is the single biggest impediment to all readers. Nothing throws up insurmountable barriers like fear. Tarot is steeped in hundreds of years of esoteric theory and rich highly structured meaning. Will knowing this add depth and richness to your readings? Absolutely. Do you need all that stuff now? Not at all.

Everything you learn from here on out is a tool for your tarot toolbox. Everything falls away the moment you start reading cards. Focus on what you see. How does the card make you feel? What messages are you receiving? Tarot is an ever-evolving art form, and you move it forward every time you read a card. Start from scratch. Toss your fear a pack of cigarettes and tell her to go outside and grab a smoke. Lock the door once she's out there. Focus on the cards at hand.

Flip a card.

What do you see?

Tarot is storytelling. You are a natural-born storyteller. Stories are universal. This is why a good astrology column feels like it was written just for you even when 14 million other people with your sign think it is just for them. It doesn't matter if you are predicting a future outcome, examining the past, or looking for guidance. No matter how you use tarot, you are telling a story.

There are two stories we constantly weave: the stories we tell ourselves and the stories we tell others. The voice inside our head is the inner storyteller. The inner storyteller chatters incessantly. It makes value judgments and assesses situations. The inner voice takes every story and makes it about us. Someone looks at us sideways or cut us off in traffic and we take it personally. The decisions we make, the thoughts we think—all spring from our inner narrator.

The second voice is the outer voice. We use this when we tell stories to others. We get home and tell our family the story of our crazy day. We are telling a story when we tell someone our personal history or glorious future plans.

If I placed a wordless illustrated child's book in your hands and asked you to tell me the story of what you see, you could easily do it. If I showed you three photographs from a recent trip to India and asked you to tell me what I was doing, you could. If I opened a magazine and asked you to make up the story behind a random editorial fashion shoot, you could do it. If I placed three tarot cards in front of you and asked you to tell me what story you see like you are reading a graphic novel, you could do it. So:

1: Shuffle the deck.

2: Draw three cards (turning reversals upright if any are upside down).

3: Tell me the story.

The story I see is...

Trust what you see. No one sees, feels, and experiences the world like you do. Tarot's power is in the abstract nature of its symbols, each of which holds particular meaning for you. Symbols like sun, moon, and skull hold universal connotation, yet how you interpret this symbol is unique to you. This is the key to unraveling the message of tarot. It is your golden ticket. This is your message.

Find your meaning the same way you catch an alluring stranger's eye from across a crowded room. Your body feels it before your intellect does. An internal tremor occurs. A spark—no matter how small—is lit. Can you figure out what it means to you? Examine the symbol the same way you'd look closer at a beguiling stranger. What intrigues you? Do you resonate with their energy? Do they look like a bowl of ice cream oozing with caramel sauce? When a symbol captures your attention in a tarot card, do the same thing. If a rainbow calls out to you, consider what rainbows mean to you. Do they make you happy and fill you with hope? If

12

the figure on the card looks confident, consider what confidence means to you. Is this card talking about confidence? Run with it!

Randomly flip a tarot card.

The thing that catches my attention about this card is...

Always go with your first instinct and watch how quickly your intuition develops. Trusting your instincts with the cards spills over into your regular life. This leads to inner and outer alignment between your authentic self and the universe. You'll make decisions faster and with more certainty. Wanna know a secret? Reading cards is no different than interpreting a snapshot of the room in front of you. One day you'll be able to read any life scene, event, and moment of anything happening as if it were a tarot card. Trust yourself. Know what you feel and feel what you know. All the answers you've ever sought are inside you.

Randomly flip a tarot card.

My instinct tells me this card is about...

Shuffling is a fun and easy way of infusing the energy of your question into the tarot. You don't need to be a Vegas dealer to do it. Go with what feels right for you.

> CARD SOUP (easiest): Spread the cards facedown on a table and mix them with your hands. Scoop them back together and begin drawing from the stack.

> CARD CUT (fairly easy): The deck is split from one hand to the next by letting sections of the deck fall into the other hand.

> CASINO SHUFFLE (advanced but worth it): Cut the deck in half so you have two small piles, one in each hand. Use your left and right thumbs to shuffle them together and combine. Repeat at least three times until the deck is mixed.

LEAPING CARDS: A card or two often leap from the deck when you are shuffling. Read these cards as extra information!

Laying out the cards can happen in many ways.

STACK OF CARDS: Traditionally, the cards are held in one hand or placed on the table. The cards are chosen off the top of the deck and flipped from left to right in order to determine if the card is upright or reversed.

HALF MOON: Spread the cards out in a half moon or rainbow shape in front of you and select cards at random.

STRAIGHT LINE: Same as half moon but in a straight line. Choose your card where the energy calls you. This is a fun system for pulling cards for chakra readings. Choose the cards from a vertical line that matches the body's chakra locations.

TABLE OF CARDS: Spread your cards out across the table like card soup and choose from where the energy calls you.

COUNTING DOWN: You can count down a specific number and then pull a card or cards. Choose a specific number to align with numerology, day, month, or age, for any reason you like.

Reversals are cards appearing upside down in a spread. Do not worry about reversals if you are just beginning. Turn them right-side up. You are not cheating. Your reading is still valid. There are many ways to read a reversal, and turning them around is one of them. To read more on the art of reading reversals, see page 75.

Read cards for yourself by writing down the messages and information as they come to you. It can feel overwhelming at first. It is natural to question yourself. Be kind. Take your time. Have fun.

Write down your answers and intuitions as they occur. Record your readings even if you only note the card and a keyword. This will help you focus your thoughts. It is helpful to read your cards aloud to someone else (even if you are reading for yourself). Reading aloud and writing it down helps you articulate the story you see unfolding in the cards.

How the cards influence each other is often described in older esoteric tarot books. These books will sometimes provide the meaning of a card and say that if it is positioned near a "good" card in a spread, its meaning is magnified in a positive way. Conversely, if it appears near a "bad" card, the meaning of the card will be subtracted or made worse.

To call the cards "good" or "bad" is an antiquated black-and-white viewpoint. Each card is a world unto itself, a literal universe with bright, shiny aspects and dark and repressive aspects—just like us!

Instead of good and bad, consider the energetic essence of the cards to be like the energy of other people. If you stood next to someone who was vibrant like the Sun card, their energy might influence you and make you feel uplifted. If you stood near a High Priestess type who surrounds herself in sacred silence, you might be inclined to lower your voice. If you stood next to a King of Wands type exuding wild, passionate charisma, he might heat you up a bit. Feel the energetic essence of the cards to see how they affect one another.

Here's a simple system for intuitive reading. Close your eyes and clear your mind by focusing on your breath for a few moments. Inhaling breath will ground you. Exhaling breath will release unneeded energy. Feel your feet flat on the ground. Root into your seat. Feel the solid foundation beneath you. Focus on your third eye center. It glows with energy. Spin this energy upward to create a gentle vortex so inspiration will infuse you from above.

Shuffle the cards. Ask a question either aloud or in your mind. Flip a card. Observe.

My message/answer is…

FINAL WORD: If you'd like one final comment from the tarot about your reading, here is a fun system: flip your remaining stack of cards over. Read the bottom card as your final word.

What I don't know about the cards is everything. Tarot students are often nervous to "get it wrong." New cartomancers don't realize that their self-proclaimed ignorance is really their strongest asset. The key to effective reading is waiting for the information to come to you.

Reading for yourself is tricky, especially when we develop habits and ways of seeing the cards. We dive into the cards and visit psychics or intuitives for information we don't know.

When reading for ourselves, how can we break out of reading ruts? How do we keep readings fresh and insightful?

Simple: Ask the cards what you don't know.

1. Clear your mind.

2. Shuffle the deck and pull a card.

3. State out loud, "What I don't know about the _____ card is that _____."

4. Fill in the blanks by selecting a card and finishing the sentence. Don't try too hard. Let an aspect of the card strike you. State it clearly. Articulate it out loud or write it down.

Once you figure out why this particular answer came to you, discover why it is relevant to your situation.

You will know your information is helpful if:

1. The information surprises you or makes no immediate sense.

2. Upon reflection, the information holds particular resonance for you.

16

Tarot Is...

Tarot is a deck of seventy-eight cards. Mysterious, hidden potential exists inside this portable, seemingly simple stack of images. To say tarot is "just a deck of cards" is like saying you are "just a person." Tarot is as complex and nuanced as you. Just as you grow and learn every day, so tarot is an ever-evolving energy. Tarot exists on the outer, visible level through its visual art and deck construction. More importantly, tarot exists in the invisible realm of your sacred imagination and psyche. Tarot is a malleable practice because each time you flip a card and shuffle the deck, you bring tarot into a new space. No one can interpret a card like you because no one experiences the world like you do.

TIPS FOR
DEEPER READING

✦

Study card definitions.

✦

*Create original meanings
of the cards.*

✦

*What song, smell,
and sound does the
card exude?*

*Look for tarot examples
in everyday life.*

✦

*Imagine what happens
before and after the card.*

✦

*Can you find a voice
inside the card? What
does it sound like?*

TAROT IS
USEFUL FOR

✦

Guidance

✦

Prophesy

✦

Magic

✦

✦

Occult Exploration

✦

Reflection & Meditation

✦

Emergent Creativity

✦

Tarot is a tool for divination. Divination is the art of prophecy, which is the foretelling of future events. To divine with the cards, one uses them to examine the past, present, or future of any situation. Ancient tribes used diviners to predict weather and determine appropriate sacrifices. Kings and queens have always kept soothsayers by their sides to advise and predict the rise and fall of their empires and armies. World's religions—from Christianity, whose biblical book of Revelation predicts the four horsemen of the apocalypse, to Tibetan Buddhism, which uses astrologers to determine an individual's manner of burial—employ divination. Modern-day divination includes storefront psychics who weave fortunes under neon signs, televised mediumship, and beloved astrology columns read by millions.

We don't know who the first tarot reader was. We don't know where the first tarot deck came from. We don't know who invented it. The only thing we know for certain is that the desire to unravel ominous portents and understand the past, present, and future is as old as humanity itself.

My first tarot experience was...

Tarot is a looking glass. Tarot is a mirror of you. Each of the seventy-eight cards sparkles like the facets of a diamond. Each reflects your personality, spirit, and soul. Tarot shows you emotional states such as the Ace of Cups, who is an outpouring of feelings. Tarot reflects your energetic reserves, like the Star, who is you at complete peace when feeling calm, relaxed, and focused. Tarot reflects your mind, like the Nine of Swords, who is a savage, negative thought pattern. Tarot reflects soul evolution, like the Lovers, who are you crashing into another and falling deeply in love. The stately Emperor is you erecting emotional and literal boundaries such as when you walk away from abusive relationships or change its parameters. The Queen of Wands reflects living your passion so brightly the world stops, gasps, and stares. Each card has something to say about you.

Flip a random card.

This card reflects me when I...

Tarot is a portal. Tarot is a mirror we can actually walk through as if we were characters in a fairy tale. Crossing the threshold moves you deeper into your own internal reserves. Once we understand how tarot reflects our personal aspects, we can move deeper into this potential. Like a witch moving through a looking glass, you can greet the card's energy on its own terms.

The Empress, for example, is a pure reflection of your creative potential. Gaze at the card and imagine how you engage in creativity. What do you love to do? How do you do it? What would you do if the sky were the limit?

When I see my creative self, I envision myself...

Tarot is a collection of archetypal imagery. An archetype is a universal idea understood by all people regardless of gender or culture. Everyone understands the concept of mother, represented in tarot by the Empress card. Every soul on the planet understands the concept of father, represented by the Emperor. Everyone grasps the nature of unexpected catastrophe contained in the Tower card. Every culture has its wise ones as represented in the Hermit, the clown figures as represented in the Fool, and so on.

Tarot archetypes are a collection of humanity and experience at your fingertips. The cards are a delicate and eloquent reminder that at our core, people are all more alike than we are different. Everyone wants love, security, and happiness. Tarot helps us chart the course toward these things, and archetypes are the time-worn concepts that bring the cards to life.

The archetype of the Hanged Man is the mystic.
Mystics always make me think of...

Tarot is a gateway into archetypal energy. You can enter the card as a portal into your deeper self (as described above), but you can also move the opposite way and cross into the energetic world of the card's archetype. For instance, you might decide to enter the threshold into the Death card. Enter the card with your mind's eye and begin to see beyond the card's borders. You see Death riding upon a horse, you hear the rushing river, you hear the cries...

Find the Temperance card and look at it. What do you think the inside of this card smells like? What sounds do you hear? Is the wind rustling the trees? Are the birds chirping? Is water lapping on the shore or are crickets chirping? If a song or piece of music was playing inside the card, what would it be? If the figure spoke, what would their voice sound like? What are they saying?

Choose a simple goal for a gateway journey. Will you ask for a message or observe some particular element? Decide what piece of information you'd like to uncover or what experience you'd like to have. Venture inside the card with your mind's eye. What do you discover?

My message from the Temperance card is...

Tarot is an energetic container. You can step inside a card and literally infuse yourself with archetypal energy. You know how being near a happy person makes you feel happy? The same empathic process works with tarot. You can access any quality you desire and infuse that quality into yourself through the appropriate card.

Let's say today you have an interview for your dream job. Select the Magician card, enter it in your mind's eye, and imbue yourself with his charisma. This will help to ensure a sparkly and impactful meeting.

Focus on the card image. What do you see, smell, and hear? Move through the borders of the card. Stand in front of the Magician and request that he share some of his energy with you. Allow the transfer to take place, thank the archetype, and exit the card.

Alternatively, you can bathe in a card's energy. This is similar to experiencing a sound bath, where students lie in a restorative position while chimes, gongs, and singing bowls are played. The sound washes over the students, thereby cleansing their bodies.

To bathe in the energy of a card, prepare as you would for a gateway experience. Study the meanings of a card and reflect on the card's image until you can feel, hear, and taste the card. Once you can picture the image with clarity, close your eyes and move into the card with your mind's eye.

A card whose energy I am drawn to is...

Tarot is a gateway to the supernatural. It's hard to stop with just one card. It keeps you coming back for more. You find yourself haunting the local bookshop. You delight in discovering any magical or esoteric system that can be placed on top of tarot's structure. The astrological alignment of each card draws you deeper. The next thing you know, you are studying Qabalistic theory and calling to the four corners with the cards under a milky white moon. You use tarot for immediate creative solutions and discover wild psychic pops are beginning to occur for you. Tarot provides an opportunity for you to create sacred rituals. You come to the cards for one reason and you end up using it for a myriad of other witchy, wonderful things.

The supernatural fascinates me because...

Tarot is an exquisite art object. The oldest tarot deck we know of was commissioned in the fifteenth century by a wealthy and powerful family in Northern Italy. The Visconti-Sforza deck was created to celebrate the marriage of two wealthy and powerful Italian families. It was painted by miniaturist artist Bonifacio Bembo in a gothic style. The deck is emblematic of its time, richly detailed and gilded in gold paint. The cards contain family members, familial symbols, and heraldic devices. You can visit cards from this deck in person at the Morgan Library in New York City. Call the museum ahead of time to see if they are on display.

Beguiling art will keep you returning to your cards. Find tarot styles resonating with your taste. The deck's theme, one that matches your aesthetic, is important, especially when learning and integrating tarot meanings. We project ourselves onto the cards. You will want a deck with a mood, style, and swagger you aspire to.

My favorite style of art is...

My usual mood is...

My aesthetic is...

Tarot is used for gaming. Tarot was used as gaming and gambling cards in taverns across medieval Europe. These decks, printed on thin paper, were cheap and widely available. Carved block stamps were inked, stamped, and crafted into decks. The flimsy and ephemeral nature of these cards meant most were destroyed by time. Every now and then, a stash of old cards are discovered inside plaster walls, tucked away in dusty European attics.

Tarot was different than a traditional fifty-two-card pack because it carried an extra suit called the major arcana. Medieval Europe's general public was mostly illiterate. The church and powers-that-be used universally recognized images such as the Wheel of Fortune, Justice, Death, the Lovers, and the World to convey the morals of daily life.

Life is often compared to a game. You play. Games of chance are transformed into the examination of personal fortune, luck, and destiny. Do you believe you can change your luck? You take your chances. You roll the dice. You play, you win. You play, you lose.

I believe I have power over my destiny because...

Tarot is the book of you. The first tarot books were published in the seventeenth and eighteenth centuries and written by male authors, many of whom used the cards primarily for magical purposes and based their work on older medieval grimoires. We know that fortunetelling, while not exclusively, is largely a female art form. It always has been. Women have not historically written esoteric books, owned publishing companies, or edited the newspapers. Therefore, the history of fortunetelling, especially fortunetelling though tarot cards, remains largely unknown and unrecorded.

MAGIC IS...

✦

Alignment

✦

*Connection to seen
& unseen worlds*

✦

✦

*Knowing you are a
conduit of power*

✦

*Simple actions =
impactful results*

✦

Magic Is...

Magic is what happens when the blueprint of who you are comes into alignment with the expanding energy of the universe. Magic is an explosion of possibility and sublime synchronicity. It is as viable and electric as lovers meeting for the first time. Like the atmosphere, magic surrounds and sustains us. Magic is an interconnected web of energy.

Physics tells us the nature of the universe is expansion and contraction. Moons, stars, and galaxies swell and compress like the inhale and exhale of your breath. Just as the cadence of stormy waves crash onto pebbled beaches and pull back to the fray only to lunge back to the shore, so do our bodies echo oceans, planets, and intergalactic space. What is true for the universe is true for us.

Life is cyclical. Day turns to night. Seasons change. Summer gardens burst forth and die back. Luminous winter nights entice us to dream as the solar system whips us around the sun. Our lives echo the seasons. Babies are born, they grow up, and they die. Death makes way for new generations and fresh possibility.

Throughout this comic interplay, beneath the sound and fury of the kaleidoscopic light show you experience every day, is your life. There is a single basic pattern, one unique imprint. It belongs to you and you alone. This imprint, like a fingerprint, is sacred, subtle, and original. Its internal energetic pattern is eternal. Like a snowflake, a seashell, or a spiral galaxy, nothing else in the expanding universe is exactly the same. Everything contains a magical imprint, a unique intelligence.

You are designed just like a garden seed containing all of the information it needs to become a vegetable or flower. Hopes, dreams, and desires are sowed deep inside of you for a reason. The longings of your soul, your talents, and personality are your magical keys. Your unique awareness is how the universe experiences itself.

Magic is the trembling strings, the electrical grid, and the field of play supporting and sustaining the visible and invisible world. It is an energy that can be weaved and worked with by anyone. Some people actively practice and engage in what is known as magical arts. You might call these people witches, shamans, yogis, or mystics.

People often engage in magic unconsciously. For these people, magic unfolds through the nature of who they are, their habits, and their actions. These people sparkle. They are unique. They look as if they have swallowed the moon.

Magic often springs from spiritual and religious practice. It doesn't matter if a person is Muslim, Christian, Buddhist, or whatever spiritual system they align with. Magic can pour through an atheist. There is no belief required. Why? Because magic is life, and life is what we all live.

Magical practice is profoundly simple. But just because it is simple doesn't mean it's easy, especially when needs, desires, and emotions tug at us. Magic will never leave or abandon you, but it doesn't mean your life will be perfect. It doesn't mean you will always get what you want by casting a spell or communing with spirit guides. We are human. Humanity means we all feel pain and experience suffering. Our hearts will break, our lives might fall apart, and we will have bad days. But magical practice teaches you to always do the best with what you have.

The word *esoteric* means "secret." The secret of magic is that it isn't actually a secret. It is right in front of you. Magic exists in plain sight. This is the secret.

Lucky for you, magic is like an ocean. You can move as far into it as you like. If it freaks you out, you can sit on the dock with your toes in the foamy surf. If the idea of magical practice excites you and you want to move further, you can set sail for uncharted lands, scuba dive into subterranean caverns, and explore harrowing depths, discovering things no other human has ever seen or experienced. The only question really is... how far are you willing to go?

Tarot is the perfect tool for magical practice. Why? Because tarot takes us out of our head and places possibility before us. Tarot provides us an opportunity for centering ourselves. Tarot is a ritual tool. Tarot asks that we reach deeper and listen to our authentic inner voice, the spirit song of the High Priestess.

Tarot images give us energy and ideals to aspire to. These energies come to us in the form of beautiful artwork. Tarot can be the focal point of magical spells. It acts as a daily vision board. The cards themselves are symbolic of the nature of the occult.

Tarot reflects the human psyche. The cards are like the partner in crime we always desired. They are always there for us, helping us to engage in conversation with our higher or lower selves. The cards help us achieve goals and cultivate solutions. The cards allow us to open up to the space of possibility. There is an inherent optimism that arrives with a tarot reading. We want to know what is possible. Tarot shows us and then gives us the roadmap of how to reach it.

RULES OF MAGIC

✦

1: Take responsibility

✦

2: You get what you give

✦

3: Everything is energy

✦

4: Like attracts like

✦

The basic rules of magic are simple:

Take responsibility for yourself. Magic is not about manipulating exterior events or other people. It is not concerned with the lot you were dealt at birth or the unfair circumstances of your life. Magic lies in how you respond to the world.

Everything in the seen and unseen world is connected. Everything is energy. Like attracts like. The quickest way to get something is to act as if you already have it.

If something exists in your imagination, it is possible. Your passions, interests, and talents are inside you for a reason. They are a personal compass.

Your attention is your magic wand. What you focus on is what you ignite with energy. Choose wisely.

Your Intuitive and Psychic Muscles

Intuitive and psychic muscles are fascinating. How do you know what you know? It is an extraordinary process to deconstruct how you interface with the material world. Tarot is the perfect tool to begin exploring your intuitive and psychic strengths. Once you identify them, you can begin the practice of making them stronger, like any muscle in the body. Honing your intuitive strengths will pay off in every area of your life as personal choices are made with ease and you come into alignment with the authenticity of who you are.

One of the unacknowledged reasons people come for psychic readings is to prove to themselves that the invisible world exists and that psychic and intuitive faculties are real. How else would a complete stranger be able to look at their cards or gaze into their palm and know everything about their life?

INTUITION: *Knowingness within the body*

PSYCHIC: *Information from outside the body*

ASSOCIATIVE MEMORY: *Mental shortcut*

THE CLAIRS

Clairvoyance: *Seeing*

Clairaudience: *Hearing*

Claircognizance: *Knowing*

Clairgustance: *Tasting*

Clairsentience: *Touching*

Clairempathy: *Feeling*

PROJECTION: *Assigning personal traits/ideas to others*

EMPATHY: *Taking on others' emotions as your own*

No one feels, sees, or tastes the world like you do. You are unique in all the world. Every human on earth shares basic physical qualities like arms and legs, brains and blood, yet how you inhabit your body is wildly different than anyone else on the planet. No one discerns, observes, and listens the same way.

We are each born with different sensate abilities. Do you and your best friend see the same color blue? We don't know. Science can't prove we all experience the same color. Human eyes respond to light reflection in varying shades. Shades determine the intensity or vibration of a color, not the experience of the color itself. No one can prove the purple I see is the same purple you see.

Each of us responds to taste, sound, and touch differently. Fresh green cilantro might be your favorite culinary herb, but to your Aunt Mary it tastes like a tin can. Jazz gives you a splitting headache, but your cousin loves it. Back scratches relax you, but your partner screams with ticklish sensibility when your nails graze their bare skin.

Our preferences stem from how we experientially feel the world. No one can jump inside your body, look through your eyes, taste through your mouth, or listen through your ears (and if they can, well, that's a story for another book). Your experience of the world is as unique as your kiss.

The invisible nature of sensate abilities makes it exceptionally hard to articulate intangible qualities. Describing how we experience sensate information is tricky business. Language fails us when expressing the ineffable. Can you explain the dimensional reality of the dream you had last night? Art, literature, and poetry serve us best when expressing the nature of experience.

It is your choice to become the Indiana Jones of your unique experience. Don't shy away from it because it is mysterious or hard to explain. I can't count how many people have confided in me after a class or lecture that they have psychic and intuitive abilities. These abilities often cause them great anxiety, scare them, or freak them out. It is hard to talk about these issues because we have not yet developed the language to aptly describe it.

It can be scary when we receive information about future events, death, ghosts, etc. The supernatural isn't separate from our life. It is the very bedrock infused around us that makes life possible. Court it, make friends with it, and play with the mystery of it.

People often ask me about scary things like demons or dark, nefarious energy. I always tell them that what is true for the visible world is true for the invisible world. All of the same rules apply. The supernatural can be as safe or as dangerous as any street in New York City at 2 a.m. In my experience, it is only real live people who have hurt or posed a serious threat to me. Regardless, it is important for you to have boundaries, show respect, offer kindness, and be safe.

Cultivate and own your gifts rather than shying away from them. Learn to use them to the best of your abilities. Align your insights with your highest possible good. Don't let someone else tell you about your gifts and natural abilities. Push further on your own. Figure it out for yourself. Invent new language and words to express how you know what you know. Own how you experience the world. Dive deeper into your experience of mystery. Embrace the supernatural creature you are.

I have always felt like my special intuitive gifts were...

Intuition vs. associative memory. Intuition is your inner witch. She is your sage, your wise woman, and the beacon guiding you to this very moment. Your intuition operates continually, like your heartbeat. It supersedes your awareness. Intuition is not something you need to get, it is something you already have. Intuition is the function of sensing or knowing something immediately, without reasoning. It is a quick and ready insight embedded within our body and springing from the soul. It is an immediate apprehension and a subtle sense that lets us know what we are experiencing and how we can best respond to it.

Intuition tells us when something is special or just right. Have you ever known just by locking eyes with someone that they would play an important role in your life? Your intuition tells you when something is deliciously right or terribly wrong. Think of those great decisions you have made—the ones where every cell in your body said yes. That was your intuition backing you up. But we have all made terrible judgment calls even when our intuition was screaming no, no, no. We may have been so attached to what we thought we wanted that we ignored our intuition and wound up paying the price later.

Children are highly intuitive creatures because they have not yet been taught to ignore their instincts. All children mature and feel their way through the world. We are often told by parents, friends, or adults that our actions and intuitions are wrong. We act in alignment with our intuition and are quieted, shushed, or made fun of. We may raise our voice in dangerous and abusive situations only to be silenced by the adults who supposedly know better. When our childhood intuition is rebuked, it becomes difficult to trust it. Lying to a child sends the message that their intuition is worthless and incorrect. The child grows up doubting themselves and their inner voice. Healing your intuitive facilities as an adult is one of the most empowering things you can do.

Reading the tarot will restore intuitive trust. Intuition is what guides the messages and your interpretations of the cards. Trust in your own ability to read the cards spills out into regular life. You make decisions with ease, move with the energy of magic, and discover marvelous synchronicities blossoming around you.

Synchronicity is two or more unrelated events occurring at the same time. The face of a friend pops into your mind's eye, and two hours later you receive an unexpected text from them saying they are in town and want to meet you for dinner. The weather forecast is dreary. You almost cancel a hike, but something tells you to go anyway. You make it to the summit and strike up a conversation with a random fellow hiker. They wind up hiring you for a dream job. Synchronicity is intuition in action. It is the universe's way of wrapping its arms around you, leaning in, and letting you know you chose well.

An amazing synchronicity happened to me once when...

Associative memory is often confused with our intuition. Associative memories are the mental shortcuts to help our brain work efficiently. Associative memory is how we learn and recall links between two unrelated items. A green light means go, while a red light means stop. Our brain makes the connection automatically. We don't need to pause while driving to figure it out. We navigate the car, listen to the radio, and carry on a conversation simultaneously.

Associative memory can affect us physically. Let's say one night you become sick from drinking one too many peach martinis. From that evening forth, you may find the smell of peach schnapps revolting. That's your associative memory. It also affects our opinions and feelings about other people in positive and negative ways. Let's say your cherished grandmother had a glistening mane of silver hair, a passion for purple, and was dripping in diamonds. Chances are, if you meet a white-haired woman in a purple dress with diamond drop earrings at a cocktail party, you'd feel an immediate sense of warmth toward this stranger. That's your associative memory in action.

Assumptions and preconceived notions spring from our associative memory. Associative memory even helps us memorize tarot definitions and make connections between the cards. Unfortunately, the same abilities, when unchecked, can lead to racism, sexism, and all varieties of moral judgments based solely on appearance and previous experience. Worst of all, an association can feel intuitive to us. How often have you made a speculation or a judgment call about someone you've just met, only to find out you were wrong? We all make assumptions about strangers with a quick glance. We chat with them and are surprised by how different they turn out to be. Assuming you know something because you made an association is quite different than knowing it intuitively. We don't want to confuse the two while reading tarot or when living our life.

How can we tell the difference between intuition and associative memory? Awareness of the gulf between intuition and associative memory is the first step. Then, understand the subtle difference between the two by pausing and checking in with the body. We can begin with the tarot.

Flip a random card and look at the image.

The first thing I notice about this card is...

It makes me think of...

Pause for a moment and consider how you made this association.

Did my association come from within my body or my head?

Is this based on a past experience or something deeper?

Psychic faculties are different than intuitive faculties, though the general public often uses the two words interchangeably. Understand the difference between the two by distinguishing where the information is coming from. Intuition comes from inside the body. It is a deep knowledge, a certainty held within the intimacy of the self. It pulses like an underground spring through the interior of the body. Psychic information comes to us from outside the body. Psychics commonly refer to "psychic pops" or a "psychic hit" because psychic information often feels like an unexpected pop or a bubble bursting into the head. It flows in from the outside world and can rarely be controlled. Intuition flows, while psychic information comes and goes.

Psychic information can be very specific and doesn't always make sense. It is important to write down and record any psychic hits you experience, for two reasons. One, it may make sense once you have more information. Two, you will more readily confirm psychic hits when the ability is honored and honed by recording them.

I have experienced psychic information when...

The five clairs are extrasensory ways a person experiences knowledge. The five clairs are not the end-all explanation but a starting point for you to begin exploration into how you are a conduit for psychic and intuitive information. Don't let the challenge of explaining psychic or mystical experience stop you from trying to move further into it. Let it make you better at conversing about such indescribable things as you adventure into the experience of life in your body. The Golden Dawn assigned eso-

34

teric functions to most major arcana cards, and some correlate with the clairs. Use their functions to move further into the card's meaning.

CLAIRVOYANCE IS "CLEAR SEEING"

Clairvoyance is the ability to see something that isn't right in front of you. A man suffers from a recurrent nightmare of watching his wife kissing the next-door neighbor. He arrives home early one day and discovers said neighbor and wife in bed together. His dreams were true. A sensitive teacher sees a charcoal darkness around troubled students and bright yellow mist around highly creative ones. A hospice nurse watches halos develop around patients who are ready to pass to the other side and she knows when they will die. These are all examples of clear sight.

The Emperor's esoteric function is "sight."

Pull out the Emperor card. Examine it and ask yourself how seeing relates to the Emperor.

> *Sight is the esoteric function of the Emperor because…*
>
> *Sight helps me understand the Emperor*
>   *in a new light because…*
>
> *Five ways that sight relates to the Emperor are…*

CLAIRAUDIENCE IS "CLEAR HEARING"

Can you accurately describe how you "hear" your own thoughts? Have you ever watched a mediumship circle where the medium claims to be listening to the voices of souls who have died or passed over to the other side? This is an example of clairaudience, where a person hears messages and voices from the invisible world. Near-death experience stories often include clairaudience when a person in between life and death hears a message or a voice tells the person why they must return to life, often for a person who needs them or a mission that must be completed. Clairaudience extends beyond voices, however. An individual may hear music, otherworldly sounds, or the sounds of things that are impossible to describe. Have you ever thought you heard someone speaking to you but they weren't? Perhaps you were picking up on their thoughts, which would also be a form of clairaudience.

The Hierophant's esoteric function is "hearing."

Pull out the Hierophant card and examine it while contemplating how hearing relates to the Hierophant.

Hearing is the esoteric function of the Hierophant because...

Hearing helps me understand the Hierophant
in a new light because...

Five ways hearing relates to the Hierophant are...

Claircognizance Is "Clear Knowing"

Claircognizance may be the subtlest and most widely available of all of the clairs. Have you ever simply known something is about happen, is happening, or did happen without direct knowledge of how or why you knew it? This is claircognizance. Twins are known for being in tune with each other in frighteningly specific ways. Having a hunch about something also falls under claircognizance. Hospice workers will often know when a patient is about to die, but even laypeople often experience a knowingness of when someone is about to become pregnant or when someone is going to die without knowing why they know such things. How often have you known you were about to receive a call or a text because you thought of the person right before you looked down at your vibrating or ringing phone? That's a classic case of claircognizance!

The Empress's esoteric function is "wisdom and folly," relating to knowing.

Pull out your Empress card and examine it while contemplating how knowing relates to the Empress.

Knowing is the esoteric function of the Empress because...

Knowing helps me understand the Empress
in a new light because...

Five ways knowing relates to the Empress are...

CLAIRGUSTANCE IS "CLEAR TASTING"

A young mother is overcome with the taste of her beloved grandmother's lemon cake. Though her nana is dead, the taste always appears as a message of love. Medical intuitives sometimes taste an illness or the disease of their clients. Drug counselors in rehabilitation centers can sometimes taste when a client begins to abuse drugs again. The uncanny sense of tasting marks clairgustance.

The esoteric function of the Lovers is "taste."

Pull out the Lovers card. Examine it. Contemplate how taste relates to the Lovers.

> *Tasting is the esoteric function of the Lovers because...*
>
> *Tasting helps me understand the Lovers*
> *in a new light because...*
>
> *Five ways tasting relates to the Lovers are...*

CLAIRSENTIENCE IS "CLEAR TOUCH"

A psychic works with a police commissioner to solve local cases. He brings her objects from the murder victim and the crime scene. She touches these objects and is able to provide valuable clues to help police solve the crimes. Massage therapists with extrasensory perceptions are able to feel their way to their client's most needed areas. Reiki practitioners feel their way energetically to heal clients.

The Hermit's esoteric function is "touch."

Pull out the Hermit card. Examine it. Contemplate how touch relates to the Hermit.

> *Touching is the esoteric function of the Hermit because...*
>
> *Touching helps me understand the Hermit*
> *in a new light because...*
>
> *Five ways touching relates to the Hermit are...*

Five-Minute Exercise to Expand the Senses

Psychic and intuitive faculties are muscles. They become stronger with exercise. Set the timer on your phone for five minutes. Begin with your sense of sight. Spend five minutes focusing on seeing. Look at what is before you. Observe the light, color, and texture. Once you've taken in what is before you, look through the wall, hill, or trees.

What can you see in your mind's eye that exists beyond?
Do this for seven days.

Move to your sense of sound. Spend five minutes a day listening to the sounds around you. Identify and pull apart every sound you hear, from wind-blown chimes to the tapping of rain at the window. Listen to the voices in your house. Can you hear the breathiness between words, the silence between the sounds of nature? Listen for sounds beyond your normal perception. Can you hear the murmur of your neighbors, the sounds inside the car driving by, the sound of the deep forest outside your window?

How deeply can you listen?
Do this for seven days.

Move to your sense of smell. Spend five minutes focusing on your olfactory senses. Can you detect the scent of cleaning products in the living room, a hint of moisturizer on your skin? Do you sense the lingering whiffs of last night's dinner or the dampness of morning grass? Move further. Can you smell the produce inside your refrigerator or the scent of the pond visible in the distance? Can you smell gas fumes on the road or your neighbor's roasting chicken and cherry pie?

Focus on your sense of smell.
Do this for seven days.

Move to your sense of taste. Spend five minutes focusing on your sense of taste. Begin by tasting the inside of your mouth. Eat one bite of food. How does it wake up your mouth? Can you taste from the different parts of your tongue? How would you describe it? Can you taste the separate ingredients that went into what you are eating? Look at or visualize something in the pantry. Can you taste it without eating it?

Focus on your sense of taste.
Do this for seven days.

Move to your sense of touch. Spend five minutes focusing on your sense of feeling. Begin with how your clothing feels on your skin. How does it feel on the back of your neck, your elbow, your back? Is the air on your bare skin warm or cool? Touch the fur on your pet with your eyes closed, noticing all the sensations. Imagine your bed: how do the sheets feel? Imagine walking through an old library, touching the bookshelves as you move. Recall the sensory feelings of your favorite childhood place.

Can you feel it?
Do this for seven days.

Once you've devoted a week to each of your senses, bring them all together on a daily basis. Set your five-minute timer and move through each of your senses. Once you've brought awareness to each sense, move deeper with them, allowing them to unfold around you, becoming stronger and more sensitive each day.

Chapter Two

Your Foundation

Ways to Study

Ways to study tarot are wide and varied. Once upon a time, it was hard to find like-minded tarotists and even harder to find a class—especially if you resided in a remote rural area. Technology has changed the tarot game. You'll find study suggestions in this section along with learning and sharing suggestions.

Self-study. Imagine yourself locked away in a tower, alone with nothing but seventy-eight cards and no outside resources. You would figure out how to use them. You already know everything about the deck because you carry all your life experience and creativity with you. How you integrate and interpret the tarot is your own personal magic, your own very special sauce.

No one reads the cards like you do. Pull a card and interpret it. Move outside the borders. Revisit the card at the end of the day. How did your intuition about the card line up? You are your own teacher. You are the guru you've been looking for. All the answers are already inside of you.

I am self-disciplined when I...

Live classes and meet-ups. Live classes are my favorite way to learn the cards and practice reading for others. Under the guidance of an inspired teacher, you are sure to learn new things while sharing personal insights and ideas. Deep bonds often develop between classmates by reading for each other week after week. You'll become close to people of vastly different interests and backgrounds. Weekly classes offer excellent support systems and community building, and you might just meet a group of people you'll know for life. I did!

My favorite class was...

Online classes and groups. Online classes operate like live ones. They are convenient when you can't leave the house or don't live in an area close to a tarot school or study group. You can also find live classes or prerecorded lessons on YouTube or purchase master class options from tarot teachers. Online experience makes it easier to tailor your study times with your schedule. Deep bonds and friendship may be born virtually as well as in person.

Online classes make me feel...

Social media study. Social media accounts often post tarot study hints and opportunities. You'll find weekly tarot spread challenges, daily card readings, interpretations, video responses, reviews, and deck walkthroughs, along with a variety of educational opportunities. You can dip into your tarot education throughout the day via your phone or computer.

Social media is...

Retreats, conferences, and workshops. Retreats, conferences, and workshops are an enjoyable way get out of the house and immerse yourself in the art of tarot and self-study. Tarot is often incorporated with other modalities such as writing, yoga, and psychic practice. It is an opportunity to travel by taking a learning vacation in exotic locales or at famous retreat centers around the world and forming connections with new people.

I would love to book a retreat in...

Correspondence courses. Wouldn't it be mysterious to walk to your mailbox and have a tarot lesson waiting for you in a crisp white envelope? If you like the idea of lessons being sent to you and being given weekly assignments, a correspondence course may be perfect for you. I personally loved looking forward to the magical white envelope appearing in the mail every week like a metaphysical gift. B. O. T. A. is a modern mystery school offering snail mail courses.

Weekly lessons sound...

Free ways to learn tarot. Libraries and the internet are your best friends when it comes to a free tarot education. You'll find loads of conflicting information online. It is okay for the information to conflict. Tarot and magic are complex subjects. You might find it confusing if random internet searches become the core of your tarot practice. Internet information offers little depth. A keyword search is no replacement for a deep dive into the riches available for free at your local library. Tarot is about you. Seek out a cohesive system that works for you.

Never forget the most important free resource: YOU. Your own intuitive reactions and interpretations of the cards will always be the most important part of your practice. All it costs you is time and attention.

How to find the right teacher. Finding a gifted teacher—a personality you respond to and someone who inspires you—is a beautiful experience. Stars often align and a teacher will appear out of the blue when you least expect it (that's magic).

Create space for an amazing teacher to enter your life by keeping a door open and putting the intention out there. Ask for recommendations, read reviews, and poke around while you are waiting for them to materialize. Discover how each teacher works and what they offer. Finding a teacher can feel a little like dating, but when you find the right one, it will become a cherished relationship.

My favorite teacher was...

Keep in mind that the teacher/student bond is a sacred one.
The Hierophant card traditionally represents the one who passes on
hidden mysteries. These mysteries are contained within the Hierophant's
key. It is worth noting that where there is power, there is abuse. Just like
abuse in clergy, schools, and clubs, so the same applies in the world of
tarot and metaphysical studies. All teachers are not created equal. You'll
find tarot teachers (and readers) with wild, oversized egos. That's not to
say you can't learn from an instructor with a ginormous sense of personal
importance, but it is in your own self-interest to be comfortable setting
boundaries. Is the course about them or you?

An ideal teacher

+ has your highest good in mind
+ wants to help you learn
+ shares their light with you
+ reflects your inner light
+ works for the greatest good of all
+ wants you to succeed
+ helps you uncover what you always knew

Stay away from one who

+ manipulates or controls
+ provokes shame or negativity
+ pits students against each other
+ is sexually inappropriate
+ claims their way is the only way
+ makes you uncomfortable
+ uses "secret knowledge" as power

Practice, practice, practice. No matter how you choose to learn, you can't simply sit back and memorize the cards. You have to practice casting them, reading them, and integrating them into your life. One of the quickest ways to learn is to perform tarot readings for all your friends. People jump at the chance to have their cards read because everyone wants to hear about themselves. You'll also cultivate and appreciate the differences between reading for yourself and another. Once your friends' friends find out you are reading the cards, they'll be knocking down your door.

Tarot Journal

A tarot grimoire or journal is an important tool. This is your record and exploration of your tarot experience. Every day brings fresh insight, new illumination, and a richer understanding of the arcana. Writing and recording your process provides you with the magical record of your life.

A grimoire is a book of collected magic, a witch's handwritten record of her work, spells, discoveries, and recipes. Magical books like the Kama Sutra, Torah, or Koran are considered powerful objects in their own right. Any book lover will tell you that books large and small, from *Frankenstein* to *Wuthering Heights*, reverberate with unique power.

When you craft a book of your own, a record of insight, learning, and revelation, you create a core reserve of personal power. You interpret the wisdom gleaned from others and give it your own unique spin. Your tarot practice is an instrument of growth. As you experiment with magical practice, you will want to reflect on learning moments, experiences, failures, and winning moments. Know what works for you so you can build upon it. Call it a journal, a grimoire, or by any other name, but relish in creating this unique record of you.

I like the idea of creating a book of myself because...

JOURNALING HINTS

✦

Write every day

✦

Keywords

✦

Card pulls

✦

Synchroncities

✦

Consider your tools. How do you typically like to write? If you are a writer by nature (you are already a gifted storyteller), you may have noticed the difference in how your writing tools inspire you. A jet-black ballpoint pen casting across a creamy white blank page may fill you with excitement. Writing with a pencil might remind you of grammar school days with warm lead and a chalky eraser to nibble on as you collect your thoughts. Handheld devices help you to compose glowing notes when an idea strikes you during your commute or in the middle of the night. Computer writing offers the musical tapping of clicks on your keyboard to lull you into creativity.

My favorite writing tool is...

Consider your writing habits. Are you a midnight owl scribbling away till all hours? Do you rise with the sun, eyes bright and shiny while nurturing a steaming mug over an open notebook? Do emotional outbursts and creative blasts bring you to the page to express yourself in a flurry of excitement and fervor? Are you an obsessive note taker or do you usually put things off figuring that you'll get around to it someday?

My favorite time of day and way to write is...

Record-Keeping Devices

JOURNAL: Perfect for those with an established love of diaries and record keeping.

ELECTRONIC WRITING DEVICE OR APP: Ideal for tech lovers and digital nomads.

THREE-RING BINDER: Satisfying for record keepers and those who like to move information around.

SOCIAL MEDIA: YouTube, Instagram, and all forms of social media can act as daily recordings and interactions regarding your tarot journey.

AUDIO: For those who like to muse aloud.

Suggested Tarot Journal Sections

A card a day. This practice is described later in this chapter. Dedicate a section to recording your daily pulls and insights. Begin with a black sheet of paper. Write your question on the top of the paper: "What do I need to know today?" Draw your card and write its name in the center of the page. Note any immediate associations leaping to mind along with ideas or blurts about what the card means to you. Answer your original question. Later that evening revisit the page. Write how the card applied to your day (or didn't). Look up the card's definition in a book and list some keywords to bridge your understanding of the card.

Card meanings. Card meanings are a place to record your personal understanding and experience of each card. Keywords spark your own interpretations. If a card reminds you of something or makes you feel a certain way, note it here. Include your favorite quotes or song lyrics applying to the cards. For instance, the song "Don't Give Up" by Peter Gabriel and Kate Bush is a lovely theme for the symbolic journey depicted on the Six of Swords. From his novel *Rose Madder,* Stephen King's quote that "It ain't the blows we are dealt that matter but the ones we survive" pairs nicely with the Nine of Wands, which often shows a bandaged figure emerging through a fence. Jeanette Winterson says in her brilliant novel *The Passion* that "Perhaps all romance is not a contract between equal parties but an explosion of dreams and desires that can find no outlet in everyday life. Only drama will do, and while the fireworks last the sky is a different color." This evocative quote pairs perfectly with the Lovers card.

CARD IMMERSION JOURNAL ACTIVITY

Clear your mind. Do not ask a question. Shuffle your deck and pull a card. In the center of a blank piece of paper or page in a journal, write the name of the card. Jot down your initial observations about the card. Write the symbols you notice. Write the colors you see. Write the sounds you hear. Once you have filled the page with observations, examine the card and what you have written. Can you give yourself a one-sentence piece of advice regarding what you have discovered about the card?

Symbolic Association and the 3 F's

Tarot speaks in symbols. We communicate seamlessly with the cards once we master the art of symbolic language. Create a personal symbolic dictionary with a technique called the 3 F's. The 3 F's stand for faculty, feeling, and functionality. Faculty is how the symbol/object is generically used. Feeling is your emotional response to the symbol/object. Functionality is the symbol/object's metaphoric operation in your current life. Let's say you choose to interpret the symbol of the Empress's chair. A chair's faculty is to provide support. Your feeling might be delight or relief it is there for your comfort. Functionality asks whether or not you currently feel supported. This includes issues of mental, emotional, and financial support. Try for yourself. Pick a random card, close your eyes, place your finger on the card, and open your eyes. Interpret the symbol you are pointing to:

FACULTY: This symbol's primary purpose is…

FEELING: The symbol makes me feel…

FUNCTION: The feeling of this symbol is operating in my life right now as…

Repeating Cards

Repeat cards are particular cards appearing again and again in your daily pulls and tarot spreads. They tend to align with the cycles of our lives. You'll find different repeat cards per season and per life cycle. Repeat cards will come to define certain life moments and important events.

For example, when my first book, *Tarot Diva*, was published, the Wheel of Fortune appeared repeatedly. This arcana about energy and revolution aligned with lots of exciting press opportunities and new business relationships. Every time the card popped up, which felt like every other day, I used it as a reminder not to question all the exciting opportunities but to roll with them.

Pay attention to how a repeat card's energy is working with you. Listen carefully to the messages they bring. Make extra space in your tarot journal and answer the following questions:

You are repeating because I need to know…

A quality I have not yet discovered about you is…

Together we will…

Creative Writing

Composing fictional or memoir-style stories about each card is a great way to become intimate with them. Inventing a story about a card or applying it to your life will help you form a unique relationship with the energy of the card. You'll never look at the card the same way again.

Creative writing prompts:

> *Flip a single card and finish this sentence: Once upon a time...*

> *Flip three cards and write a children's story with a clear beginning, middle, and end, beginning with this sentence: It was a dark and stormy night...*

Memoir writing prompts:

> *Flip a card and look for the first symbol that you notice. Use it to fill in the blank: When I was young, my _____ was...*

> *Flip a card and let it remind you of something from childhood, then answer this: I'll never forget the day I...*

> *Pull the Death card and place it in front of you, then answer this: The first time I encountered death was when...*

Additional Journal Sections

PSYCHIC AND INTUITIVE DIARY: Record psychic and intuitive pops.

CARD OF THE YEAR/MONTH/WEEK: In addition to your card of the day, it is fun to pull a card for the week, the month, and the year.

SPREADS AND READING RECORDS: Record your spreads and the information gleaned from them.

QUESTIONS: Create a space in the journal where you write your most evocative and important questions. Creating an excellent question is the first step toward gaining the outcome you desire. It takes time to formulate a really good one. Keeping a list will help you refer back to them. Use them again when needed. See the Master List of Questions at the back of this book.

WRITING PROMPTS: A great place to answer questions posed in this book.

SKETCHING: Regardless of skill level, the act of sketching your cards will bring your attention to details you might have overlooked.

MAGICAL RITUALS, SPELLCASTING, AND RESULTS: If you use tarot in magic spells, here is a wonderful place to record the spell, ingredients, details, and results.

DREAM INTERPRETATIONS: Dreams are a direct door into your subconscious and intuitive life. Writing about them deepens the meaning and experience. Interpret dream symbols as you would a tarot symbol.

SHADOW WORK NOTES: Shadow work is powerful and transformative; record your work here.

Daily Practice

Daily practice, often called "a card a day" or a daily pull, is a profound devotional tarot act. It can be done every day in less than five minutes. It is remarkable that something so simple has such life-altering effects. Ingraining this pleasurable habit fosters an intimate relationship with card meanings. It is a moment of contemplation that gives you an opportunity to step back, set up your day, and consider what is really important for you. It also helps you learn the cards.

To perform the daily practice, pull a single card every morning from a shuffled pack of tarot cards. Select a time of day you are most likely to pull a card. Ideally, pull your daily card when you can spend some time contemplating its meanings and implications. Habitualize this process. Make it part of your daily routine. Lots of people enjoy pulling their card in the morning along with tea or coffee. Morning is ideal because upon waking you are closer to the unconscious state of sleep and thus aligned with your contemplative inner state.

My quietest time of day is...

Formulate your question or intention by articulating your desire before pulling a card. What are you looking forward to or needing help with in the coming day? Are you seeking a particular piece of wisdom? Working toward enhancing your psychic muscles? Manifesting your wildest dreams to fruition? State what you need before pulling a card.

Conversely, you might want to peek at the energy your day has in store. Perhaps you are just learning the cards and want to experience a single card's significance throughout the day in comparison with the card's traditional meaning. Whatever and however you choose to use your card a day, do it with intention and integrity.

My intention for today is...

DAILY PRACTICE

✦

Compose a question

Clear your mind

Pull a card

Write your interpretation

*Check in with the
card at night*

✦

Clearing your mind is the most important part of daily practice. Close your eyes. Take a few deep inhales and exhales. Ground yourself and root into the earth below. Imagine the flower of your third eye opening. It will give and receive information. Imagine the day in your mind's eye. Articulate your question or intention aloud. Approach the card from a peaceful, alert state.

The best way for me to calm my mind and feel at peace is...

Shuffle the deck and pull your card. Let the image greet you. Allow it to wash over your consciousness. Let the story, observation, or impression come to you. Write your experience down in your tarot journal. What is the message you receive? What advice does it give? Did someone or something burst into your head? Did you feel a psychic pop? How is this card advising you? What does it tell you to focus on?

I am most open to receiving messages when I...

Evening check-in is an opportunity to check back in with your morning card. Grab your journal. Look at the notes and impressions you made about the card at the beginning of your day. Did you forget about the morning message? Did your card relate to how your day turned out? Did the essence of the card manifest in your experience of the day? Do you feel like you embodied the card? What new observations did you uncover about your card?

A note for beginners about your daily pull. Each card is a broad ecosystem with high and low points, as complex and nuanced as any person you know. Tarotists eventually come to recognize there are no "good" or "bad" cards. You might wake up in a delightful mood, feeling glorious, and the last thing you want to see is the spooky Nine of Swords. Take out the scary cards or any cards you don't want to see when selecting your card a day. Don't feel like you are sticking your head in the sand. Incorporate challenging cards when you feel ready. Daily cards are about maintaining the pleasure of your practice.

Pull only from the major arcana if pulling from the whole deck feels daunting and overwhelming. Once you become comfortable interpreting these cards, you can begin to add other suits, court cards, "spooky" cards, etc.

Reversed cards can be completely ignored during daily practice (or anytime). The only catch is that you decide how to interpret a reversal before you begin reading any cards. Don't worry about the reversal if you don't want to. I never use reversal interpretations in my morning pull. It is also fun to pull cards from the deck until an upright card appears as your card of the day.

A choice card is an optional addition to your daily practice when you get a message making you feel trapped or uncomfortable. Pull a choice card. This card is a choice or option that is available to you all day. The choice card message does not replace the original message but adds nuance and gives you an option of how to work with the energy of your day.

Example: You wake up on Tuesday unexpectedly happy from a delicious dream lingering in your subconscious. The Five of Swords appears as your daily card and dampens your mood. You feel like it means a disagreement is imminent. You pull a choice card: the Eight of Cups appears. You gaze at the figure on the card who is walking up a mountain. You decide the message of your choice card is that you can take the high road and walk away from any person or thing that doesn't feel right to you. You take its advice and have a wonderful day.

Acquiring and Caring for Your Deck

I'm a sucker for old wives' tales. They are chock-full of wisdom and humor. But there's a difference between listening to a story and believing in it as literal truth. A famous myth states that you can only read cards with a tarot deck someone has gifted you. It's a mysterious idea, isn't it? But this old wives' tale simply isn't true; sometimes you have to make your own luck. That's what using tarot is all about.

I bought my first tarot deck when I was twelve years old. It would have been ideal if someone had given me my first deck, but if I had waited around for that perfect deck, I may never have flipped a card in my lifetime.

You can acquire your deck any way you like as long as you aren't stealing it. Speaking of stealing decks, be sure to purchase tarot from your favorite metaphysical bookshop and reputable sellers at every opportunity. Overseas companies are now scanning and selling low-resolution versions of popular tarot decks. Replica decks and stolen PDF book downloads rob authors and artists of royalties. It is theft.

Tarotists often become avid deck collectors. Visit shops, purchase unique decks in romantic and exotic locations, order them from your favorite neighborhood bookshops, and enjoy all that the world of tarot has to offer you.

Opening/initiation ritual. Rituals forge sacred bonds between reader and deck, and you'll find more about them in the next section. An opening ritual with a new deck is a special occasion.

Don't worry if you have already opened a deck and are reading with it. You can still perform the ritual. Place your deck in numerical order (refer to the booklet that came along with your cards to find the alignment of suits) and arrange all cards right-side up.

Set aside at least an hour where you will not be disturbed. Turn off all electric lights. Light some candles and a cone or stick of incense. Open your deck if it is unwrapped.

Sit before the incense with your deck in hand, slowly turn over each card. One by one, with care and thought, observe the picture on each card as you pass it through the smudging smoke. Say its name aloud. Move through the entire deck. Perform any additional ritual work.

Touching the deck. Decide whether you will choose to allow other people to touch and handle your cards. The general idea is that other people place their energy into the cards when they touch them. This works well when you are reading for others. However, it is beautiful to keep a sacred tarot deck that has never been touched by anyone but you. Most card slingers keep a sacred deck for themselves and another deck that is touched by others.

Storing the deck. Storing your deck in a beautiful place is a mark of respect. Pay attention to how you store your favorite and most-used deck. Cards can be wrapped in silk scarves or a fabric of your choice. You can also find beautiful tarot reading cloths that will unfold into something you can spread out and read the cards on. You may store your cards inside a beautiful carved wooden box, a designer box (like Fendi or Dior), or something that feels especially magical or appropriate to you and your aesthetic.

Give your cards an extra power punch by storing them with a favorite cleansing stone, gem, crystal, or any other magical item you feel adds to the energy of your deck.

SUGGESTED GEMS

✦ *Black Tourmaline:* A grounding stone great for both yourself and the deck, it soaks up and disperses negative energy.

✦ *Clear Quartz:* Use to shield yourself and your deck against undesirable influences.

✦ *Fluorite:* Protect your psyche and cards from others' emotional energies.

Cleaning and cleansing. You can always energetically cleanse your deck by ordering and smudging the cards as suggested in the initiation ritual above. Charge your cards by the light of the full moon by placing them on a window ledge. You can empower the cards with solar energy by leaving them near the window for at least eight hours on a sunny day. Use a soft rag and baking powder to erase fingerprints and grease smudges on the cards.

SUGGESTED INCENSE

+ *Sage:* General clearing and cleansing.

+ *Palo Santo:* Spiritual healing.

+ *Cedar:* Repels negativity and attracts clear, affirming vibrational energy.

New deck interview. This is a way to get to know your new tarot deck. After all, your relationship to tarot is a two-way street between yourself and the energy of the cards. Shuffle your deck thoroughly after performing your opening ritual. Ask the following questions of the deck and provide the answers in your journal:

1: What do you want me to know about you?

2: What is your greatest strength?

3: What is your greatest weakness?

4: Why are we a good match for each other?

5: What can I expect from you?

6: What do you expect from me?

7: What can we learn together?

Ethics and Boundaries

An ethical code is essential because reading tarot is a magical endeavor. Magic is power, and with power comes responsibility. You are bound to tiptoe across ethical boundaries every now and then. It is helpful to figure out these foggy gray areas ahead of time. Should you peek into someone else's business? Is it a good idea to craft tarot magic to bend someone's free will? Would you give others medical advice based on the cards? These are just a few ethical questions you will rub shoulders with when reading tarot.

Boundaries are essential for yourself and when reading for others. As a beginner, there's no better practice than reading tarot for friends and family. The good news is, you'll never run out of people to practice read-ing for. Everyone's favorite subject tends to be themselves. You'll find no shortage of willing victims. Once people find out you are reading cards, certain people will seek you again and again to use your card-reading skills as a chance to obsess over things like their romantic relationships. You need to know when to say enough is enough.

One way to set boundaries when reading for friends is to...

Boundaries also consist of what you will ask of the cards for others and yourself. How you use tarot depends on your particular sensitivities. This is a highly subjective area. A hospice nurse who reads tarot will likely have a different relationship with the energy of the Death card than a superstitious Italian grandmother, and therefore each will offer different interpretations of the cards. Each of us has a different cultural context and different set of gifts and sensitivities. What is true for one human is different for another. Therefore, the information each person can pull from tarot will be different. Consider your pre-existing skills and talents.

I have always had a talent for...

The witch's threefold law states that what you put out into the world returns to you times three. Let me rephrase this important con-cept: The energy you put out is what comes back times three. It applies to everything in your life. Simply put, do not do something that you wouldn't want done to you.

Would you like it if a person used tarot to peek at your secret, private thoughts? Would you enjoy being manipulated by magic? Would you want to do something against your will? How would you feel if a tarotist read cards for your pregnant mother and told her you would be an ill-fated, problematic child? When it comes to ethical dilemmas, simply put yourself on the receiving end of the scenario.

On a deeper level, the energy you exude is what you are already immersed in. To put negativity, cruelty, anger, and manipulation into the world, you must first be filled with it (whether justified or not). This

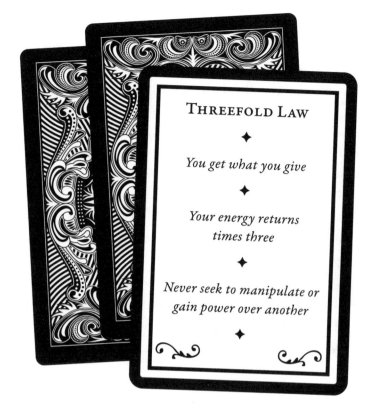

Threefold Law

You get what you give

*Your energy returns
times three*

*Never seek to manipulate or
gain power over another*

intensity returns to you *times three.* Think of how life transforms if you respond to every slight or injustice with kindness and peace. What would your ultimate result be?

The magical rule of three means when I give love, I get...

Predicting the future is a tricky business that can return to haunt you. The archetypal gypsy fortuneteller who gazes into your future is beguiling. Wouldn't you love to find a mysterious woman to give you all of life's answers? If we would literally see the future, most fortunetellers (myself included) would be sipping a chilled glass of bubbly rosé in the South of France with our lottery winnings. It beats the hell out of sitting under a neon sign hawking ten-dollar card readings to sweaty teenagers at the Jersey shore.

The more you work with the cards, you will discover there is no past or future. There is only the infusion of all possibility right now. Tarot helps you uncover all the answers you seek. These answers are inside you. Your future is not contingent on other people, situations, or outcomes. It is up to you.

We read energy when we read the cards. We are all energetic beings floating through the energetic magic of the universe. Can we look at patterns in the cards and detect the most likely outcome of a given situation? Absolutely. Can you predict a future event with tarot? Only you can answer that question. I certainly can't, and I've never met anyone who could, but that doesn't mean psychic, intuitive, and mysterious things don't happen with the cards. They do!

People will always sit down with you and ask to know their future. The question is, will you give them what they want to hear? Will you tell them with certainty what is going to happen?

I think predicting the future with tarot is...

The power of suggestion occurs when a person is presented with an idea or declaration about the future and they turn in into a reality by making it happen. Imagine the power of suggestion when you are sitting with a deck of tarot cards in your hands—especially if the person you are reading for believes the cards predict the future or always tell the truth!

Consider a person's feelings and sensitivities when reading the cards. Never blurt a frightening prediction. For example, the Tower card appears. It would be neither kind nor helpful to scream "Collapse! Ruin!" There's no point in frightening someone. They would walk out the door looking for collapse and ruin around every corner.

To protect yourself and others, always make an effort to read for the highest good of everyone involved. This doesn't mean all of your readings will be perfect. We are human, and we all fumble and make mistakes, yet we can strive to give the souls we read for empowering information. We can gift them with words that will elevate, inspire, and provide clarity and confirmation.

The power of suggestion is...

Peeking in on other people's business is tempting. Don't. Do. It. It is not ethical. It is not okay. It is none of your business. To avoid this pitfall, bring the responsibility back to yourself in the question. Instead of asking "Is that guy I'm crushing on thinking of me?" rephrase the question. Ask "What can I do to spark a relationship between us?" Refer to chapter 3 for extended advice on creating proactive questions.

Confidentiality is paramount in tarot readings and when casting magic. When you read cards for another person, you are holding sacred space for that person. No matter how juicy and delicious their inner secrets, thoughts, and desires are, it is not your place to broadcast it; refer to the threefold law. Keep their trust. Never ever discuss a person's tarot reading with others.

Keep the nature of your magical work private, especially when it comes to spells. This doesn't mean you can't collaborate with covens or friends and work together magically. In fact, collaborative energy raises vibrational magic. But when casting solitary spells, the energy of an intention changes when it is shared by talking about it after the fact. Always keep a little magic for yourself. Never disclose the purpose of a spell once you have worked it.

Medical, legal, and financial advice should be avoided even if you are a medical professional, lawyer, or finance expert. Your advice coupled with the tarot cards has the potential to deeply imprint the person you are reading for. States in the U.S. have varying degrees of laws against fortunetelling. The last thing you want to be responsible for is affecting a person's decision about litigation, their bank accounts, and their health. If someone asks about these areas, politely explain that you do not answer such questions. You may choose to read the general energy of a situation, but hold back on offering any specifics. Avoid giving anyone a reason to sue you.

Reading for pregnant women is something to consider before an expectant mother shows up in front of your cards. Are you willing to say or show something that could frighten a woman who is soon to be in the hospital? Consider the power of suggestion. The image of the Death card can be terrifying to one unfamiliar with its nuanced meaning.

Do not run the risk of frightening or stressing out a pregnant woman. Avoid it altogether. Would you really want to bear the weight of responsibility for a woman in her last trimester to see the Eight or Nine of Swords or something equally spooky that she might internalize? I have made it a personal rule to never read for a pregnant woman and highly advise you to do the same.

Alcohol and drugs should be avoided before or during a tarot reading. The point of cartomancy is to gather your highest self while harnessing your deepest intuition. It is challenging enough to clear your intuitive channels without having them affected by drugs or alcohol. You also run the risk of saying something hurtful or damaging, which you will regret. Stay true to your brilliance and avoid the hooch while reading your cards, especially for others.

Nonjudgment and listening are essential. How would you feel if you asked an intimate question during a reading and the reader looked at you cross-eyed? The job of a reader is to read the cards, not insert their personal opinion. Listen to the person sitting across from you. Examine the cards. Answer their questions, rephrasing the questions when needed. The space you hold for another during a reading is sacred. Do not betray this trust.

Sample Code of Ethics

+ I read for myself or another's highest good.

+ I reveal information in a kind, empowering manner.

+ I understand what I put into the world comes back to me by the rule of three.

+ I will not perform readings wishing harm, seeking damage, or maligning another person, place, or thing.

+ I will not use the cards to peek into someone else's life or private thoughts.

+ I will not offer myself or another medical information or advice based on the cards.

+ I will not offer myself or another legal or financial advice.

+ I will not discuss the contents of any tarot reading to outside parties without express advance permission.

Create your own code of ethics. It can and most likely will change as you grow and evolve as a reader, so adapt as need be.

My code of ethics is...

Chapter Three

Magical Readings

Preparing for a Reading

Selecting your primary deck is like falling in love. The deck of your dreams may hit you hard, fast, and early. You might already have it in your hot little hands. Perhaps you have yet to discover your perfect partner in crime. Cast a wide net if you are still on the lookout for the perfect deck. Look online at deck reviews and video unboxings, but most importantly seek out brick and mortar metaphysical shops and bookstores. Holding a deck in your hand, even if it is unopened, is the best way to determine how you will respond to the deck's innate sensual quality. When you find the deck meant for you, you will know it.

The tarot of my dreams would be...

Multiple decks are fun to have on hand because the relationship between you and your primary deck evolves like any other relationship. You will grow, and your tarot tastes and needs will grow as well. Using multiple decks expands your tarot palate and helps you become tarot fluid.

Choose your decks according to mood. Use dark gothic vampire decks when you are feeling subversive and working out deep internal issues. Use nature decks when you feel inspired and connected to the weather. Use whimsical decks when connecting with your inner child. Every tarot deck has a unique personality. Pull one out when you want to hear its particular voice.

Choose decks for specific actions. For example:

+ You might reserve one deck only for spellcraft.

+ You might reserve a single deck for you alone that no one else is allowed to touch.

+ You might reserve a deck exclusively for reading for other people.

+ You might select a "last word" deck to offer the last word on a tarot reading.

Think of your tarot decks as a circle of advisors there to aid your every need.

Build your practice step by step and card by card. If learning the entire deck feels overwhelming to you, remove the minor arcana and read with the major arcana, the Fool through the World. Add additional cards like spices into a stew when you feel comfortable. Alternatively, you can read with only a suit at a time.

Remove scary cards if they freak you out. Tarot should not feel frightening. If something bothers you, remove it until you are ready to integrate it. You might consider removing scary cards when reading tarot for the public. Remove the Death card when reading for strangers since people tend to take that card at face value. You never know who is going to walk up or what experience or assumptions they hold about tarot cards. What if an eleven-year-old with a sick mother walks up to your table and pulls the Death card? Do you want to be responsible for putting that image in a child's mind? There is no right or wrong answer, but it is something for you to consider.

Questioning Well

Questions are essential. A good question has the power to change your life. They are the salt and pepper, the PB and J, the bread and butter of reading. A powerful question is an act of pure magic. Questions set your brain on a direct course of discovery. They will provoke the highest, most creative answer. Our brains are hardwired to find solutions. A good question opens possibility, fosters flow, and helps your brain, heart, and gut operate at their highest potentials, moving you toward desirable experiences and outcomes.

I normally avoid adjectives like "good" and "bad." Life is far too complex. When it comes to crafting powerful questions for your tarot practice, there is a distinct line between good and bad. Good and bad questions are like the difference between gazing at a postcard of the beach and actually lying on a towel, feet in the sea, golden sun on your glistening skin. Nothing compares to the real thing.

The difference between good and bad questions is as easy as drawing a line in the sand. Bad questions box in the brain without room for expansion. A person asks, "Will I ever fall in love?" Reversed Lovers appear: the answer is a resounding no. What then? Will you pack your bags? Take the card at its word? Stop desiring romance and companionship? No way.

A bad question leaves no room for action. A person asks, "Will I be rich?" The Wheel of Fortune appears: the answer is a resounding yes. What then? Quit your job, hop back in bed, and wait for a bag of money to knock at the front door? You could...but is that the best course of action?

Bad questions can leave you feeling hopeless. A person asks, "Why am I unhappy?" The reversed Ace of Cups appears: the answer is "Because you are depressed." Okay, we already established that, so now what?

Powerful questions are magical. The first rule of magic is acknowledging the role you play in your future. It is easy to blame other people, outer situations, and events as the cause of unhappiness or discomfort. Power increases when you choose how to react to any outer circumstance.

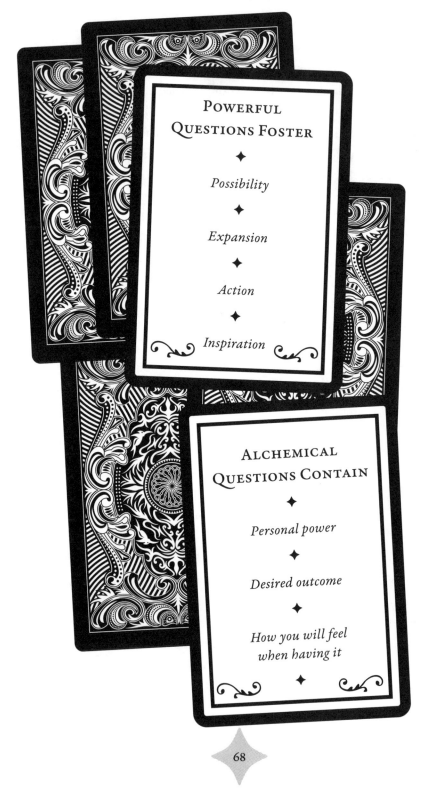

POWERFUL QUESTIONS FOSTER

✦

Possibility

✦

Expansion

✦

Action

✦

Inspiration

ALCHEMICAL QUESTIONS CONTAIN

✦

Personal power

✦

Desired outcome

✦

How you will feel when having it

✦

A good question includes personal responsibility. They begin with "How can I..." or "What can I..." Instead of a love question that asks "Will I ever fall in love," transform the question into "How can I attract the highest possible romantic relationship?" or "What can I do to fall in love?" The reversed Lovers appear, suggesting the inability to be vulnerable and open due to past heartbreaks. You can mend your broken heart by opening up to the world around you and thus will attract new love.

Powerful questions include your desired outcome. Be specific. "Will I be rich" is vague. That matter of riches is highly subjective. Instead, ask "What can I do right now to improve my financial situation?" The Wheel of Fortune appears, suggesting that you've had some financial highs and lows in life but things are looking up. Make the most of what you have by creating a savings plan that helps you save more when you are making more. It helps your financial energy evolve.

Look at the transformation of bad into good questions:

+ "Why is this happening to me?" becomes
  "How can I set myself up for success?"

+ "Why does my life suck?" becomes
  "How can I change the pattern in my life?"

+ "Why am I depressed?" becomes
  "How can I create positivity and change?"

My biggest question at the moment is...

*I acknowledge my power in stating my desire
and the question becomes...*

Unethical questions occur when you peek into another's life without their permission. Unethical questions include "Is (insert name) thinking about me right now?" Rephrase this question into "How can I bring my highest self to my relationship with (insert name)?" Unethical questions pry into other's personal business: "What is my daughter doing at college?" If you have to ask the cards and can't ask her, there is a bigger problem at hand. Transform the question into "How can I best support my daughter?"

Reading the energy of a situation is helpful in knowing how to respond to a situation without specifically peeking inside other people's lives. It's like walking into a room and taking a survey of what is going on.

We intermingle, read, and exude energy all the time. The world is electric connection. The essence of a sacred temple is a different vibrancy than that of a crowded football stadium. We have all been in the uncomfortable space between a couple who is fighting; we know it even if they aren't speaking. We all feel the energetic difference between a morning commuter train versus the clamoring electricity of evening rush hour.

We observe and respond to other people's vibes all the time. You will often be drawn or repelled by another person within the first few minutes of meeting them. We often fall in love with a person whose energy feels familiar and comforting. We respond to the intensely beautiful feeling of having known them our entire life, even if we've just met.

Every card in the tarot deck contains its own unique vitality. Shuffle and pull a card at random from your deck. Rather than looking to a particular symbol or color, allow yourself to feel the energy pouring out of the card. Do this by allowing yourself to have an all-over body/physical response to the card. Write this observation down. Once you have noted the energy of your situation as reflected by the card, you are free to formulate the next question.

Shuffle and pull a card without a question:

The energy of this card feels like...

Ask a question about a particular situation. Include your power and desire. Shuffle and pull a card by reading the energy of the card:

The energy of my situation is...

Rephrasing questions becomes an integral part of the tarot reading process whether you read for yourself or a partner. Crafting a question is like sculpting a work of art. You are clarifying, becoming clear, and getting rid of what you don't need in order to craft a question that sets you on the path of evolution and success.

There are times in life when you or people you read for do not know exactly where discomfort is coming from. I once performed a reading with a petite blond woman whom we will call Jennifer. She arrived at my reading table and revealed how she was in a slump. She felt icky and depressed. She had no question other than "What do I have to look forward to?"

I saw two options. My first option was to shuffle the cards and lay a colorful multicard spread. I could begin reading away, telling her what I saw in the cards—a valid and acceptable choice.

My second option was to move deeper. I asked her what felt frustrating. I inquired about her hopes and dreams. Jennifer sprang to life and sat up straight as she answered. She described her dead-end advertising job. Her creative talents were smooshed by all the busywork and efforts to please others. She described the same dynamic in her romantic relationship too. She was so busy taking care of others, she had nothing left for herself. A light bulb went off: she saw the cause of her unhappiness. We hadn't pulled a single card.

The two of us crafted questions such as "What simple action can I take every day to set me on the path back to my authenticity?" The King of Cups (the master dreamer) appeared. She decided her daily action was to write a paragraph a day of the novel she dreamt of writing. We asked, "How can I change the dynamic in my romantic relationship so I can receive as well as give to my partner?" The Star appeared (opening and clarity). We decided it meant she needed to carve self-care time for herself (massage and yoga) out of the time she usually spent cheering her mate for his favorite things (hockey and baseball). The Emperor (structure and boundaries) appeared as the final card of her reading, and she decided erecting boundaries was the medicine required to steer her life in a positive direction.

Alchemical questions create change. Alchemy is the medieval art of metamorphosis. Ancient alchemists worked in the tireless pursuit of turning base metals into gold. It is the forerunner of modern chemistry. Alchemy perfects what nature has left unfinished.

Spiritual alchemy is the transformation of one's life into a vein of gold. It is the possibility of renewal, unification, and divine perfection. The base metal reflects a human, imperfect and unbalanced, who is transformed into gold via the transfiguration of the soul.

The alchemical process is reflected in the procession of the major arcana. The Fool, who is the soul, is channeled into the material world by the Magician and so begins a series of actions and lessons reflected by the oncoming cards. The entire process results in the final transformation into the World card.

Alchemical questions are a magical process invoking transformation simply by asking it. It includes the elements of a powerful question but adds a third element provoking enchantment:

ALCHEMICAL QUESTIONS

+ Acknowledge the role you play.

+ State your desired outcome.

+ Identify and align with the emotional feeling you'll have once your desire is attained.

The rules of magic state that like attracts like. The quickest way to court what you desire is to act and feel like you already have it. This is why when you include the emotional feeling you'll have upon receiving what you want, you will bring it toward you faster. The brain doesn't know the difference between imagining it and actually having it. Therefore, the act of adding your feeling encourages more of those feelings and puts you in alignment with your desired outcome. Magic!

The beauty of stating your desired emotional outcome is that you don't have to bother with the specifics of what something will look like or how it will manifest. How do you know the universe doesn't have something better in mind for you than you can even possibly imagine? One of the Tower card's many excellent gifts is that it allows us to release predetermined expectations. How often has your heart's desire been standing right in front of you and you missed it because it didn't show up the way you expected?

Let's say you want to make money doing what you love, but you aren't sure what career is right for you. Create an alchemical question: "What can I do right now so that I am getting paid well for doing what I love and it brings me happiness and joy?" State the question out loud. Imagine yourself doing what you love to do. How does it feel? How do you look? How do you spend your days? Repeat the question and pull a card.

Think of something you desire right now. It could be as large and luminous as starting a new job in a foreign country or as simple as cultivating daily happiness.

What I want more than anything is…

My alchemical question is…

The card says…

One easy thing about tarot is that it offers us something simple to focus on. Lots of information flies at you during a reading. Life bombards us with enough distractions. The smallest shifts in life have the biggest side effects. Make it a habit to walk away from any tarot reading, any question, with a piece of advice from the cards. What is a single solid thing you can do?

Shuffle the cards and flip one.

One simple thing I can focus on to give me pleasure is…

Fun Exercise

There are times when you will want to work with your cards but are completely out of questions. No worries! I have you covered.

Let the cards create the question. Lay out a single card. Describe what you see. Figure out what question in your life this card is answering. For example, you flip the Sun card. You say, "I see a woman on a horse under a glowing sun. She is moving out into the world in freedom, bliss, and health." The question is "How can I move forward at this point in my life?" The answer is in freedom, bliss, and health. What one thing can I focus on? Moving ahead and taking action; even if you're unsure, keep moving.

Shuffle and flip a card.

The card is...

I see...

The question is...

The answer is...

TAROT REVERSALS

✦

Opposition

Blockage

Attention

Challenges

Patterns

✦

Reversals

Tarot reversals occur in a reading when cards appear upside down. These are cards who are shuffled and drawn and appear upside down to you from your point of view. When dealing cards for any spread—even a one-card spread—place the deck to your left and flip the cards over to your right. It should look like you are turning pages in a book. This is an important habit because you will avoid confusion. You will always know if a card is reversed no matter if you choose to read it as a reversal or not.

Your wild, beautiful life is not cut and dried, and neither is the upside-down world of tarot reversals. You'll eventually become a reversal renegade, selecting when and how you feel like working with them. Choose from the following list of techniques. Employ only one at a time at first, but be sure to try all of them out. Always decide ahead of time how you will read reversals before casting your cards. Adapt the techniques as you like so they work for you. Remember, your tarot practice is not about doing the cards the "right" way, but rather about reading cards in a unique style reflecting who you are, your deepest and highest self.

1) Reversal as opposite from regular meaning: This traditional take on reversals gives the reversed card the opposite meaning from its regular meaning. If the Ace of Cups means an emotional opening, a reversed Ace of Cups would mean being emotionally closed off. If the Wheel of Fortune suggests luck changing for the better, a reversed Wheel would suggest luck changing for the worse. If the Three of Swords reflects heartbreak, the reversed Three of Swords means heart healing, and so on.

Craft reversal meanings that are as rich as regular meanings by making space for them in your tarot journal. Continue to expand upon the reversed keyword meanings.

Pull your Ace of Wands and observe.

> *If an upright Ace of Wands reflects the spark of desire*
> *and new beginnings, a reversed Ace of Wands*
> *with the opposite meaning is...*

2) Reversal as blockage: The reversal reflects an energetic blockage that can be tended to once identified. You will become like an energy doctor when working this way. Once a block is diagnosed, you can figure out how to restore and heal it.

The Three of Cups usually shows three figures dancing, and its keywords are pleasure and friendship. Using the blockage technique, the reversed Three of Cups card indicates unexpressed feelings inside a friend relationship.

You've identified the block; now you can take action. In the Three of Cups example, let's say a close friend has hurt your feelings. You've garnered resentment, and there's some anger spilling into other relationships. You can decide then and there to forgive that person and pull an additional advice card on how to do it.

A beautiful magic action is always available to you with reversals: unblocking by turning the blocked card right-side up. As you turn the card, make a statement such as this one: "With this action, I open the flow of energy."

Pull your Seven of Cups and observe.

> *If an upright Seven of Cups means choices,*
> *options, and imagination, the blocked*
> *energy of the Seven of Cups means…*

3) Reversals screaming for attention: Reversals in large spreads become part of a pattern of cards. Reversals become indicators of cards that are dying for your attention. It is easy to gloss over the tough stuff when you are reading for yourself. Read reversals as a gasp for help in a spread. Let the reversal lead you to the root of an issue or challenge.

For example, a reversed Hermit appears in a seven-card spread between the Five of Pentacles (suggesting financial hardship) and Knight of Swords (suggesting swift action). The reversed Hermit should become the focal point of the reading. The Hermit usually holds a lantern, symbolizing shining your light of knowledge after a period of deep introspection. The reversal indicates that financial hardship is due to refusing to examine the situation from your true self. It suggests taking time to figure out what finance and responsibility mean to you; only then will you have the wisdom to salvage the issue at hand. Once this action is taken, the Knight of Swords suggests the problem is quickly alleviated.

Shuffle the cards and lay them out until you have a reversal with two upright cards on either side. Put the rest of the cards away and focus on these three. Read them as indicated above.

The reversal means...

4) Every card in the spread is reversed: This is a message that can't be ignored! Always take note when all cards are reversed. It implies the need for a deep and introspective dive into the root of your question. Find the solution to these blockages by flipping cards until an upright card appears. The upright card will hold a viable solution to the reversals.

Interpret the story of the cards as it refers to a deep-seated, subconscious issue. For instance, I pull the Four of Cups, the Two of Cups, and the King of Wands all upside down. It looks like the love and companionship I desire (represented by the Two of Cups) is being held back due to the lack of seeing opportunity (Four of Cups) because my eyes and attention are distracted by something else (as seen in the gaze of the King of Wands). I flip the remaining cards until an upright card appears. It is the Knight of Pentacles. He advises me to create something solid in the real world that can be implemented (the pentacle in his hand) as I move forward into the future (reflected by the plowed field waiting its seed), but to take it slow as it won't happen overnight (the speed of his horse). I decide to schedule a romantic dinner every Tuesday night, either homemade or out at a cozy restaurant with no phone, no distractions, so my husband and I can focus on each other.

Shuffle the deck and place three cards in front of you. Turn them all to the reversed position.

It looks like the story of these cards says...

Pull from the remaining cards until an upright card appears.

The advice is to...

5) Reversal as challenges overcome: A reversed card can be interpreted as an issue that was once challenging but no longer holds you back. If the Page of Cups reflects listening to one's intuition, a reversed Page of Cups shows it used to be hard for you to follow your instincts, but now it is a natural and easy process for you. If the Ten of Wands is a challenge overcome, the reversal indicates you are now easily able to carry a heavy workload.

Pull a card and reverse it if it appears upright.

*This card says I used to have an issue with...,
but now I...*

6) Reversals as the light and dark sides: Life is a mixture of light and shadow, expansion and repression, yin and yang. Sometimes you are up to greet the greatest challenge with vim and vigor, while other times you'd just as soon crawl under your covers and let the cards fall where they may.

+ An upright card holds the expansive qualities of the card like a balloon growing larger.

+ A reversal holds the contractive qualities of the card like the air leaking from a balloon.

The Empress reflects creativity and abundance flowing outward (expansive), while the reversal would reflect so much creativity and motion that it blots out the light of day (contractive). This marks the difference between a productive artist and a manic artist or a caring mother and a depressed mother.

The Devil reflects manipulation and control flowing outward (expansive), while the reversal would indicate so much internal force and cruelty that it literally destroys him (contractive). A reversed Devil, therefore, loses his power, literally sets the chained lovers free, and vanishes.

Pull a card.

If an expansive _____ means...,
then a contractive _____ means...

7) Ignore reversals: A reversal can be ignored and simply flipped right-side up. This is the best technique while you are learning. Move at your own pace. Don't overcomplicate your readings. Get comfortable with the deck. Ignoring reversals is an option for anyone, anytime, regardless of reading experience or level.

Major vs. Minor

This is an important distinction. The first clue to understanding the difference between the majors and minors is found in the name. The majors reflect big, huge life moments while minors express our day-to-day lives. Majors mark growth and evolution while minors express normal occurrences or things we do. Majors do not only express external, obvious life-marker moments such as graduations, birthdays, weddings, etc., but, more importantly, majors mark moments of internal growth and/or essential components of your consciousness as a soul expressing itself in the material world.

Major arcana moments are those big lessons and turning points. If you see lots of major cards in a spread, it means you are at a crucial life junction. Major arcana cards have broad implications and sweeping effects on our lives while the minor arcana are small day-to-day activities. The minor arcana are the seemingly insignificant things we do—although remember big magic springs from small actions. These are our touch-and-go moments, things we do regularly, and the stuff that makes up the routines and perspectives of daily life. Minor arcana issues occur inside the greater scope of the majors.

The Fool's Journey is a helpful way to examine the cards. The Fool is traditionally the joker or the wild card in a regular pack of playing cards. The Fool is special in tarot because his number is zero. Zero represents all

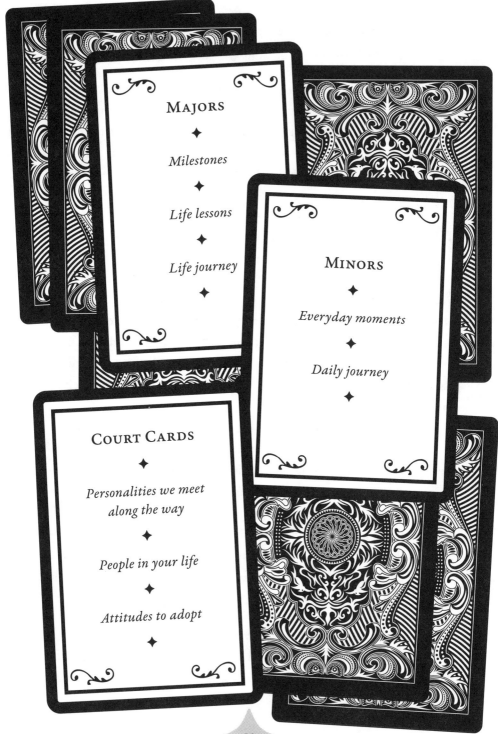

MAJORS

✦

Milestones

✦

Life lessons

✦

Life journey

✦

MINORS

✦

Everyday moments

✦

Daily journey

✦

COURT CARDS

✦

*Personalities we meet
along the way*

✦

People in your life

✦

Attitudes to adopt

✦

things, all potential, and all possibility. Therefore, just like the joker in a deck of regular cards, the Fool has extra-special superpowers.

Did you ever play the game Candy Land? Think of the Fool as a token on a game board who moves from card to card and learns a lesson at each turn. Each card is a learning experience, an expression of the Fool (or yourself), or a suggestion or solution. The only difference between Candy Land/tarot and your personal journey is that the Fool is you and the game board is your life.

Major arcana is:

+ a learning or growing moment

+ past, present, future experience

+ expressions of the soul

+ suggestions, ideas, and solutions

The last time I experienced an essential life lesson was when...

Yesterday the highlight of my day was...

The thing I want most right now is...

Tomorrow I hope to...

My soul shines out into the world when I...

The solution to my current challenge is to...

Hero's Journey

Author Joseph Campbell identified the Hero's Journey as a narrative pattern found in ritual, religious myth, and storytelling. Tarot's structure aligns itself perfectly with the narrative pattern Campbell describes. The Hero's Journey structure is embedded within great works of art, literature, and theater. This storyline is a metaphor for growth, lessons, and life experience, and you'll find it inside tarot's major arcana.

The Hero's Journey is symbolic, eternal, and archetypal. An archetype is a collective human idea and original model on which similar things are patterned. Plato's Theory of Forms states that the essence of a thing is its underlying form or idea. Jungian psychology explains archetype as an innate universal prototype.

Archetypes can be simple recurring symbols like the dove reflecting the idea of peace. An archetype can be a recurring motif in literature or painting. Lover's archetypes include Adam and Eve or Shakespeare's Romeo and Juliet.

Each of us embarks on a Hero's Journey in our life. Our triumphs and tribulations foster personal growth as we become closer to who and what we really are. It is the journey of wisdom and understanding.

The major arcana is a symbolic representation of this voyage. The cards will always graciously indicate where we are in our journey on a daily, monthly, or yearly basis. Reading cards or having your cards read, you become the Hero. The cards reflect your journey. Reading for a friend or client, the friend or client becomes the Hero, and the cards reflect their journey.

Just as the universe is chock-full of stars and galaxies, so tarot is filled with symbolic and literal archetypes. They are the underlying pillars of tarot. Tarot's major arcana reflects an ideal example of the Hero's Journey through three distinct stages: the earthly journey, the spiritual journey, and the heavenly journey.

The Earthly Journey

Major arcana cards zero through seven reflect the earthly journey. The Fool (0) sets off in search of adventure and experience. He encounters a series of terrestrial authorities, each more powerful than the previous one: a street Magician (1), a virginal High Priestess (2), a maternal Empress (3), an authoritarian Emperor (4), a pontificating Hierophant (5). Once finding true love (the Lovers, 6), the Fool becomes as powerful as is possible for a human being (the Chariot, 7). From an earthly point of view, the journey is finished. However, the journey has just begun.

THE SPIRITUAL JOURNEY

Cards seven through fourteen reflect the spiritual journey. The Fool understands power resides beyond mere material dominance (Strength, 8). Removing himself from society (the Hermit, 9), he intuits the mystical mechanics of reality (the Wheel, 10) and discovers there is a higher power and purpose in the universe (Justice, 11). Facing a difficult test (the Hanged Man, 12), the Fool loses everything (Death, 13). During the process, the Fool discovers the true meaning of life (Temperance, 14). This concludes the Fool's spiritual growth.

The Heavenly Journey

Cards fifteen through twenty-one reflect the heavenly journey. Having overcome and faced profound fears (the Devil, 15), then having broken and destroyed pride (the Tower, 16), the Fool ascends to the heavens (the Star, 17; the Moon, 18; the Sun, 19) to face one final test (Judgement, 20). Passing the test, the Fool is worthy of the greatest possible reward (the World, 21).

Pulling apart the deck is a great way to get to know the cards. Tarot, like the body, connects with a specific skeletal structure. Grasp the basic structure and you'll be on your way to card meanings. The cards work together like the four seasons. Each suit and number carries its own special characteristics that interrelate in a spread.

Learning tarot is like learning how to cook or bake. Once you grasp the basics of flavor and purpose of ingredients for your chosen style of cuisine, you can begin to create endless options.

Pull out your tarot deck and place it in front of you.

+ MAKE A MAJOR ARCANA PILE: The majors have fancy titles such as Empress, Star, and World.

+ MAKE A MINOR ARCANA PILE: The minors are the ace through ten of each suit (pentacles, swords, wands, and cups).

+ MAKE A COURT CARD PILE: The court cards are titled page, knight, queen, and king of each suit.

It is normal to get a little confused when you are first pulling apart your deck, especially if it has been shuffled. Take your time and enjoy the process. Feel free to repeat this as often as possible, and time yourself to see how quickly you can do it.

Tarot Suits

The suits and their corresponding elements are essential in tarot reading and magic. It is said in the West that there are four classical elements interplaying with one another to make up the world as we know it: earth, air, fire, and water. These four elements are used in ritual and assigned to the four directions on a map: north, south, east, and west. Animals, both real and mythical, are assigned to each element. Winged creatures and fairies align with air, fish and mermaids to water, lizards and dragons to fire, and burrowing animals and gnomes to earth. Astrology assigns an element with each sign of the zodiac so you will know if you are an air sign, a water sign, a fire sign, or an earth sign. It is enormously helpful for your practice to understand how the four elements relate to the four suits.

Swords (mind) are air. Air is invisible; it is felt but not seen. Air can move quickly or be staid. Air makes life possible, provides us oxygen, and fills our lungs. It is the delicate surface sustaining our human life and saving us from the cold, bleak death of outer space.

Air connects to the suit of swords because our thoughts move quickly. Our brain can feel like a flurry of activity. When we try to quiet the mind, thoughts come rushing in to fill the empty space. Air connects to the suit of swords because it moves things along and our thoughts are contracted to help us figure things out. Physically, the mind is reflected by the brain in the highest point of the body. Air reaches to the highest outer limits of planet Earth.

Many tarots will include air visuals on their sword cards. This will help you identify a sword card, and it will also offer you information about that card's energy. For example, in the Rider-Waite-Smith deck, readers will find many cards with bodies of water and clouds. The water and the clouds are sometimes still and calm, reflecting air energy that is slow moving, and other times stormy or wild, reflecting tumultuous or quick-moving energy like that felt on a windy day. Sword court cards will often include air symbols such as birds, butterflies, and big skies.

Consider for a moment what air feels like. Bring the qualities of air to your mind. List them in your journal.

Swords and air are...

Cups (heart) are water. Water is in constant state of flux, just like our emotions. Water is liquid; it evaporates, turning to mist and cloud, fog and ice, before transforming back into water again. Water is rain, snow, sleet, and hail. Bodies of water—lakes, ponds, rivers, and muddy creeks—flow with unique energy. Water makes up 60 percent of our bodies and 71 percent of Earth's surface.

Pentacles = Money,
objects, people

Swords = Thoughts,
stories, ideas

Wands = Passion,
energy, career

Cups = Emotions,
dreams, love

SUITS & ELEMENTS

Earth = Pentacles

Air = Swords

Fire = Wands

Water = Cups

Water has incredible depth (especially ocean waters), and this connects to qualities of empathy and compassion. Think of how dangerous people with the inability to feel emotion or empathy are (i.e., sociopaths). Water and our emotional state are imperative to human life.

Tsunamis, thunderstorms, and snowstorms are indicative of storms of emotions. Consider the phrase "my heart is frozen" or "bursting." Think of how quickly a piece of art, book, or song will bring an emotion to the surface. And when emotions surface, it literally feels like they are rising up from the depths of water. Our tears are made of flowing water droplets when we laugh hard or cry.

Many tarots will include water visuals on their cups cards. This will help you identify a cups card, and it will also offer you information about that card's energy. You might see aquatic animals, mermaids, and the sea or flowing water. Cups court cards will often have water symbols in the court's clothing or have a seaside environment to express the element of water.

Consider for a moment what water feels like. Bring the qualities of water to your mind. List them in your journal.

Cups and water are...

Wands (gut) are fire. Fire is as nurturing as it is dangerous, just like intention and desire. A flickering candle illuminates a room with a mysterious glow. A cracking fire provides heat and cooks food. Wildfires can rage out of control, consuming everything in their path. Fire must be fed; it must consume in order to maintain itself. The sun is a symbol of fire at the center of our solar system. Fire is the most volatile of elements, and humankind's mastery over fire was a game changer in evolution.

Fire is related to everything about us that has to do with energy. It is will and intensity. You have heard expressions like "fire of the soul" or "I am totally burned out" or "hot under the collar." Lovers often describe how their bodies heat up just thinking about the object of their affection. Crowds at protests, concerts, and group events get excited and feel "fired up."

Many tarots will include fire visuals on their wands cards. This will help you identify a wand card. You might see actual fire, torches, and candles on the card. You may spot fire elementals like lizards or dragons. Court cards may include desert scenarios, hot suns, and fire symbols like pyramids and sunflowers to help you identify them as wand cards.

Consider for a moment what fire feels like. Bring the qualities of fire to your mind. List them in your journal.

Wands and fire are...

Pentacles (body) are earth. Earth is rich and fecund. It is the grounding sustenance we take refuge in. It is where we plant crops, make our homes, and craft our lives. Earth is alive and rich; everything springing from the dirt is at our fingertips. The earth is the resource we all require and contains the building blocks of life. Earth is what we are made of and what we are. We are part of nature, not separate from it.

The suit of pentacles and earth is everything that is at our fingertips, from money in the bank and in our wallet to our flesh and bones. It is soft pillows, the car in our driveway, and the dream house we will some-day inhabit. You may have heard the expressions "she is a very grounded person" or "it's a muddy situation" or "we'll move heaven and earth to get this done." These all spring from the nature of elemental earth.

Many tarots will include earth visuals on their pentacles cards. This will help you identify a pentacle card. You might see plants, flowers, trees, and vegetation; you will often see a crowded card as things accumulate. Court card figures will often be seated in lush gardens, sprawling king-doms, or display wealth to help you identify them as pentacle cards.

Consider for a moment what earth feels like. Bring the qualities of earth to your mind. List them in your journal.

Pentacles and earth are...

You Are the Unfolding Eyes of the Universe

The four suits of tarot are very simple to interpret when you understand how they directly relate to you inside your body and in your experience of living. You experience all four suits all the time even if you are unaware of this. The key to unlocking tarot is to observe your expression of the cards.

You are the universe. Divinity. Pure consciousness. Everything you see, notice, observe, listen to, eat, laugh at, make fun of, enjoy, dislike, resist, and surrender to is the universe seeing itself, understanding itself, and recognizing itself. What is true for you is true for the universe. What is true for the universe is true for you. As above, so below.

You, like the Fool, are on a journey, a quest, an adventure. The journey of who you are, like a sacred circle, will lead you back to yourself. The World circles back to the Fool and begins the journey again. Your journey begins with you. It ends with you. You may travel to the edges of your backyard or to the far-flung reaches of the world. The exterior world is energy changing form—a mere illusion. Your interior life and your inner roads bear the mark of eternity. It is the internal journey that matters. Everything else? Shadows and dust.

Each day as you wake, the mystery of who you are unfolds a bit further. You move forward, backward, or sideways on your respective path, closer to or further from your goals. You speed along on cruise control. Other times, you become lost in thorny thickets, gasping for air in quicksand. We instigate cause and effect with our actions and deeds. We fill the world with our energy. We give energy away to other people and things or we spend it wisely on what we love, reinvesting energy in ourselves.

You are the active observer of everything that has ever occurred in your life. You are the sole experiencer of your life. We are each centers of our own universe. Humans are like glowing, fiery suns. We float in the center of a personal solar system made of life events, family, friends, jobs, school, pains, and pleasures. Inside this constant revolution, some people and events come closer while others move away only to return in a future cycle as our gravitational energy pulls them back in. We respond to each experience, to what we draw near and what we press away.

You wake in the morning to sunlight streaming across your pillow. You feel the aliveness of the body inside your skin and humming bones. You are a child who loves to play, you are a teenager who yearns to break free, you are a young adult who is scared but bold, you are middle aged with responsibilities, you are old with a softening body and the mark of wisdom on your face. You smile with eyes twinkling because beneath it all, you are still YOU.

This piece of you, this observer, remains unchanged from when you were three to your current age to your ninety-eighth birthday and beyond.

> *My earliest memory is...*
>
> *One of my favorite childhood foods was...*
>
> *A funny early memory from childhood is...*
>
> *I remember being small because...*

The active observer is you beyond the thoughts and judgments forming in your mind.

The active observer is you beyond your emotions, which come and go, rise and fall.

The active observer is you beyond your passions, desires, and habits.

The active observer is you beyond your body, your age, and your possessions.

Bliss is your natural state. It is the essence of who you are. Babies, toddlers, and small children engage in complete immersion with presence on a moment-to-moment basis. Infants do not consider the past or future. Toddlers are not preoccupied with how they appear to others. Children find wonder and delight in blades of grass and cardboard boxes. This is bliss.

When you look at a brilliant orange sunset, the universe sees through your eyes. You hug your best friend, and the universe is hugging too. You dive into the foamy ocean, rise up, and splash the saltwater around you, and the universe sees and feels it too.

The bliss body is illustrated in the World card. The World dancer moves in rhythm with the universe. She attains loss of ego, freedom in the moment, and complete awareness. The dancer's choreography is ingrained; she need not think of it. She transcends her thoughts, feelings, and desires by responding to each string of music as if it is the first time she has heard it.

Understanding the active observer and nature of bliss helps you discover how the four suits operate in your life. The four suits are literally like layers of a cake sitting on top of your active awareness. Your active awareness is the creamy center of an indulgent cake. It's the sweet spot you want to get to.

The layers—wands, swords, pentacles, cups—are not bad; quite the contrary. These layers are essential to who you are and your development. But once you know and identify these different layers, you will learn to respond to them rather than letting them control you. This will dramatically alter all relationships. Knowing how to do this also places your destiny into your graceful hands.

The ultimate goal is not to secure a constant, continual state of twenty-four-hour bliss as exists inside the World card. That sets up an unattainable ideal. The goal is to become aware of what is happening inside your brain and body. Tarot will give you many clues, like a roadmap. Once you are aware, you create a space of observation. This is conscious awareness.

Awareness, space, and attention encourage
magic to unfold by…

Swords (mind)—If tarot is storytelling (which it is), then swords are the stories themselves. Swords are the library inside your brain—every book, story, lesson, movie, and fairy tale you've ever read, watched, told, or retold. The suit of swords reflects your mind and everything you think.

Swords are every word you've ever uttered. Swords are the sentiments you write in an email, a letter, or a text. Swords are the manner in which you speak to others. Swords are the voices inside your head. They are the words of others falling out of their mouths and into your ears. It is the mental images, mind games, and scenarios you create about the past, present, and future. Now you know why the suit of swords looks scary.

Beyond the words we speak, swords reflect all mental processes behind the articulation of our thoughts. It is the conditioning of your mind based off of previous experiences. Swords are calculations, judgments, and decisions. Swords are how you interpret experiences. Swords are ideas and plans you have laid. Swords are the reasoning and rationalization behind what you do and how you act. It is the idea of who you are. They are the decisions that shape and mold the ego you have created.

Cups (heart) are pure emotion. They represent everything you have ever felt and will ever feel, from excruciating visceral pain to exhilarating happiness. Cups are profound sadness, sun-shining hope, and bright optimism. Cups reflect depression, gloom, and joy. Cups are the entire emotional scale as it exists inside of you. Cups hold tears, laughter, happiness, and, above all things, love.

Cups are everything the heart is capable of feeling. Cups reflect the luminous imagination and all the waking and sleeping dreams you've ever experienced. Cups reflect empathy and are the ability to feel compassion for what another person is feeling. Cups reflect the instinct and expression of all forms of art. Cups reflect flights of fancy, overwhelming laughter, and the deep intrinsic affection you feel and express. Cups are the sense of love and connection between yourself and others. Cups are the feeling you are experiencing right now.

Wands (gut) reflect the driving force of energy and the intensity of desire. Wands wake you up in the morning. Wands get you out of bed and put a spring in your step as you slip out the door. Wands are the spark of romance, sensual desire, and spicy erotic attraction. Wands are spiritual rapture.

Wands are pure inspiration and the energy that makes anything you put effort behind grow and flourish. It is what keeps you focused. It is also what can spiral out of control when it's allowed to run wild.

Wands reflect career and life choices. Wands reflect your energy levels and hot, boiling blood racing through your veins. Wands tend to get things done but can also wear you out because they tend to run so hot and so strong. Wands are the stamina and charisma you express to the world.

• • • • • •

A note about wands and cups: It is important to differentiate between the desire reverberating inside wands and the fluid emotion spilling out of cups. They should not be confused. Desire and love intertwine like vines of woven wisteria and honeysuckle, but they are two distinctly different things. Desire requires action, while love requires feeling. Love moves mountains, but it can also be a passive experience. Desire and the suit of wands always carry a physical, visible side effect: the spark of flirtation that brings people together, a flash of passion moving a person or crowd to action, the fire ignited when injustice is witnessed or experienced. The element of longing—that toe-curling, sweet ache of painful deliciousness that is never satisfying, that deep-in-your-bones longing—comes straight from wands.

• • • • • •

Pentacles (body) reflect everything you can see, smell, taste, observe, and feel. Pentacles are the material elements in the world. They are the soft, cozy blanket wrapped around you as well as your body itself. Pentacles are other people, places, and all things on the planet with physical form, mass, and structure.

Pentacles represent resources available to us and the results we reap. It is the stuff we surround ourselves with, the food we eat, the things we purchase, and the stuff we create. Pentacles represent money and all issues surrounding your financial life. Pentacles are all the ways the physical and tangible world appears to us in its ever-changing forms.

Active Awareness Meditation Exercise

Perform a meditation where you notice what crosses your mind and you identify it as sword (thought), wand (desire), cup (imagination), or pentacle (physical reaction).

Sit quietly where you will not be disturbed. Have a timer (either on your phone or an alarm) with you. Pull all four aces out of your deck and place them in front of you from left to right in the following order: Ace of Swords, Ace of Wands, Ace of Cups, and Ace of Pentacles.

Focus on the Ace of Swords. Observe it. Notice every single detail. Close your eyes and bring to mind an image of a sword. Perhaps it is silver, sleek, and sharp. This is a thought. Become aware of your thoughts for the next minute. How does it feel to listen to your inner voice? Clear your mind and become alert for the next crossing thought. Come back further and watch your thoughts coming and going without interrupting or repressing them. Just notice.

You have just experienced the nature of swords and thoughts.

The thoughts repeating in my mind like crazy today are...

Focus on the Ace of Wands. Observe it. Notice every single detail. Close your eyes and bring to mind the image of a wand. Perhaps it is vibrant, glowing, and pulsating with power. Consider what you desire in this present moment. What is the focal point of your energy right now? What consumes your attention on a deep internal level? What are you after? If you were a character in a novel, what is your goal, your aim? Are you striving to attain something professionally? Are you lusting after someone? Who is it? What purpose are they serving for you? Does it serve your highest good?

You have just experienced the nature of wands and desire.

The thing I desire more than anything right now is...

Focus on the Ace of Cups. Observe it. Notice every single detail. Close your eyes and bring to mind the image of a cup. It may be a golden chalice or a sleek wine glass. Consider how you are feeling. What is your emotional state? Are you feeling giddy, excited, creative? Sad, gloomy, annoyed? Move deeper. Pick your feelings up, roll them out, and examine them. Are they distracted, imaginative, or excruciating? How have you been feeling lately? How do you feel right now?

You have just experienced the nature of cups and emotion.

My feelings right now are...

Focus on the Ace of Pentacles. Observe it. Notice every single detail. Close your eyes and bring to mind the image of a pentacle. It might be a witch's pentagram or a shiny coin. Bring your awareness to your physical body. Feel the respiration of your breath moving in and out. How do you actually feel on a physical level? Are your muscles tight? Is the air a pleasant temperature on your skin? What part of your body begins asking you for attention through a twinge, an itch, or restlessness? What feels good and expansive?

You have just experienced the nature of pentacles and the physical body.

My body feels like...

0 = Possibility

1 = Origin

2 = Duality

3 = Birth

4 = Stability

5 = Challenge

6 = Harmony

7 = Mystery

8 = Equilibrium

9 = Manifestation

10 = Culmination

Numbers and Patterns

Humans are hardwired to recognize patterns. Children are taught to discover patterns through mathematics. Patterning helps us make predictions, understand relationships, and arrive at conclusions. Numerical relationships may seem cold and abstract, but a subtle and powerful magic governs the nature of numbers. A deeper examination of numbers will help you cultivate meanings of the cards while giving you clues to the foundational building blocks of the universe.

ZERO
Key: Possibility

No. Thing.

Creation stories and myths are apt to begin the same way: "At first there was nothing." Nothingness is associated with the number zero. Zero contains the potential of all things. Zero is formless space of all possibility and the expansiveness supporting earth, air, fire, and water. Zero is the space between cards in a reading. Zero is the nothing that contains absolutely everything.

Zero's symbol is a circle. Zero is an egg before fertilization. Zero is the shape of the sun, moon, and all planets, including our own Earth. Zero's circular shape is Earth's track as it revolves around the sun. The circle is the shape of the molecules making up our bodies, the shape of our eyes, the wheel.

Mandalas and temple circuits echo the pattern of the universal circle. Tibetan Buddhists walk temple circuits around sacred sites. For example, when pilgrims come to Lhasa, the Holy City, many come after spending months on foot. Once they arrive, they walk clockwise around a sacred temple as part of their worship. As they move, they spin prayer wheels both in their hands and golden prayer wheels around the buildings. This action is quite beautiful and adds a vortex of energy around structures and sacred mountains.

Imagine sitting alone inside the darkness of the red velvet jewel box that is Broadway Theater on opening night. Listen to the quiet before the stage door is unlocked. Feel the vibrating silence before the stage lights are thrown. Observe the stillness before the actors spill into their dressing rooms laughing and chatting. Imagine the calm before the ticket operator hangs his coat and pulls opens the window. Sense the spaciousness before the perfumed crowd pushes up to the bar and finds their seats. Hear the expansiveness before the musical overture's crash, waves of laughter, and a swell of curtain applause. This complete darkness and silence of an empty theater is akin to the feeling of zero. It is nothing yet contains everything. Zero is infused with all things. Inside its depth and potential is the humming motor of the universe.

Observe the Fool card.

> *The Fool is assigned the number zero because...*
>
> *The Fool's "empty head" is a gift because...*

ONE

Key: Origin

One is the beginning. A flame in the dark. A dot on a horizon. The first star in the evening sky. It is the moment you are birthed. Your first gasp of air. The first drop of paint on a canvas. A drip of water from the faucet. The hot tear falling from your eye. The first snowflake of a blizzard. A flower shoot poking through the earth. A cumulus cloud forming in the sky. One is connected to the root chakra, located at the base of the spine, which is also the first part of the human body to develop in utero.

One is the beginning. The original. It is the first thing appearing inside the field of cosmic possibility. The number one bears origin on all the cards it appears upon.

Pull the Magician and all four aces.

> *The Magician is numbered one because...*
>
> *I can see the Ace of Wands begins the suit of fire because...*
>
> *I can see the Ace of Cups begins the suit of water because...*
>
> *I can see the Ace of Swords begins the suit of air because...*
>
> *I can see the Ace of Pentacles begins the suit of earth because...*

Two

Key: Duality

The number two acts as a reflection, as clear as a looking glass. Two is a double. Two is the essence of duality like a cell dividing itself in mitosis. Energy now radiates back and forth between the relationship of two things. Lovers gaze at each other. A pair of friends sit beneath a moonlight sky confiding in one another about their wildest dreams. A person, place, or thing absorbs and reflects energy back to the other. This is why our personal attention and focus (as exemplified by the Magician's wand) is powerful. We choose to focus on something and light that thing up with power and energy. We magnetize it. We enter into partnership with it. The number two bears duality upon all the cards it appears upon.

I am currently focusing most of my attention on...

I would like to focus more of my attention on...

Pull the High Priestess and all twos out of the minor arcana.

I can see these cards reflect the nature of duality because....

Pull out the Justice card (11 = 1 + 1 = 2).

Pull out the Judgement card (20 = 2 + 0 = 2)

Justice and Judgement contain duality because...

• • • • • •

Bonus exercise: Inspect your tarot cards to discover the graphic nature of two. Go through each card of your deck and pull out any card with a mirror or reflecting image of two similar things. Do you find two sphinxes on your Chariot card? Two towers on the Moon card? Two pillars on the High Priestess, Justice, and Hierophant cards?

• • • • • •

Three

Key: Birth

Three is the universal number of creativity. Three occurs from the collision of the first two objects. Birth is the metaphor for the emergence of something new. Partners create a home. A couple creates or adopts a child. Famous triads in history and mythology reflect the significance of number three: the Celtic triple deity, Maiden/Mother/Crone, Christianity's Father/Son/Holy Ghost, the philosophy of Mind/Body/Spirit, the triad between our two physical eyes and our invisible third eye. Ayurvedic medicine is based on the balance of three bodily humors (Vata, Pitta, and Kapha). The graphic triangle is used to represent the channeling of divine energy. This is seen in church steeples, temple towers, and the witch's cone hat.

The number three is a tiebreaker during competition: "Best of three wins!" Psychology makes use of the Id, Ego, and Super Ego. There are three primary and three secondary colors. Human special relations (how we find our sense of space) include height, width, and depth. We see trilogies in books and movies as the basic narrative line of the human brain moves from beginning, challenge, and resolution. The universal basis of any story contains three sacred elements, beginning, middle and end. The number three bears creativity on all the cards it appears upon.

An important triad in my life includes...

I feel creative when I...

Pull the Empress and all threes out of the minor arcana.

I can see these cards reflect the nature of creativity because....

Pull out the Hanged Man (12 = 1 + 2 = 3).
Pull out the World card (21 = 2 + 1 = 3)

The Hanged Man and World reflect creativity because...

Four
Key: Stability

Four points create a square, stable cubic space. We move from the creativity of three into the solid nature of four. A skyscraper could not stand upon a triangle. Stability and grounding require the number four. It is the shape of a house, a box, a chair, a cube. Look around the kitchen and find squarely shaped potholders, tables, windows, stoves and, if you are lucky, square-cut chocolate brownies.

Stability in the material world springs from the number four. We experience four elemental directions (north, south, east, west), four elements (earth, air, fire, water), and the four suits of tarot (cups, swords, wands, pentacles). Hebrew lore claims God spoke the world into existence by uttering "Yod, He, Vav, He." The national mantra of Tibet is the sacred four-word expression "Om mani padme hum." There are four deadly horseman spreading doom and gloom in the Christian end-of-days story. There are four gospel writers in the Bible (Matthew, John, Mark, Luke) as well as four creatures found in the tetragrammaton (man, lion, bull, eagle), displayed clearly in the four corners of the RWS Wheel of Fortune and World cards. Your tarot deck is a set of four corner cards that, when stacked, create a rectangular pile not unlike a small brick. The number four brings stability to all the cards it appears upon.

Pull the Emperor and all fours out of the minor arcana.

I see the nature of stability on these cards because...

Pull out the Death card (13 = 1 + 3 = 4).

The Death card reflects stability because...

• • • • • •

Bonus exercise: Move through every card of your tarot deck and look for square and rectangular shapes. Where do you find them?

• • • • • •

FIVE

Key: Challenge

Five is a sticky number representing challenges and stumbling blocks. Stability is achieved in the four, and now it is time to explore the environment. A restlessness and energy permeate the number five. Opportunities and struggles appear. Five lets us know what we are up against. Five is the halfway point to the number ten. Logic dictates this is where things fall apart and get tough. Lessons are learned at the number five; obstacles are tackled that lead to growth and progression. It is the challenge of the five that creates the energy needed to see your way to the finish line.

Five is the number of complexity. We have five fingers and five toes. There are five senses in our body (smell, taste, touch, hearing, seeing). There are five points to a magic star also known as a pentagram. There are five vowels in the English language and five major oceans on our planet. The number five bears energy and strife across all the cards it appears upon.

Pull out the Hierophant and all fives out of the minor arcana.

I see the nature of challenge in these cards because...

Pull out the Temperance card (14 = 1 + 4 = 5).

The Temperance card reflects challenge because...

Six

Key: Harmony

Six is the big beating heart of tarot. It pulsates with love because it is found at the center of the Tree of Life. It is the number of expansion. Six is three (the number of creativity) twice (3 + 3) and looks like an upside-down 9 (which is 3 + 3 + 3). The heart is the mechanism that purifies and pumps the blood to all areas of the body. Consider the sixes of tarot as being the place where restorative energy is distributed after the upheaval of the challenging number five. The number six is harmonic energy.

Examine the minor arcana sixes in the Rider-Waite-Smith deck and you'll notice a visual hierarchy. A single character rises above others. The feminine suits of cups and pentacles reflect a character offering gifts to those below him, and the masculine suits of swords and wands depict figures in motion above others. Once the experience of the five has been satisfied, a sense of love and sharing pervades, and social harmony and evolution blossom. The number six bears harmony across all the cards it appears upon.

Pull out the Lovers and all sixes out of the minor arcana.

I see the nature of harmony in these cards because...

Pull out the Devil card (15 = 1 + 5 = 6).

The Devil reflects the nature of harmony because...

SEVEN

Key: Uncanny

The material world is established in the physical and emotional sense. The seven begins contemplation of the self inside the known universe. Strangeness emerges when we deeply analyze past experiences and present situations. Developed skills must be perfected in order to gain a desired future. Physical rest is important while mental work abounds.

Seven carries mystical qualities like a cloak. We move through a repetitive cycle of seven days until the week resets itself. Seven glowing energy chakras spin inside the human body, each with its own precise function. Seven visible planets (moon, Mercury, Venus, sun, Mars, Jupiter, Saturn) can be seen by the naked eye and have been known since antiquity as the classical planets. Christian traditions preach of the seven deadly sins countered and paired with seven heavenly virtues, one of which is even found inside the tarot deck (envy/kindness, lust/chastity, gluttony/temperance, sloth/diligence, wrath/patience, pride/humility, greed/charity). People have been naming and renaming the Seven Wonders of the World since ancient times. The number seven bears the uncanny across all the cards it appears upon.

Pull the Chariot and all sevens out of the minor arcana.

I see the nature of uncanniness inside these cards because...

Pull out the Tower card (16 = 1 + 6 = 7)

The Tower card is uncanny because...

EIGHT

Key: Equilibrium

Sensual number eight swoops into the sublime shape of the female figure. Write the number eight and you see the hourglass symbol. Place it sideways and it becomes the lemniscate, the symbol of infinity, of yin. Look to the Magician and Strength cards and discover the infinity symbol above the characters' heads. Eight suggests the perfection of the journey before its culmination in the number ten. Personal effort is reflected in reward. You have come so far. You now have something to show for your work. It would be enough to stop the journey now, but tarot reflects life, and in life there is always a delicious surprise waiting past the next turn.

There are eight limbs of yoga, and Buddhism cherishes the Noble Eightfold Path to enlightenment. Judaism ordains circumcision be performed on the eighth day of a boy's life, and Hanukkah is an eight-day holiday. The Wiccan calendar marks eight sabbaths and festivals. Spiders spin webs with eight legs. Eight p.m. was the traditional resting time of prime-time evening television programming, while 8 a.m. is traditionally the time we leave the house for work and school. Eight is karmic energy, where we reap what we have sown. The number eight bears equilibrium across all the cards it appears upon.

Pull the Strength card and all the eights out of the minor arcana.

I see the nature of equilibrium inside these cards because...

Pull out the Star $(17 = 1 + 7 = 8)$.

The Star reflects equilibrium because...

NINE
Key: Manifestation

The number nine is the place of release after learning the cyclical nature of life. The light of wisdom shines, and all that was gained is now given back. Everything becomes richer. Rewards are enjoyed and distributed.

The number nine is three to the third power. The number nine holds a unique position in the Qabalah. This is the spot on the Tree of Life where the invisible funnels into the material world. It is being the number of manifestation. The Tree of Life is graphically represented as three intersecting triangles, thus it echoes a triad of creativity powerful enough to manifest any desire, wish, or idea.

Nine is release and results. Your dream comes true. The check arrives. The house is yours. The keys are placed in your hand. The invisible becomes embodied in the physical world. This is the culmination card.

The number nine bears the nature of manifestation on all the cards it appears across.

Pull the Hermit and all the nines out of the minor arcana.

I see the nature of manifestation inside these cards because...

Pull out the Moon ($18 = 1 + 8 = 9$).

The Moon reflects manifestation because...

TEN

Key: Culmination

The journey has concluded. The story is over. The credits roll at the end of a film. The hero rides off into the sunset. The year circles back around. You leave your home only to return once again. Day falls to night as night fades to day in the endless cycle.

Add up the first ten numbers to arrive at the number 55. Reduce 55 by adding 5 and 5 and you'll find yourself back at the number 10. Here inside the number 10 we reduce it further to discover the 0 and 1. At the end we find the beginning and renewal of a fresh story. The number 10 bears the nature of culmination on all the cards it appears across.

Pull the Wheel of Fortune and all the tens out of minor arcana.

I see the nature of culmination inside these cards because...

Pull out the Sun ($19 = 1 + 9 = 10$).

The Sun reflects culmination because...

Finding Numerical Patterns in Tarot Spreads

Numbers come in handy for card interpretation as well as when you are reading multiple cards. The numbers are a shortcut to reading because they will tell you where the situation is and where and how it is developing. For example, if you cast a spread containing many aces, it suggests there are a lot of new ideas and opportunities. It also suggests the situation is in beginning stages because number one means a start. Conversely, if multiple tens appear in a spread, it suggests the situation is ending and winding down.

✦ 1's = beginnings and fresh ideas

✦ 2's = multiple choices to be made before you proceed

✦ 3's = creativity and cooperation are required

✦ 4's = stability supports you

✦ 5's = multitudes of challenges

✦ 6's = gifts and generous feelings

✦ 7's = luck and synchronicity

✦ 8's = ease, flow, and results

✦ 9's = getting what you asked for

✦ 10's = the situation reaches its conclusion

If a multitude of court cards appear in a spread, it suggests many people and personalities are involved in the situation. You may be listening too carefully to the opinions of others rather than following your heart and inner instincts.

Intuitive Shorthand

Here's a simple formula to aid you in number and card interpretation.

Looking at the linear progression of the numbers from one to ten, you will see that one is the beginning, five is the middle of the challenge, and ten is the ending. All the other numbers fall into the timeline accordingly. Therefore, if you plug the number of the card into the suit's meaning, you can interpret the card using number and suit alone.

1	5	10
BEGINNING	MIDDLE	END

✦ Pentacles = Money, objects, people

✦ Cups = Emotions, dreams, love

✦ Wands = Passion, energy, career

✦ Swords = Thoughts, stories, ideas

Using this easy formula, you will discover the following examples:

✦ Ace of Pentacles = One (beginning) + Pentacles (money) = Beginning of money

✦ Five of Cups = Five (challenge) + Cups (love) = Challenges in love

✦ Ten of Swords = Ten (end) + Swords (thoughts) = The end of mental agony

Your turn:

Ace of Wands =

Five of Swords =

Ten of Cups =

Colors can be interpreted just as you would interpret a symbol. Colors offer sensory energy to the card. The key to interpreting any color lies in your experience of that color. Does blue lift you up and make you feel dreamy or does it make you feel sad? Does yellow fill you with annoyance or optimism? Does red get your blood pumping and heart racing and fill you with warmth? Do copper and gold make you feel luxurious while silver feels mysterious and precise?

My favorite color clothing is...

The color of my bedroom walls are...

My hair color is...

My favorite color flower is...

My favorite color crayon is...

If I was a color, I would be...

Reading colors as messages is fun, especially if you have a colorful tarot deck. Here's an example of how to read color as a message: Judy asks the cards, "What can I focus on to have the best day ever?" She shuffles, flips, and receives the Six of Pentacles. The rich green cloak of a beggar catches her attention. Green makes Judy think of summer grass. She had already pulled the brilliant Sun for her card of the day. Vibrant yellow plus green reminds her of summer. She knows in an instant what her message is: "Focus on manifestation and growth. Be productive today; help things grow like your garden."

Judy examines the rest of the card now that she has received her color message. Pentacles reflect manifestation. She knows being busy and productive will make her feel awesome. She sees the figure on the card doling out money and interprets this action as an opportunity to share what she does with others via gifts. She decides to create a fun giveaway for her business.

To read a color as a message, compose a question. Shuffle your deck. Flip over a card. Read the first color popping out to you. Don't look at the scene, story of the card, or suit. Read the color's message first. Then incorporate additional information.

> *My question is...*
>
> *The color standing out to me is...*
>
> *The message of this color is...*
>
> *I now look at the other information on the card, and I see...*

Create a page for each color in your tarot journal. Add additional colors and nuances like shadows, reflections, and gradients. Craft a painter's palette to divine with.

BLACK

Deep space, deep earth, deep time. Pregnant starless night. The birth of the universe. Sleep. Black is boundaryless, borderless expansion. Black is charcoal, sable, and smudge. Spicy licorice, coffee, and loose-leaf tea. Black trumpet mushrooms, black beans, and black cats crossing your path at midnight. Black is all possibility and what gives all things definition.

> *I like black because...*

I don't like black when...

Black makes me feel...

BLUE

Dive into naval blue. Blueberries, Indian corn, and Concord grapes. Churning oceans with murky blues the deeper you dive. Sandy beaches kissed by azure waters. Big blue whales, dolphins, and singsong bluebirds. Bright wide skies. Soft denim jeans and blue hydrangeas. Blue is cobalt, azure, lapis, and sapphire.

Blue is associated with water and the suit of cups.

I like blue because...

I don't like blue when...

Blue makes me feel...

Blue represents the suit of cups because...

GREEN

Lush and rich. How many tender shades of green can you detect on a June morning? Pickles, mint, limes, and leafy greens. Sharp rosemary, spicy basil, and jubilant parsley. Tree leaves exhale oxygen back into the planet's atmosphere. Green colors the American dollar bill. Lawns, forests, and mountains blanketed with rich greens. Green is emeralds and sapphires, crocodiles and shamrocks, olives and sage.

Green is associated with the element of earth and the suit of pentacles.

I like green because...

I don't like green when...

Green makes me feel...

Green reflects the suit of pentacles because...

ORANGE

Citrus orange juice, August sunrise, and monarch butterflies. Basketballs and cheddar cheese. Fall gardens bear sweet potatoes and juicy carrots ready to be roasted for hearty autumn meals. Carved pumpkins lit with glowing candles, orange candy corn stuffed into glowing Halloween bags. Orange is peachy, salmon, cantaloupe, and coral.

Orange is traditionally associated with fire and the suit of wands.

I like orange because...

I don't like orange when...

Orange makes me feel...

Orange represents the suit of wands because...

Purple

Royal robes of ancient queens, thorny vineyards of bursting grapes, the intuitive glowing gem of a gypsy fortuneteller. Angry, bruised storm clouds piling into the sky with purple fury. Eggplants, lilacs, and lavenders add mystery to the summer garden. Mauve sunsets, smart periwinkle, and gentle violets. Purple is orchids, amethyst, and pomegranate.

I like purple because...

I don't like purple when...

Purple makes me feel...

Red

Sweet juicy cherries, ripe strawberries, ruby red popsicles dripping down your wrist on a hot summer day. Red is rosy ladybugs, stop signs, and July picnic watermelon. Red is the color of a roaring fire, crunchy autumn leaves, and spicy hot cinnamon candy. Red sunset at night is the sailor's delight, while ruby red lips and cheeks suggest the flush of sexual desire. Red is cardinal, scarlet, lit, and torrid.

Red aligns with the energy of fire.

I like red because...

I don't like red when...

Red makes me feel...

Red reflects the suit of wands and fire because...

WHITE

Pure potential, a painter's canvas, and crisp, creamy white sheets of writing paper. Silver jewelry, full moons, and vanilla whipped cream. Frozen snowscapes, cherry blossoms, and freshly painted farmhouses. Pale candles, pallid porcelain, and intricate lacework. Linen sheets, light bulbs, billowy clouds, and mysterious mists creeping into deep valleys. Ivory tusks, oyster pearls, and sea foam. White is a luminescent, vacuous void reflecting light.

White is associated with the suit of swords.

I like white because...

I don't like white when...

White makes me feel...

White represents the suit of swords because...

YELLOW

Creamy butter, bananas, and citrus lemon zest. Number two pencils, egg yolks, and omelets. Golden rays of sunshine and expansive August days lasting forever. Shiny, reflective, and dazzling coins implying wealth and splendor, golden crowns and thrones, jewelry and decorations. Yellow is sandy, golden, flaxen, and fair. It is shiny bows and ancient scrolls.

Yellow is associated with fire and the suit of wands.

I like yellow because...

I don't like yellow when...

Yellow makes me feel...

Yellow represents the suit of wands because...

Symbolic divination is integral to tarot reading. Symbols are the shorthand of tarot knowledge. You can read anything as a message or sign once you learn to interpret symbols. Symbolic value is powerful because it transcends spoken word. Advertisers learned the power of symbolic logos as a shorthand to building brand identification. Symbolic reading is as powerful as finding the truth in someone's face. Symbols move past the analytic, thinking mind and enter your interior directly.

The power of any given symbol reverberates on how deeply you resonate with the symbol. You likely have a powerful relationship with the sun as a symbol. If I asked what the sun means to you, a slew of associations would probably roll off your tongue: "Fire, summer, warmth, heat, life, pleasure, gold..." Learning to "speak" tarot is like learning a new symbolic language. Build your association to the symbols found inside the deck. Once you sort out these associations, you will interpret them with ease.

SWORD/BLADE

A sword is a sharp object used to defend and protect as well as to wound and kill. It traditionally bears two sides and was often a symbol of military might. In magical ceremonies swords reflect the element of air. Swords are considered masculine due to their external shape.

A sword makes me think of...

A sword makes me feel...

The words I free-associate with "sword" are...

The message of the sword is...

CUP/CHALICE

A cup is a container; it can be filled with anything. Cups are used to collect and hold objects, food, and drinks. They can be musical, decorative, or functional. In magical ceremonies the cup reflects the element of water and is feminine due to its internal nature and the ability to hold.

A cup makes me think of...

A cup makes me feel...

The words I free-associate with "cup" are...

The message of the cup is...

WAND/STAFF

Wands are used for magical spells, a tool for fairy godmothers and magicians alike. Wands can be walking sticks or even weapons. Tarot wands are often living wood with leaves sprouting from the top. In magical ceremonies the wand reflects the element of fire and is masculine due to its shape.

A wand makes me think of...

A wand makes me feel...

The words I free-associate with "wand" are...

The message of the wand is...

PENTACLE/COIN

Pentacles are circular and represent money and the material world. Pentacles can be placed in your pocket or buried as seeds that will germinate and sprout. Tarot pentacles often contain a witch's five-pointed star, and in magical ceremonies they reflect the element of earth and are feminine due to the earth's receptive ability.

A pentacle makes me think of...

A pentacle makes me feel...

The words I free-associate with "pentacle" are...

The message of the pentacle is...

Make a page for symbols in your tarot journal. The bigger and deeper your expanded understanding, the better. Keep adding. The more you list, the more you will know!

1. Write the symbol's name in the center of the page.

2. Write the things you free-associate with the image.

3. Write how it makes you feel.

4. Write a message to yourself from the symbol.

SYMBOLS FOR YOUR TAROT JOURNAL

KING	QUEEN	KNIGHT	PAGE
EMPRESS	POPE	DEVIL/DEMON	THRONE
CROWN	LANTERN	STAR	MOON
SUN	RAINBOW	CLOUD	SNOW
LIGHTNING	GLOBE	SKELETON/SKULL	WHEEL
FLOWER	TREE	CITY	COUNTRYSIDE
HOUSE	KEY	TOWER	BOAT

FENCE	POND	OCEAN	STREAM
DESERT	MOUNTAIN	GARDEN	HORSE
BIRD	DOG	CAT	WOLF
BUNNY	SNAIL	FISH	

Reading for Others

Artful readings for others is a process that will develop over time. You will most likely begin performing readings for practice using a book or the internet for reference. Once you are what actors call "off book," meaning you have memorized basic tarot meanings, your readings will evolve. You'll develop your own personal style. Storytelling, psychic pops, and intuition will likely kick it into high gear. Watching people's eyes grow wide with wonder as you read for them is a delight that never grows old.

Client, sitter, querent, and seeker are all common names for the person who is receiving the reading. You assume the role of "reader." Seekers ask you questions that you will answer for them based on the cards.

Setup: It is best to sit across from the person you are reading for. The cards should be read facing you, the reader. Any card upside down, or facing the seeker, can be considered a reversal. Read more about reversals on page 75. At the beginning of your practice, feel free to ignore the reversal and turn the card to face you.

Crafting a gorgeous atmosphere adds to a reading. Light some candles, sprinkle essential oils around the room, and make your reading one they won't soon forget. The more special the reading, the more they will remember what information and guidance is given to them.

Offering options: Explain the type of tarot readings you give and your tarot philosophy. People bring a lot of opinions about what tarot is and how it can be used. Most people fall into one of four categories: 1)Never had a reading before; 2) Are intrigued by the cards and can't wait to hear what they say; 3) Have enjoyed card readings in the past and love all things paranormal and mysterious; and 4) Have fear and a horror story about receiving a reading from a cruel, controlling, or dark reader. Never force a reading on anyone who holds or expresses fear about the cards. This is doubly important because during a reading, it isn't just what you say. It is also what they might see or project into the cards.

Opening: It is nice to have a prayer, intention, or mantra at the beginning of a reading for another person (or even for yourself). You might tell them this reading will be for their highest good or you may take a moment and quietly intend this from your own higher powers. You may create a personalized prayer to speak at the beginning of your reading or keep the entire process completely casual.

My friend Claudia, a professional Brazilian tarot reader, has a beautiful way of opening her readings with new clients. She paints a visual picture for her clients about what to expect. She tells them, "I will see a path for you as I read the cards. Along the way we will see options: rivers, trees, high and low points. We are free to move anywhere you like and explore anything that interests you. Know that you are in the driver's seat of this reading and can move deeper into any space you are curious about." This gives her clients a gorgeous opening context of what a reading with Claudia is like and also gives them a sense of control about the information they want or don't want.

Question or skip the question? This is the question: Sitters can ask questions, choose to remain silent, or enjoy a combination of both options.

If the sitter chooses to discuss their situation and concerns, you can help them formulate a great question based on the information provided in Questioning Well on page 67. Phrasing questions is a helpful act in and of itself. I once had a client who came to me upset and dissatisfied with her life; however, she couldn't say why. She didn't have a question but simply felt the discontent smothering her. We began talking, and by the time she articulated her question, she realized exactly what she needed to do. We didn't even need to pull cards, although we did.

Reasons people might avoid questions during a tarot reading may include any of the following:

SECRETIVE: Some people have an issue so personal, embarrassing, or complicated that they would rather not say anything to you. Honor their wish and forge ahead by trusting your instincts and the story of the cards.

CURIOUS: Some people have no idea what to ask. They just want to see what happens when someone reads cards for them.

TEST THE PSYCHIC: Some people want to "test" you and your cards, even if you don't call yourself a psychic or make future predictions. It is easy to roll your eyes at such people and delightful when you prove their assumptions wrong. Testers tend to be male (but not always), and it's deliciously fun to see their mouths drop open in astonishment once you begin reading for them.

Good readings begin by reading for a person's highest self. If you wouldn't want to hear what's about to come out of your mouth, don't say it! Offer solutions and advice and never, ever pass judgment on another, no matter what they might ask you. If a question or topic falls outside your comfort zone or boundaries, feel free to explain it is not a subject you cover and politely decline.

Reading for children: Whenever I have the opportunity to read for a child, I always turn the tables and ask the child to read for me. I ask them to pick a card and tell me what they see. Children's stories and interpretations of the cards are unsurprisingly wild, creative, and mind blowing.

Artful readings are transcendent. I've read tarot next to a caricaturist, behind henna artists, and with casino games all around me. I've read cards next to tattooed circus performers who were swallowing swords and juggling fire. It is not unusual to find yourself working alongside other party entertainers as a card reader. However, "entertainment" is not an adequate word to describe what we tarot readers do. Profound exchanges occur between reader and sitter between music-blaring speakers. It often qualifies as more than mere entertainment. I would call it art.

Profound art, literature, and painting address the soul on spiritual and emotional levels. Good art feels like it was created just for you. Writers, poets, and filmmakers seem to peek inside your mind, providing you with words, images, and ideas to express who you are and how you feel. This is art that flattens you, leaves you breathless, and helps make sense of your existence. Great art inspires us and provides connection to something greater than ourselves. It makes us feel like we are not alone. Excellent tarot readings do exactly the same thing.

All art is a psychic exchange. Intention is channeled by the artist into their chosen form. The experience is interpreted through them into you. Right now you are reading the sentences after they have streamed through my fingers on a keyboard and tumbled silently out of my head. You are reading my words while I am off doing something else—gardening, swimming, sitting on an airplane or whatever. I communicate silently to you from the past.

Tarot reading, like art, is subjective. Artful tarot doesn't happen with each and every guest, client, or friend who sits with you. But when the right person comes along, the connections are made, and the tarot reading rises above entertainment. It becomes sublime.

Long-distance readings can be performed using any sort of technology, and all of the same rules apply. Let the client see you shuffling the cards by holding them up to the camera. Ask them to tell you when to stop shuffling and begin to pull cards from that point. Instead or additionally, you can ask them to give you a number between zero and ten.

Once they give you the number, count off that number of cards and begin the reading.

Tarot scams are successful because of the perceived power/control between reader and client. People unfamiliar with tarot or psychic arts often have the perception that a reader or psychic can completely "see" them. They feel in awe of anyone called a psychic. Proceed with extreme caution when someone shares a traumatic psychic/tarot reading experience or a fear of the cards. You've probably seen news stories or even personally encountered fraudulent tarot readers and psychics. These are criminals who actively seek to dupe clients out of money. These readers bait passersby with cheap five- or ten-dollar palm, energy, or tarot readings. The reader quickly describes a "bad" energy or an evil spell lingering over the seeker. They will frighten the seeker with wild stories and dark portents. Once the sitter becomes frightened and nervous, the reader suggests a solution: for a fee, they will offer to cast magic, remove the curse, or pray the evil spirits away. If their plan works and the sitter agrees, they will be encouraged to return week after week. The reader will not stop until they have sucked as much money as possible from their clients.

Chapter Four

Tarot Spread Magic

Tarot Spreads

Tarot spreads are the pattern in which you lay out cards for a reading. Tarot spreads assign meanings for each card position. The meaning informs you how to interpret the card appearing in that spot.

For example, in a traditional three-card past/present/future spread, the first card is assigned the meaning of the past, the second card is the present, while the third card reflects the future. You can use spreads readily available in books and online. You can also invent your own tarot spreads.

You can construct an entire story out of a single image. We do this when looking at paintings and photography. We also interpret real-life images and actions as they unfold before us and relate them back to ourselves. A beautiful sunrise occurs and we look to it as a harbinger of delights to come. You walk down the sidewalk and flirt with a handsome passerby and realize you are lookin' cute today! We are constantly taking internal cues from the exterior world. We interpret what is happening before us in the context of how it relates to us (even when it doesn't). Do the same thing when you are reading a spread.

Reading the cards is storytelling. We are all natural-born storytellers. Begin with a single card. We look to the image on the card and tell the story of how the images on the card—the symbols, colors, or characters on the card—relate to your question or the assigned meaning of the position in the spread.

The simplest way to read a spread is to read the cards like you would read a graphic novel. Take your time. Begin with a single-card spread and move to spreads in a single lineup that can be read from left to right. This echoes the way we read sentences in a book (unless you read from right to left, in which case feel free to reverse). Move from single-card spreads to two- and three-card spreads and eventually to complex spreads.

No spread, no problem. You don't have to use spreads if you don't want to. State a question and flip a card for each curiosity. There are also readers who shuffle the deck and move through the entire stack of cards for their reading. They turn the cards like pages in a book, weaving together a long-form narrative and offering advice in a stream-of-consciousness fashion.

Perfect beginning spreads tend to be one- to three-card spreads. Nothing beats their clarity and specificity.

One-Card Spread

A one-card reading is clear and concise. It moves you straight to the heart of the matter, and you are less likely to confuse yourself when you refrain from pulling multiple cards.

To cast a one-card spread, compose a question, shuffle your deck, and flip a single card.

Possible meanings for a one-card spread:

+ What I need to know today
+ What I can focus on to have the best day ever
+ An element in my favor is
+ Something to keep a lookout for is
+ Theme of the day
+ Lesson of the day

- ✦ Blessing of the day

- ✦ Surprise of the day

- ✦ What can I count on today

- ✦ Spirit guide/animal message

- ✦ Daily reminder

- ✦ Piece of magic

- ✦ A possibility is

- ✦ An answer is

Two-Card Spread

Two cards offer duality. Space appears between the two cards, and you'll explore the synergy of the cards working together. You can examine them like bookends, a mirror, yin and yang, or two options.

Possible meanings for two-card spreads:

- ✦ Works for you and against you

- ✦ Light and dark side

- ✦ Option 1 and option 2

- ✦ Beginning and end

- ✦ Plus and minus

- ✦ Before and after

Three-Card Spread

Three card spreads come easily and are intuitive because the human mind moves in a linear, three-point fashion. Stories, novels, and films have a beginning, middle, and end. Apply this to a card reading and receive helpful context to the situation (what has happened in the past), what is challenging now (the present), and the most likely outcome (the future). To cast a three-card spread, compose a question, shuffle your deck, and flip the top three cards from left to right.

Play with the three-card spread by providing different meanings to the three positions:

+ Beginning—middle—end

+ Hindsight—insight—foresight

+ Opportunity—challenge—outcome

+ Working for you—working against you—unseen solution

+ Situation—focal point—direction

+ Weakness—strength—suggestion

+ Situation—action—consequence

Making Your Own Spreads

I love inventing my own spreads. I even wrote a book called *365 Tarot Spreads* where I created a spread for every single day of the year. Crafting your own spreads is creative and fun, but most importantly, you can tailor them perfectly to exactly the situation at hand.

Tarot knowledge is like life knowledge. It isn't what you know; it's what you do with it that really counts. Even if you are still using books to aid in card interpretations, you can and should create spreads. Why? Because of what happens beneath your fingertips as you flip, shuffle, and work your cards.

The tarot journey begins as a study in symbol, magic, and metaphysics and soon blossoms into an inadvertent cultivation of innate problem-solving skills, delicate intuition building, and a fascinating study of the self. Once you become adept at creating spreads for yourself, you'll be able to do it for loved ones, strangers, and or even clients. I often craft unique tarot spreads for people. It makes them feel special, and I can give them all the information they require about their situation.

The first step of creating a spread is deciding what your spread is about—the general question or topic. Grab a pen and paper, and begin jotting down your thoughts, questions, and the overall goal of the spread.

Often, when pondering the question/issue/problem that our spread will be about, we must work through myriad attachments to get to the heart of our desires. Our emotions (cups) are often hampering—blurring, coloring, and filtering our basic truth. But articulating your questions and writing them down help you to streamline your thought process through any emotion. This process gets you out of your head and moving toward where you want to be going. It forces you to articulate the most important thing: What do you want?

The second step is creating the questions for your spread. "Functional fixedness" is a term psychologists use for when a person sees things only in the manner they are accustomed to. Everyone falls into ruts of thinking and habitual ways of understanding and interpreting life. This prevents anyone from stepping back to observe their situation from a larger view.

Creating a spread forces you to examine your issue/topic/situation from every possible angle because you must come up with the questions to populate the spread. These questions are the bones of the spread. Different angles are examined, and your issue or concern is now out of your mind and spread on the table before you. Simply getting it out of your head is worth the price of admission. You can play with them, examine them from new angles, and even build upon them, creating new and better questions that, in turn, provide excellent answers and insight.

Here are some starter questions to consider:

- ✦ What do you want?
- ✦ Why do you want it?
- ✦ What is standing in your way?
- ✦ What is aiding you?
- ✦ What will happen if you receive it?
- ✦ What don't you see?

And don't forget to acknowledge the role you play in your future!

The third and final step is the shape. Creativity unleashes new possibilities. Creativity may be defined as the ability to transcend traditional ideas and create meaningful new ideas, forms, methods, and interpretations. Tarot spreads are created to solve problems and offer guidance; we rarely ask about things we already know. A meaningful new idea is exactly what you'll seek in a tarot reading.

Getting creative about the design of your spread paves the way for innovative solutions and helps your synapses fire in unexpected ways.

Pyramid Spread

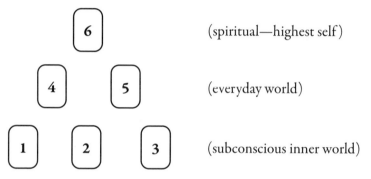

6   (spiritual—highest self)

4   5   (everyday world)

1   2   3   (subconscious inner world)

Straight Line

A straight-line tarot spread will tell you exactly how possibilities play out in a linear fashion. This is super simple and helpful. Once you become proficient at reading straight-line spreads, see what happens in a three-card spread if you push the middle card up a little further than the others.

For example, lay out a past/present/future spread and interpret it. Now push the "present" card up so it is higher than the others. This puts more focus on the issue of the present. The past and future cards seem to support the present, don't they? Does this alter your interpretation?

Now, without changing the cards, move the "present" card in the center lower than the others. Do you see how the energy of past and future now funnels into the present card? Does this alter your interpretation?

CIRCLE

The sacred circle is the first and last form in the world. It is the beginning, the dot, the cell, the eye, the plate, the ball, the wheel, the planet, the sun, the solar system. It is the endless form, it never breaks, and all parts are equal.

Create circle tarot spreads when you want to examine the holistic view of a situation. Circle spreads are helpful when you want to tie things up and seek completion. You can place the final card in the center of the spread to make it super important. You could place cards outside the circle as an example of outside influences that you either want to embrace or reject.

It is fun to sit on the floor and lay the cards out in a circle around you for meditation and ritual work.

Here's an example:

Full Circle Full Moon Spread

1. What is working in my favor?

2. What energy arrives soon?

3. What opportunity should I embrace?

4. What opportunity should I pass?

5. What is grounding me?

6. What lunar magic infuses me?

7. How can I be stronger?

8. How can I complete this cycle in the best way possible?

SQUARE

The square gives shape, form, and stability. Think of the foundations of a house or the shape of blocks. Once you have four corners, you have structure. Create square-shaped spreads when you are focused on building something in your life, be it a career, a family, a house, or a body of work. Utilize the four corners as the four things you might want to "nail down" for success.

Four Corners Career Spread

1. What keeps me focused?

2. What keeps me passionate?

3. How can I shine even brighter?

4. Why is it so important to do this work?

More Fun Shapes for Spreads

+ Five-pointed star for magic

+ Sun for inspiration and growth

+ Flowers for potential

+ Path for pathways

+ Staircases moving up or down

+ Anything you can imagine!

Taking your cards into the world will transform the way you read. Read matters of spiritual import in the attic and cast a spread in your basement to converse with your shadow self. Don't confine yourself to exclusively reading cards inside the home. Take your tarot into the garden and converse with the veggies, flowers, and herbs. Read tarot for graveyard ghosts as you listen to the whispers of those buried beneath stone slabs. Take tarot to a historical place, a museum, or an architecturally inspired building. What do the buttresses of a cathedral have to say? Lay your cards at the roots on an ancient willow tree to divine its wisdom.

Reading the space between cards is an element often overlooked by readers, yet space is what holds all potential. Space is the field of energy you entered into at the moment of your birth. Space is required to build anything your mind dreams up. The space between cards in a tarot spread is electric with possibility.

Space is the place where questions fall away and instinct becomes paramount. Intuition becomes our torchlight. If a line exists between our creative imagination and reality, it is a fluid one. Does it move like the ebbing sands of the ocean? Or is the line gauzy and thin, like the earth's delicate atmospheric membrane? We become the fecund earth, and the sustaining oxygen bubble becomes the boundary between us and the possibility of an ever-expanding universe.

NASA tells us that 68 percent of the universe is made of a mysterious force called dark energy. Dark energy counters gravity and causes the universe to expand. Could it be there is an accessible energy inside a tarot spread that we've been ignoring all along?

Einstein pointed out that empty space is not empty. Space holds more space. Space is not diluted as it expands; like a growing flower reaching to sunlight, space itself becomes more space. This means the space between your cards in a tarot reading is as potent and full of potential as the cards themselves.

The entire point of reading tarot is to widen our perceptions. When reading tarot it is helpful to keep in mind that invisible, unrecognizable things often stand in front of us before we recognize them. Just as humans once thought the earth was flat, we may discover the most wondrous possibility was in front of us all along.

CONSIDER THE SPACE

✦ Between tarot cards

✦ Between the words

✦ Between the music

✦ Between inhale and exhale

✦ Between molecules

✦ Between thoughts

✦ Inside silence

✦ Between you and me

Make use of all the space inside a tarot spread. The field your cards appear in, the space between those cards, is anything but empty. It is chock-full of possibility.

Move deeper into any tarot spread by adding three cards to the spread when you are finished interpreting the cards. Perform the following exercise at the end of any of your tarot readings and spreads:

Reading Space Between Cards

1. Examine your tarot spread as a whole and make note of the spaces between cards. Remind yourself that there is more at play than you can currently see.

2. Place one card facedown to the left of your spread and one card facedown to the right of your spread. Turn them over at the same time. These cards are read as the polar extremes, the dichotomy of the invisible yet potent field surrounding everything in and around your current situation. Re-examine your spread in the context of these two polarities. Is the field evenly balanced? Is it erratic? Are the two cards compatible or are they at odds with one another?

3. Finally, pull a last card to reveal an invisible yet present possibility you have not yet seen.

If we discern the subtle difference of sacred space and creative imagination, we realize how powerful we are. We recognize how our singular point of consciousness is the filter of what passes before us. We easily see that what we focus on becomes a reality.

SEVEN-DAY SPREAD

Craft an alchemical question as described on page 72. Make it a really important, really good question—one with the ability to change your life when you receive the answer. Acknowledge your power, state your desired outcome, and include how you will feel when receiving it.

My alchemical question is...

Ask the same question every day for seven days. Use a single pack of cards. Leave each day's card out. Place the cards where you can see them through the day in an ascending line like a stairway moving up. Contemplate the cards often in the context of your question. This becomes an evolving seven-day meditation.

Read the stairway as advice to gaining your heart's desire, which lies at the top of the stairs.

ARCHETYPAL ALLY AND SPIRIT GUIDE SPREAD

An archetype is pure energy and form, while a spirit guide and ally is a special friend or force that wants to help you. This may come in the form of a repeating card or it may be a human, angelic, or animal energy. Use manners as you would in any relationship. To discover who your archetypal ally is:

1. Shuffle the deck.

2. Ask aloud, "Who is willing to be my ally?"

3. Flip over the top card.

Keep flipping until you get an upright major arcana card. If no upright majors appear for you, your ally is the Fool.

Once you have found your archetypal ally card, place it in front of you. Focus on the image. Answer the following prompts.

I am here to teach you...

The best way to work with me is...

My message for you is...

THE EMPRESS.

Chapter Five

Tarot Magic

Art of Ritual

Sacred space is the pliable and expansive place where creative possibility exists. Like a crossroads, it is a threshold where multiple possibilities converge. The place where forest meets field. Where cultivated vegetable garden meets wild thorn bushes. Where lips conceal unspoken words. Where inside meets outside. Where the known and unknown collide. It is the membrane, the very skin of our psychic reality. It is where we pass into the interior of a tarot card to interface directly with the arcana. Sacred space is found in holy temples, yoga studios, theaters, museums, etc. Cultivate sacred space for transformative readings by crafting simple rituals.

Ritual is an action or series of acts repeated in a set, precise manner to bring about a desired outcome. A gardener places her golden hair into a knot behind her head, reaches down to take a handful of dirt, sniffs the rich-smelling earth, then pulls on her gloves as she does every day before tending to her herb and vegetable farm.

Spiritual practices are grounded in ritual and rite. A Buddhist nun rises at 4:30 a.m. and observes the pre-dawn darkness filling her chamber. She listens to the silence, washes her face, pulls on her jewel-toned robe, and files into the nunnery to begin morning mantras.

Ritual activities activate our senses. The writer enters her office at 10:15 a.m., sets a classical music playlist, turns her phone to silent, places a sugar pastry at the upper right-hand edge of her desk, pulls out the scraps of notes she's scribbled with ideas that came to her during the night, and begins the task of writing.

Rituals breed pleasure. The young mother snuggles into the soft skin of her baby fresh from his bath. She sprinkles her hair over his face, causing him to laugh and coo. She places him on the changing table, secures his diaper, snaps him into jammies, and brings him close for a feeding. He hungrily sucks as she feels warmth overwhelming her body, and his eyes gaze up at her. His lids grow heavy, then close with sleep, and she tucks him under his fuzzy blue blanket, clicks on his nightlight, and exits the room. She watches her favorite show before drifting into a deep sleep. Their nightly ritual is complete.

Ritual calls deep attention to the present moment and what you are doing. It sets the mind for work, whether productive, spiritual, or pleasureful. Ritual is a mindfulness practice where action aligns with intention. Sports figures employ pre-game huddle rituals. Royal families abide by them. Your own cultural holidays are populated with rituals that mark the passing of time and our place in the wheel of the year. Crafting tarot rituals, whether it be a card-a-day practice or selecting a special space to perform readings, will encourage your subconscious and intuition to open for your readings.

Gestures are movements, usually with a hand or finger, that express particular meaning. Catholics make the sign of the cross by touching fingers to forehead, heart, left, and right shoulder. The Hierophant and Ten of Swords in the RWS deck make the sign of benediction. Yogis and Buddhists place their palms together at heart center and bow their heads to display reverence. A mudra is a ritual hand gesture.

Create a meaningful tarot gesture by placing your hands on top of a tarot deck to infuse it with energy. Take a moment to clear your mind and align with the energy of the deck in the midst of such a gesture. Either place your hands side by side with palms down over the deck or cross your hands with palms down while focusing on the cards. Imagine a line of energy moving between you and the cards.

Create a cleansing gesture by crossing your hands over the deck like an X with your palms down. Swipe out, left hand left and right hand right, to finish the clearing or to mark the completion of shuffling. Perform this gesture to clear your energy from the deck before passing the deck on to a person who will shuffle for themselves.

Words and phrases performed in a prescribed manner are useful in ritual. Ashtanga yoga begins with a specific mantra at the beginning and end of practice. Religions utilize specific prayers during a devotional service or sermon. Witchcraft employs rhyme for inherent power in their incantations—think Shakespeare's "Double, double toil and trouble."

The same set of opening words is often used to call the elemental corners or invoke the four elements of tarot. To call in the elements, say:

I call to the suit of wands.
I call to the suit of pentacles.
I call to the suit of swords.
I call to the suit of cups.

Calling in the elements is like opening a door. You will want to thank and release the elements when you are finished, thereby closing the door. Work in reverse and thank each element when you finish:

I thank the suit of cups for aiding me in my work.
I thank the suit of swords for aiding me in my work.
I thank the suit of pentacles for aiding me in my work.
I thank the suit of wands for aiding me in my work.

Ritual may seem ornate and intimidating, but look closer: everyday life is littered with ritualized actions. We brush our teeth in the morning and night. School is ritualized for organizational reasons and to help students remain on track. Meals are ritualized according to culture. It might sound as if a ritual is a habit, and often rituals do become habitual. Spiritual, meditative, and magical rituals are meant to seduce the senses so the soul flowers open to begin the process of transformation.

Ritual accessories are a delight to collect and have at your disposal. They can be found anywhere from nature to a gift shop.

Candles are a treasured ritual object and a tarot reader's best friend. Candles set a mood and transport us back to a time when we relied upon sunlight and fire as sources of light and heat. Candles cast a sense of intimacy for a tarot reading. They make everyone more mysterious. A candle's flickering environment can be used for magic and aromatherapy. Purchase scented candles or add a few drops of essential oils to fill the room with scent.

Make magic out of the simple ritual of lighting a candle:

1. Clear your mind and focus on your candle.

2. Fill the candle with intention while holding it in your hand and visualizing your goal. Your intention can be anything from an insightful tarot reading to the goal of finding your heart's true love.

3. Light the candle and as you do so, imagine it is the start of making your intention come true.

4. Observe the flame. Watch it dance and shimmy. Observe the glow. Look for the heat waves moving up and out. Imagine the flame as the point of light that attracts what you need.

5. When you have finished the reading, ritual, or meditation with the cards, either snuff the candle or blow it out. If you blow out the candle, imagine the lingering smoke as your final word to the forces that be—for your guides, angels, ancestors, and invisible helpers.

Use flameless candles if open fire is an issue, as it is sometimes when reading tarot in public spaces. A flameless candle isn't as sensual but still creates a lovely ambiance.

Choose a candle color to align with the intention of your reading or desired result:

BLACK: Possibility and depth

BLUE: Peace and healing

GREEN: Prosperity and finance

PINK: Friendship and family

PURPLE: Psychic, spirituality, dreams

RED: Love and passion

WHITE: Purity and protection

YELLOW: Creativity and manifestation

Incense is a fragrant material that creates an aromatic smoke when burned. It is crafted from plant materials and essential oils. It is widely used in religious practices. Egyptian hieroglyphs depict priests using incense to fumigate tombs and sacred ceremony. Eastern Christian and Catholic churches often swing ornate incense burners that look like the RWS Queen of Cups' chalice.

Loose incense can be burned in many different ways and has been since the beginning of time. Dried and fragrant herbs can be tossed onto midsummer fires. Tibetan pilgrims burn incense bundles in giant kilns that billow fragrant smoke up to their deities.

TYPES OF INCENSE: Loose, cone, coils, thread, stick, incense matches

Choose an incense to align with the intention of your reading and desired result:

CINNAMON: Raising energy

FRANKINCENSE: Any magical work

LAVENDER: Relaxation

MUSK: Sensual attraction

NAG CHAMPA: Enlightenment and meditation

SANDALWOOD: Peace and positivity

VANILLA: Luck and knowledge

Essential oils, made from plant and botanical extracts, are a delicious way to seduce the self into ritual work. Align the oils and blend or mix and match to suit your mood. Essential oils can be dropped in candles, boiled in water, spritzed into the air, and anointed on the skin.

Check to be sure you are not allergic to the oil before anointing your wrists and temples. You can vaporize or diffuse their scents as an addition or alternative to sacred smoke.

BASIL: Harmony

BERGAMOT: Strength

EUCALYPTUS: Clarification

GRAPEFRUIT: Uplifting senses and mood

LAVENDER: Psychic work

LEMON: Clear thinking

PALO SANTO: Blessing

PEPPERMINT: Raising energy

ROSEMARY: Remembrance, love

Note: Certain oils can cause irritation and should not be used on pregnant women. Please see the safety guidelines on the bottle and/or consult your doctor before using.

Music heightens any mood you'd like to create. Choose music you love that aligns with your ritualistic goals. Classical, ambient, and film soundtracks are excellent for getting into the mood. You'll find endless chanting, world music, and assorted spiritual music from around the globe on streaming services. Turntables and vinyl records offer the richest quality listening experience.

Bells and singing bowls are useful for clearing spaces and attuning yourself to a higher vibration. Ring a bell in the four corners of a room to clear the space. Singing bowls create a rich tonal sound when used correctly (it might take you a little practice) and are used by Buddhist monks for meditational practice. Once the bowl begins to sing, you can align your energy with its otherworldly vibration.

Fresh flowers and herbs bring vibrancy to a table. Fresh flowers and herbs are infused with archetypal energy. Pull a tarot card to communicate directly with an herb or flower. Ask it how it would like to work with you. Select according to season, personal pleasure, or magical alignment.

DAFFODILS: Fortune

LILACS: Beauty

LILLY: Purity

MOTHERWORT: Comfort

PARSLEY: Luck

ROSEMARY: Memories

ROSES: Love (align the color as you would with a candle)

SAGE: Fresh start

SUNFLOWERS: Abundance

THYME: Honor

TULIPS: Prosperity

YARROW: Psychic powers

Sacred bathing and cleansing are pleasurable ways to embark on a ritual. It is a highly symbolic act as we are born from birth waters. Use sea salt to sanctify bathwater or enter nature's sacred waters if you are near a pond, river, lake, or sea. If indoors, fill your bathing space with candles and music. Remove your clothing as a metaphor for letting the outside world and all problems drop away. Enter the tub and let the water remove tension while you meditate on an aligning tarot card such as the High Priestess for intuition and self-knowledge or the Star for inspiration and the muse. Exit the bath and dress yourself in soft, silky clothing—or wear nothing at all.

Third Eye Activation Ritual

Here is an opportunity to put all the suggested ritual accessories together. All ritual items are suggestions. Feel free to swap out, change, add, or delete accessories to suit your personal taste.

NEEDED:

+ High Priestess card

+ 4 candles and a lighter

+ Moonstone

+ Freshly cut lavender

+ Third eye chakra singing bowl track

1. Gather all spell materials. Preset your space so all items are easily on hand. Place High Priestess card, candles and lighter, moonstone, and fresh lavender on the table.

2. Turn your music on and the lights low. Prepare a ritual bath by adding bath salts and a few drops of lavender essential oil to the running water. Once you are in the tub, use your mind's eye to imagine the High Priestess as if she were floating above you. Imagine the water you are floating in is High Priestess water. Imagine that moonlight illuminates the water and fills your bathroom. Bring her image closer to you and let her image merge with your body so the two of you become one. Close your eyes and imagine all the moonlight gathering and pouring directly into your third eye, which is located above your nose and between your eyebrows.

3. When you are ready to exit the bath, drain the water yet stay in the tub. As the bathwater drains, allow all negativity, angst, emotions, and feelings you don't need to run down the drain with the water. This restrictive

energy will be released back into the earth so its energy can be regenerated into something else. Air-dry your skin without a towel.

4. Go to your ritual space and light four candles in four directions. As you do so, dedicate each candle to a suit of tarot by saying, "I invite the suit of cups and the element of water, I invite the suit of wands and the element of fire, I invite the suit of pentacles and the element of earth, and I invite the suit of swords and the element of air." You have now opened a sacred space.

5. Place the High Priestess card in front of you on the table or on the floor (depending on where you are working). Bring her up and in front of you in your mind's eye, but rather than merge with her, speak to her, converse with her. You might record your conversation; you may have a list of questions you would like to ask her. Know when you speak to the High Priestess that you are really speaking to the deepest, truest, most authentic part of yourself. She is you, and you are her. She works through your third eye and intuition to see the path, alignment, and information for your greatest good, highest power, and deepest self. Just as your entire life spills forth from your dreams, instincts, and desires, so does all water in the tarot deck spring from the High Priestess. Nothing is accidental. You are never given a circumstance you can't overcome. Your challenges are there to forge you into the creature you were meant to be. Speak with the High Priestess; open a conversation that will never end. Find yourself in her gaze. Ignite your third eye and let it bring you to magic each and every day.

6. Slip the moonstone under your pillow and sleep with it for the next seven days to increase your psychic power.

Family history and personal DNA should be mined for rituals and items that will resonate with you. Your personal ancestry carries ritualistic heritage. For example, if you have Irish ancestors, study up on Celtic rituals and mythology. Dive into history, visit the library, and read up on ritual legacy work that is already ingrained within your body. Seek out the rituals of your ancestral history in addition to the wonderful ritual tools that are available for everyone. Create your own unique ritual work, openings, and closings.

SPELLCASTING
ESSENTIALS

✦

visualize

✦

feeling

✦

action

✦

Spellcasting is as sensual and fun as it is profound and life changing. Spellcasting requires you to raise energy and direct it toward a specific goal. It leaves you feeling marvelous. Tarot spellcasting basics are described here, but please note there is no better guide than your own creativity and instinct.

Perform a spell anywhere at any time. Cast spells inside your house, in the woods, in your yard, or at the beach. Cast spells with others or you can cast them alone. Align your spell with unique moments like new moons, full moons, and solstices or perform them on the spot when the impulse strikes you. Spellcasting allows you to direct all your supernatural power into a specific goal.

The essentials of spellcasting are the same as an alchemical question. You will want to take responsibility for yourself by directing the magic toward yourself and intended goal and never bending the will of another. You want to clearly visualize and feel yourself in the space of receiving your magical results. You will take action by the physical mechanics of the spell, which are the actions you take, the words you speak, and the cards you choose to work with.

It is important to let go of any expectation once you have cast the spell. The universe will always give you exactly what you need, nothing more, nothing less. Just because we want something doesn't mean it is best for us. Imagine if everything you ever wanted came true! Trust in how magic unfolds. Let go of expectation. You will know if what you desire is in alignment with your highest good by observing the results of your magic.

1. Select and Write Your Magical Goal (Visualize and Feel)

The most important part of spellcasting is articulating exactly what you want. Spells work the best when desire and emotion align with natural energy.

The spell begins the minute you decide to cast it. Writing out and planning your desired intention is in advance of casting the spell. It doesn't have to be poetic or grammatically correct. You never have to show it to anyone. The point is to get detailed. Write about how you feel, what does life look like, what do you see in your mind's eye as your desire comes to fruition? Once you've described everything in detail, craft your intention into one sentence. Do this just as you would create a question for a tarot spread (see page 67). Place this sentence at the top of the page.

2. Choose Location and Time

Cast spells when alone or when you are least likely to be disturbed. Think of it as a date with yourself. Spellcasting is a sensual process. You will seduce yourself into the highest energetic state possible. Spells can be aligned with helpful outside forces such as the waxing moon (whose energy helps attract) and the waning moon (whose energy helps repel). Cast a spell at the stroke of midnight, twilight, or sunset as the visible and invisible worlds intertwine.

Consider your location. The kitchen table is a perfect choice. It tends to be the heart of the house, functional, and carries the metaphor of manifestation (like cooking). You may enjoy the privacy of your bedroom or attic space. Magic outdoors is sublime, especially if you have a special grove of trees or an opportunity to cast deep in the forest or at the sea. Winter is a marvelous time to cast because you can take over an open field and carve acre-wide symbols in the snow! Think big, get creative, and have fun.

3. Gather Needed Items and Appropriate Cards

Tarot is ideal for spell work because of the visual component of the cards. Spells work on your subconscious just like tarot symbols do. Choose candles, clothing, flowers, and essential oils whose colors align with the intention of your spell. Select appropriate music, a symbolic food to eat, or essential oils to complement your spell. Once you have articulated your magical goal and chosen one or more tarot cards illustrating your desired goal, you will use the cards symbolically inside your spell by laying them out and entering them to visualize your goal.

4. Ritual Cleansing

A ritual salt bath, shower, or outdoor bathing is a pleasurable way to prepare for your spell. Prepare a candlelit bath and throw salts, flower petals, and herbs in the water. If you have access to a river, pond, lake, or ocean, bathing outside is an incredible way to align yourself with the natural energy of the earth. A simple shower is excellent as well. Imagine the waters cleaning away unneeded energies and attitudes. The water will drain any negativity or blocks and allow yourself to open to possibility.

5. OPEN SACRED SPACE

Move clockwise to open sacred space for your spell. Call to the elements, directions, and tarot suits to aid you in your spell work. For example:

Face east, lay the Ace of Cups, and say, "I call to the suit of cups and element of water to aid me in my spell."

Face south, lay the Ace of Wands, and say, "I call to the suit of wands and element of fire to aid me in my spell."

Face west, lay the Ace of Pentacles, and say, "I call to the suit of pentacles and element of earth to aid me in my spell."

Face north, lay the Ace of Swords, and say, "I call to the suit of swords and element of air to aid me in my spell."

6. VISUALIZATIONS

Once you have officially opened the space, it is time for the action of the spell. Read your sentence. Take your written goal and read every word. Lay out your chosen tarot cards, seeing everything taking place and happening as you envision. Perform any other activities or meditations you like. This is the space where you raise your energy and direct it toward your chosen goal.

7. CLOSE

Close your sacred space as carefully as you opened it. Do this with gratitude. This time, move counterclockwise to close the space:

Face north and say, "Thank you to the suit of swords and element of air for aiding in my spell."

Face west and say, "Thank you to the suit of pentacles and element of earth for aiding in my spell."

Face south and say, "Thank you to the suit of wands and element of fire for aiding in my spell."

Face east and say, "Thank you to the suit of cups and element of water for aiding in my spell."

Let go of all expectations and attachments to your end result. This act gives the universe an opportunity to play its part. It will also give magic an opportunity to surprise you. The culmination of magic often manifests in vastly different ways than you might imagine. Mind-blowing side effects, fringe benefits, and silver linings that you never could have imagined often unfold. Don't stand in its way and miss out because the apple you were expecting shows up as an orange. That orange might be bursting with treasure. Trust and let go. Be patient. Know that if something does not come to you, there is good reason for it. The universe will always give you what you need. Watch miracles unfold. Expect the unexpected.

stay open

stay present

prepare to be dazzled

Here are three spells from my book *365 Tarot Spells* to get you started.

Spell to Attract the Highest Possible Romantic Relationship

INGREDIENTS

Rose petals and distilled water

Two of Cups

The Lovers

The Star

Ten of Pentacles

Ten of Cups

Roses aid in protection and true, lasting love. Bathe your hands in rosewater before casting your cards. This will intensify the effect of laying your hands on the cards.

The spell begins with the preparation of rosewater, which takes over twenty-four hours. Use this time to meditate and ponder all the ways in which you share love in your life. To prepare rosewater, pick or select a cup's worth of red rose petals. Set petals with just enough distilled water to cover them in a saucepan. Simmer until petals lose their color. Strain liquid into a glass jar, set in a sunny windowsill, and leave for twenty-four hours.

The Two of Cups is the arrival of your perfect heartfelt match. The Lovers represents the electric jolt of attraction—the sensual, physical jolt that lets us know we are alive, that we are here to love and create. The Star card funnels the Two of Cups' good feelings together with the Lovers' passion and openly channels each with her water. She is the integration of passion and feeling. The Ten of Pentacles is the physical manifestation of all things loved and adored. The Ten of Cups represents the arrival and manifestation of a happily ever after ending and the joy that a well-rounded life brings.

METHOD, VISUALIZATION, AND MEDITATION

Lay the Two of Cups and recall the feeling of meeting a perfect friend. Recall the feeling of simpatico and the recognition of oneself in another. Feel the warmth of two hearts coming together. Lay the Lovers card next to the Two of Cups. Feel the fire and flames of desire radiating out of this card. Explore the implicit sensuality of this card and the attraction between the two bodies who are revealing themselves. Note that each card is blessed from a higher source above and between them.

Place the Star card underneath with a corner touching each card. Imagine you are vulnerable, free and open to channel this greater higher passion and love, a passion and love that is so right for you, so full of what and who you are; feel it flowing. Imagine yourself naked under a constellation-filled sky. Each star above you is twinkling at you. One star in particular contains the love energy to bring your perfect match to you. Imagine the star's light washing over you, and in your mind's eye pour water from the canisters at your feet. The moment you do this, you begin to manifest this love into your life.

Lay the Ten of Pentacles. See all the material things love brings to your life. Imagine your friends and family around you, celebrating the happiness you have cultivated. Ancestors surround you, and there is money, more money than you will ever need. Lay the Ten of Cups and feel the lightness of spirit that love brings. See the children dancing and feel yourself childlike and free. A rainbow crosses you because the storm clouds have passed. You are free to move forward with love.

LAYOUT

This is an especially powerful mandala spread and one that may be left out to ponder for days.

Two of Cups   **The Lovers**

The Star

Ten of Pentacles   **Ten of Cups**

Spell to Attract Positive People

INGREDIENTS

2 cups chamomile and honey tea

Three of Cups

METHOD, VISUALIZATION, AND MEDITATION

Honey is an ingredient used in many drawing spells, which brings things we desire to us. Chamomile is a bright, cheerful flower and was a sacred herb for the Druids. The qualities of chamomile are likely similar to the qualities of people you'd like to attract into your life.

Infuse your tea and add honey. Sip and enjoy your tea while leaving a full steaming cup across the table from you. This is an offering to your future friends. Place the Three of Cups card before you. Enter the card and feel the warmth of good feelings surround you. Feel the celebration and camaraderie of being among people who make you feel good. See their cups lifted in the air and then feel how high other people can bring you when they shine the light on your positive qualities and you do so back.

Note that the three friends on the card are also like flowers in a garden, each with their own unique beauty and talent, inspiring one another to do better and be greater. Each member of the circle is better for knowing each person. Know these people—people with warm hearts and good intentions—are heading toward you as you work this spell.

When you are finished, take the tea and spread it around the outside of your home, letting it seep into the earth and attract your new friends.

AFFIRMATION

Three of Cups with love and light
Bring wonderful people to my sight.
My circle surrounds me honest and true
A sweet, delightful witch's brew.
Friends, come to me—Come quick! Come soon!
We meet before the next full moon.

Grow My Money Spell

INGREDIENTS

Fresh mint

A penny, nickel, dime, quarter, and dollar bill

Page of Pentacles

Seven of Pentacles

Small box

METHOD, VISUALIZATION, AND MEDITATION

Mint is the herb reflecting money. Use a bag of mint tea if you can't find fresh mint. The Page of Pentacles represents a person about to plant a seed, while the Seven of Pentacles represents the manifestation and harvest of that seed.

Place mint in a box. Place the Page of Pentacles before you. The ground is fecund. The scent of sweet poppies fills the air. You can smell the rich, upturned earth waiting to be filled with seed. Hold the quarter in your hand and feel its weight. Know that this coin represents the beginning of manifestation. Place it into the box with the mint. Add the rest of the coins and the dollar. Close the box.

Place the Seven of Pentacles next to the Page of Pentacles. See how the single pentacle has divided and multiplied. It is the singular nature of growth that all things innately want to expand when you give them proper attention. In your mind's eye, imagine the money in your account growing and multiplying. Make a promise to do one single thing that will aid in the multiplication of your finances.

AFFIRMATION

Pentacle, herb, coin, and bill
Your multiplication is my will.
My money grows and builds up high
My riches nearly touch the sky!

153

Tarot charms are small pieces of portable magic that you cast and create for yourself to carry and infuse yourself with all day long. Traditionally a charm is a verbal spell. The incantations of witches are charms, such as "Double, double toil and trouble." Children's rhymes, when used as petition, are magical charms: "Star light, star bright, first star I see tonight, I wish I may, I wish I might, have this wish I wish tonight."

The word *charm* means to be alluring, attractive, and magnetic. This is the essence of sparkling energy that the world will take notice of. Like sunlight or moonlight sparkling in the water, so too will you shine.

Create a tarot charm in the morning and infuse yourself with its energy all day long. Use a tarot charm before an important occasion, job interview, presentation, etc.

For example, you have a big project due at work and it requires a weekend of preparation and focus. You decide to charm the Emperor card because he represents stability and laser attention. He also all but guarantees success.

To charm a tarot card, choose the archetype and tarot card with the energy you'd like to exude. Here are some suggestions:

- ✦ Ace an interview = Magician
- ✦ Focus = Chariot
- ✦ Love = Lovers
- ✦ Mastery = Emperor
- ✦ Money attraction = Ace of Pentacles
- ✦ Peace at home = Ten of Cups
- ✦ Peace of mind = Four of Swords
- ✦ Privacy = Hermit
- ✦ Sexy vibes = Queen of Wands
- ✦ Success = Sun

Remember, your own associations and connections to symbol and image are the most powerful magic! Make your own master magic list of tarot charms. Move through your tarot, flipping a card at a time. Select a piece of magic you think the card best embodies.

If you could use each card for a specific piece of magic, what would it be?

Tarot Spirit Card

There are three ways to find out what your tarot spirit card is.

1. Thumb through your deck and pull out the card that is your absolute favorite. This is the card that fills you with elation when you pull it, whose image is soothing to your soul, the card you simply adore.

2. Enter into meditation and ask for your spirit card to appear to you.

3. When you pull cards on a daily basis, you soon discover the same card popping up over and over again. Your tarot spirit card is the card that keeps appearing for you like crazy.

Every time we invoke magic, we really invoke ourselves as we have always been intended to be: sensitive, brilliant, inventive, authentic, unique, powerful. Knowing this, it is possible to weave sacred space beyond mere spellcasting and into every aspect of our daily lives.

A note on magic and spell results...we don't always know what is best. Imagine if everything you ever wished for came true!

QUEEN ofPENTACLES

Chapter Six

Bringing Magic to Life

The Intelligence of the Body

Somatic tarot is how we bring tarot into the body. You will consciously become aware of how you are a living and breathing embodiment of the cards. Just as tarot is a gateway that can be entered, you will discover how the cards enter and animate you. It is the ultimate understanding of yourself in the context of the cards and vice versa. Somatic tarot work also helps you disseminate where psychic and intuitive information occur in your body.

Reading with the intelligence of the body will break your tarot practice wide open. It also acts as a lifeline when you find yourself in a reading rut. Did you know your body is worth MORE than nine million dollars? That's right. Your flesh and blood is a miraculous machine science is unable to re-create or duplicate. It performs a myriad of functions that you don't have to think about. Your brain fires electrical synapses. Your digestive system pulls the nutrients you need. Your lungs and breath inhale and exhale like rhythmic ocean waves.

Body intelligence is a unique wisdom in any chosen part of the body. To understand the intelligences inside your body, imagine you are standing before a breathtaking mountainscape. You feel the mountain's energy while admiring its peaks. If you've visited more than one mountain, you'll recall that mountains, like people, contain their own unique energy, or

157

vibe. You decide to hike to the top of the mountain. You discover different elements making up the mountain as you move higher on the path. You observe grass, flowers, and trees. You see streams, animals, and insects. These separate intelligences, merged together, create the energy of the entire mountain. Each different element of the mountain contains its own unique intelligence and function.

The three intelligences of the body begin with the head, heart, and gut. These are the three places we regularly access when making decisions.

Place your hand on your head. Consider how you make decisions with your brain. Observe yourself thinking, calculating, and observing. The phrases "I'm stuck in my head" or the adjective of being "heady," which means to "affect the mind or senses greatly," refer to the intelligence of the head.

Place your hand on your heart. Have you ever made a decision from your heart? It feels different than a decision from your head, doesn't it? The phrases "heartfelt," "heartwarming," and "heart opening" all refer to heart intelligence.

Place your hand on your lower belly. Consider how you make decisions with your gut. Observe how you sense, feel, and know from inside your gut. The phrases "gut reaction" or "gut wrenching" refer to the feelings associated with the gut.

You'll arrive at different information as you focus on each of the three intelligences of the body. Example: Imagine the following scenario. You walk out of your favorite restaurant and are confronted by an angry mob of people (this situation could be represented by the Seven of Wands card). The crowd mistakenly thinks you have blocked another person's car in. Leading from your head, you might yell back at the crowd or try to reason with them intellectually. If you lead with your heart, you may try to appeal to their emotional side or burst into tears. If you lead with your gut, you may run back inside the restaurant to find safety and call the police.

Consider the following scenario: You uncover solid proof that your monogamous life partner has been cheating on you behind your back with your best friend (a situation that could be reflected by the Three of Swords or a reversed Lovers card). If you respond from the head, it might take a while to fully understand the implications as you sort out the mind-boggling news. You will likely respond with shock and disbelief. If you respond from the heart, you might have a severe emotional breakdown, screaming and crying. If you respond from the gut and your partner is sitting in front of you, you punch them in the face.

Consider how you might offer differing advice based on the three intelligences of your body. Suppose your favorite teenager comes to you in tears because they did not gain acceptance to the college of their dreams. If you respond from the head, you might explain how competitive certain schools are based on the number of applicants. If you spoke from the heart, you might respond by telling them how intelligent, beautiful, and unique they are and that any school would be lucky to have them. If you responded from the gut, you might tell them how they can become a transfer student and be safe and sound inside a dorm room at their dream school in no time. Three intelligences offer three valuable solutions.

Everyone would respond uniquely to each scenario, but you can begin to understand the difference in feeling and responding out of the body's intelligences. Knowing how your energy centers operate is helpful when moving toward your goals. Head intelligence is helpful when studying, making decisions, and figuring things out. The head aligns with the suit of swords and the quality of air. Heart intelligence is helpful when embracing life and finding compassion and empathy. The heart aligns with the suit of cups and the quality of water. Gut intelligence is useful when you need to respond with bodily safety, for healthy food and eating choices, and for rooting into truth. The gut aligns with the suit of wands and the quality of fire.

Making decisions from my head feels like...

Making decisions from my heart feels like...

Making decisions from my gut feels like...

Three Intelligences of the Body Reading

Reading from the three intelligences of the body is useful for three things:

1. It breaks you out of your reading ruts. We fall into habits of how we read and how we interpret each card, especially once we've been reading tarot for a long time. Interpreting the cards from three different parts of the body offers new information.

2. You can respond from these intelligences when making decisions and responding to external issues and relationships.

3. Checking in with your body is the best way to move from your authentic and High Priestess self, which holds all personal authenticity. How do you know you are responding from your highest wisdom and deepest knowledge? By checking in with your body.

Craft a question.

Shuffle and pull a single card.

Bring your energetic awareness into each part of the body as you answer:

My head says...

My heart says...

My gut says...

Third eye opening occurs when you employ intuitive powers. The third eye is said to be the place of concealed wisdom, thus aligning it with the High Priestess tarot card. It relates to psychic power, remote viewing, and astral travel. Third eye opening is a natural side effect of using tarot.

The third eye is the space between and slightly above your eyes. If you were to draw a triangle with your eyes at the base, the tiptop of the triangle would be your third eye. Indian, Hindu, and Buddhist women often wear a beauty mark or decorative bindi jewel at their third eye.

The third eye is not a literal eyeball hidden behind the skin of your forehead. The phrase is a metaphor for the center of higher wisdom and psychic power. It is a reminder that there is more to the world than meets the eye. To look with the third eye is to use every psychic sense you possess. It is to see and know beyond "normal" ways of knowing something.

You already use your third eye to intuit the outside world. It is likely an unconscious action when you see, imagine, and feel what is around you. The third eye transforms when we look on others with envy, jealousy, or anger. It becomes the dreaded evil eye.

Mediterranean culture is rife with blue, white, and black evil eye amulets used to deflect the energy of dark thoughts. Anger, jealousy, and hatred are emotions harboring intense power. Everyone experiences nefarious thoughts. Having them does not mean you are evil. The trick is to notice the feelings and let them go. Become conscious. Keep from using your energy toward others in a nefarious manner. It will make you feel better because wishing harm on another is the quickest path to putting yourself in harm's way. Do not align with energies you wouldn't want coming toward you. It is the witch's rule of three.

One of the most powerful ways to use the third eye is to turn it inward. Use it to examine your interior self. Use your third eye to examine dreams (cups), passions (wands), ideas (swords), and the physical layer of your body (pentacles). Engaging your third eye to explore your inner layer is to explore a vein of gold.

Observe the inner nature of your heart and feel your guts. Converse with different parts of the body to heal what is damaged (keep in mind this should never substitute actual medical advice). Gaze into the space inside your body holding memory and experience. Use your strings of breath, your inhales and exhales, to travel back in time. Meet the generations who came before. They live inside of you. Their memories, ways, habits, and talents are buried within us.

Chakra Reading

Chakras are energy centers inside the body. We all hold memories, trauma, and pleasure inside the body. Explore and expand the power pulsing inside you. Perform the chakra reading to assess your internal state. It begins at the base of your spine and moves to the top of your head.

Close your eyes and sit straight in your chair. Take three deep inhales and exhales. Feel your feet root into the floor and feel the roots extend into the earth below. Pull energy from the earth up and to the base of your spine. Bring it up to your stomach, your heart, your throat. Bring it up to your eyes and to the top of your head. Open your eyes and cast your cards as follows:

Questions

1. Root: *What keeps me grounded?*

2. Sacral: *What makes me feel alive?*

3. Solar Plexus: *What gives me power?*

4. Heart: *How can I expand my heart?*

5. Throat: *How can I communicate better?*

6. Third Eye: *How can I see my truth?*

7. Crown: *How do I best connect to my highest good?*

Five Sense Journaling Exercise

Shuffle the cards while focusing on the awareness of the body. Pull a card for each sense and answer the question posed.

Smell is associated with the root (first) chakra: self-preservation, heredity, vitality, and identification with the physical body. Smell is a very distinct quality and can evoke intense emotion. Olfactory senses bring the world inside you. Humans are able to detect over one trillion distinct scents. Smell brings pleasure while keeping us safe.

I take better care of myself when I...

Taste is associated with the sacral (second) chakra: self-gratification, sexual fulfillment, and nurturing. Your tastes are what intrigue you—your likes and dislikes. Your tastes can be refined and made more discriminating. This card will provide information on how you take care of yourself and how you identify with your emotional body.

I nurture myself when I...

Sight is associated with the solar plexus (third) chakra: self-definition, ego identity, thoughts, and willpower. Your capacity to actually look at what is ahead for yourself and others, how excellent you are at interpreting what is right in front of you, and how to clear your vision so that you see what you need to.

I can see myself in a new light by...

Touch is associated with the heart (fourth) chakra: self-acceptance, social identity, love, and peace. Touch is how you literally feel the universe and the world around you. Touch extends to how you make a difference in other people's lives and your own emotional state. Touch infiltrates every inch of our body inside and out.

I make the world a better place by...

Hearing is associated with the throat (fifth) chakra: communication and creativity. How well do you listen to yourself and those around you? If you sit with a friend or client, do you really take their needs inward or do you launch into your interpretation straightaway? How can you better open up to hearing what is around you?

I express myself well when I...

Your Sixth Sense

How much do you trust your inner voice?

I can hone my psychic and intuitive abilities by...

Applying sense meditation to a card is a fabulous way to enter a tarot archetype. Sit comfortably with your deck in a calm and centered space where you will be undisturbed. Select a card to explore with your five senses. You can either choose the card you would like to work with and place it before you at the start or shuffle the deck so you can flip the card at random when the time comes. Place a small piece of dark chocolate (or your favorite small one-bite food like a nut or a berry) next to you and within hand's reach.

Close your eyes and focus on your breathing. Fill your body on the inhale and empty yourself on the exhale. Allow your breath to become like the rhythmic crash of waves on a shore—the push and pull, the inhale and exhale, the expansion and contraction.

Sound: Once you have connected to your breath, keep your eyes closed. Focus on the sounds surrounding you. What do you hear? Perhaps birds are singing, the fridge is humming, or maybe you detect music playing from some far corner of the house or from a car passing by. Try to identify each sound, list them as you notice them. Once you are listening, can you move deeper into each individual sound? If you hear birds, can you differentiate the multiple bird songs? If there's music playing, is it a radio or a record? If it's from a car, can you connect to the throbbing bass of the speakers? Does it sound like the beating of your heart?

Smell: Keeping your eyes closed, shift your focus to your sense of smell. What scents do you detect? Is there a trace of therapeutic essential oil or earthy incense in the room? Do you smell a lingering lemon scent from a cleaning product, are savory food smells wafting from the kitchen, or do you detect yummy green grass and flowers? Is the wind bringing the scent of soil from an incoming rainstorm? Can you smell your own skin? Move deeper into whatever you detect. Can you pull apart the scent?

Taste: Your olfactory sense is intimately connected to taste. Moving from the sense of smell, what do you taste? What does the inside of your mouth taste like? What do your teeth taste like? Is there a remnant of a drink, food, or toothpaste across your tongue? Focus on the muscle of your tongue and try to notice and taste every part of it. Reach out to your chocolate or one-bite snack and pop it in your mouth, slowly savoring it before you swallow.

Feel: Focus on your tongue. Trace the inside of your mouth. Slide your tongue across the roof, the cheeks, and the spaces between your teeth. Move your awareness to your delicate fingertips and lightly touch them together. How is this sense of touch in your fingertips different from the touch of your tongue? Move through your body and find every place of contact between your body and the outer world. Feel where your skin meets the fabric of your clothing. Feel where the pressure of your skin sits against the chair or the floor, and in every square inch where you find contact, explore it through your awareness.

See: Open your eyes. Gaze in front of you. Look only at the colors surrounding you. Do not identify anything. Observe your peripheral vision and allow everything to come into focus. Look at the wall (if there's a wall) in front of you. Can you see through the wall? What lies beyond? Can you see with more than just your eyes? Can you see with your entire body? Can you observe with your whole body? Can you sense with your entire body?

Enter the card: Take the card you have chosen to enter and place it in front of you where you can observe it. Stare at the card for 2 to 5 minutes. You can preset a timer on your phone if you like. Look at the card with your entire body. Observe it carefully with your eyes. With a soft gaze, enter the card. Allow the borders of the card to dissolve. Let the card fill your entire line of vision.

Third Eye Activation Exercise

Pull your Ace of Pentacles card and sit with it in a comfortable spot where you will not be disturbed. Set a five-minute timer. Use a soft gaze to observe the Ace of Pentacles, noting every detail of the card. Close your eyes when the timer goes off. See the pentacle in your mind's eye. Turn the pentacle a bright golden yellow. The pentacle glows with the intensity of the sun. Spin the pentacle clockwise and watch it glow, spark, and rotate. Imagine the glowing pentacle at your third eye center.

Bring your vision through the third eye by gazing through it with your eyes closed. Observe whatever's in front of you. Push your vision past it. What lies beyond? If you are sitting outside, allow your vision to expand as far as you can go.

Bring your vision back into your head and switch to look out the third eye through the back of your head (because chakras exist through the body, front and back). Observe whatever's behind you. What lies beyond it? If you are sitting outside, allow your vision to expand behind you for as far as you can go.

Bring your vision back to your head and use your third eye to see the landscape to your right without turning your head. What is next to you? Expand your third eye vision further. See the landscape to your left. What is at your left side? Expand your third eye vision further.

Bring your vision back to your head and turn it inside yourself so you are gazing inside the body. Your third eye is now moving inside of you. Examine the inside of your face, your cheeks, your mouth. Look at your ears and through your nose. Turn your third eye vision straight down and peer down your throat.

Examine your neck and shoulders. If you notice any tension, release it with your gaze. Move deeper into the muscles and help them relax. Journey into the bone and deeper into the marrow. Use your vision to slide down your spine. Move it into the center of your heart. What do you see? What do you feel? Peer into your lungs. Watch them expand as you breathe in. Notice them contract as you breathe out.

Move your vision into your stomach, then into your guts. There is so much sensitivity and history packed in there. What do you notice? Move to the bottom of your thighs, look out the front of your knees. Bring your vision down to the space between your big toe and the second toe. Stretch your feet. Look out the bottom of your feet. What do you see?

Look outward from different parts of the body as you work your way up to your head. Once you reach your head, look through the top of your head, through your skull. Open to receive light and inspiration. Feel the energy pulsing through you.

Return to the space of the third eye. See the bright yellow pentacle glowing at your forehead, activated and alive. Bring yourself back to the room you are sitting in and open your eyes.

Bringing Tarot into Your Yoga Practice

Bringing tarot and yoga together deepens your experience with the cards and your yoga practice. Tarot and yoga can be seamlessly intertwined and become a powerful force of transformation and evolution. Tarot and yoga are both practices that aid your soul in its unfolding of itself. Tarot is a visual practice, operating symbolically and inspiring the reader's creative imagination and intuition, while yoga is a physical practice, where the student moves the body through postures called asanas. Each push us forward in unexpected ways and unleash possibilities we can scarcely imagine.

Sacred space: Tarot and yoga both allow the practitioner to carve out sacred space amidst the daily noise and distraction of day-to-day life. The practices often, but not always, involve the use of sacred objects such as incense, candles, and a dedicated space. A tarotist clears and quiets the mind as she draws cards. A yogi settles down and focuses on the breath to quiet the mind at the beginning her practice.

Flow: Both tarot and yoga reflect life as a constant state of flow. In yoga we move from one asana, or pose, to the next, while in tarot the cards move in numerical sequence, the minors from ace through ten and back around. The majors run from zero (Fool) to twenty-two (the World) and circle back to begin the cycle anew.

Intuition and answers: Tarot and yoga are practices that quiet the mind. The tarotist centers herself so she can focus on the messages coming through the cards while the yogi focuses on her breath and brings attention inside the body. Both activities bring us into a state of higher listening and help us become the active observer of our present experience. Doing so allows intuition to blossom, and we become adept at finding answers to life's biggest, smallest, and most interesting questions.

Sublime structure: Tarot contains a gorgeous internal structure, just like the delicate bones of your human skeleton. Each of us are made up of the same essential body parts from blood to belly, yet who we are—the signature of our soul, the way we inhabit our body—is as unique as the snowflakes in a storm. Individuality graces our skeletons, muscles, and soft internal organs. No two people move in exactly the same way; even identical twins are different. Tarot's structure is so well organized and simple that a multitude of spiritual systems and themes can be placed on top of it and make perfect sense. Yoga's structure comes through its shapes, which embody archetypal energies just like tarot.

Archetype and asana: Yoga asanas imitate the archetype of animals (down dog) and objects (boat pose). One can hold an asana while breathing and meditating on the lessons of the pose just as we may contemplate a tarot card. Placing a yoga asana with each major arcana card offers the tarot reader an opportunity to experience and embody the archetype in a fresh new way.

Readers are who are used to entering the cards via guided meditation or role-playing in a classroom or workshop situation will find a new way of embodying the cards through yoga postures. Combining asanas with the majors and calling the major archetypes to mind while inside the posture is a powerful new way to embody the eternal lesson of archetypes. It also merges the archetype with chakras, breath, and motion, thereby filling them and yourself with energy and the universal life force.

> FOOL = Mountain/tadasana, which begins the practice. The Fool is pictured on a mountaintop. Both pose and card offer balance, presence, and spiritual clarity. Consider the heights and depths we aspire to ascend. The card and the pose also prepare us for the looming adventure ahead of us both in our practice and in our life.

> MAGICIAN = Sun salutation/surya namaskar. The sun salutation is a dynamic pose matching the Magician's energetic stance. Sun salutation channels solar energy from above and invites it into the body, just as the Magician channels spiritual energy through his body and into the material world via his magic wand.

> HIGH PRIESTESS = Intention/opening chant. The yogi quiets the mind, settles into her practice, focuses on her breathing, and begins devotion to her practice. This posture is often accompanied by an opening chant/mantra/stated intention. These actions align the inner and outer selves.

> EMPRESS = Triangle/trikonasana. The Empress is number three, the number of creativity, a triangle with three points. The posture offers expansion. The body opens like a flower soaking in solar energy while the heart expands for deeper love, expansive compassion, and unbound creativity.

EMPEROR = Four-limbed staff pose/chaturanga dandasana. *Chaturanga* means four limbs, and *danda* means staff. The Emperor is number four and traditionally holds a staff. This dynamic pose requires strength, control, and agility—all Emperor qualities. Chaturanga builds the stability needed for a demanding physical practice.

HIEROPHANT = Pyramid with reverse prayer/utthita parsvottanasana. This eloquent, devotional posture reflects gratitude in the presence of divine holiness. A prayer is a symbolic gesture uniting polarities as the left and right palms come together. Bowing is the act of ultimate reverence. The reverse prayer reflects duality, opposition, yin and yang, and balance and harmony of the heart. The triangular shape of the legs and ultimately the entire body echoes the graphic trinity of the Hierophant.

LOVERS = Camel/ustrasana. The yogi balances on her knees and reaches back for her feet, offering her heart to the sky. This heart-opening pose is a gesture of extreme vulnerability and tenderness. The Lovers card reflects how we offer ourselves to another when we engage in acts of love and creativity.

CHARIOT = Chair/utkatasana. This dynamic pose reflects the charioteer and his vehicle. Chair pose is often held for long periods of time. The arms reach skyward while bent legs and seat move down. Oppositional energy speaks to the Chariot's fortitude. Power and balance is required. It invokes the effort utilized to set a goal and move directly toward it without distraction.

STRENGTH = The Strength card aligns with yoga's warrior II pose, or virabhadrasana. The yogi forms the posture of an advancing warrior. The Strength card reflects internal vitality and the warrior pose energizes the body. Like the Strength card, it combines stunning power with soft, pliable gentleness.

HERMIT = Plow/halasana. The yogi lays on her back and swings her legs over her head, keeping them straight while the top of her feet rest on the floor behind her. Plow pose brings the practitioner directly to the heart chakra. There is no avoiding it. What happens when you are confronted by the nature of your own heart's attitude toward itself?

WHEEL OF FORTUNE = Wheel/urdhva dhanurasana. It is a standing backbend emulating the shape an archer's bow or a wheel, connecting it to the symbolic shape of the Wheel of Fortune. It aligns with the wild energy of universal forces. Backbends work the nervous system, the network connecting the brain, spinal cord, and nerves. It can feel like a roller coaster: intense, scary, and even terrifying, precisely why it aligns with Wheel of Fortune energy.

JUSTICE = Eagle/garudasana. Eagle requires complex balancing ability as leg and arm wrap the body while knees bend into a sitting position on one leg. The balancing aspect aligns the yogi with Justice's sword and scales.

HANGED MAN = Supported headstand/sirsasana. Inverting the body encourages balance and strength while flipping the world in its head. Examine the nature of the universe and your location on the planet. There is no right-side up or upside down. See through the illusion.

DEATH = Corpse/savasana. In this pose the yogi literally assumes the posture of Death's deep sleep and lies like a corpse on the yoga mat at the end of the practice. Rest and stillness are as important as effort and output, ebb and flow.

TEMPERANCE = Seated spinal twist/ardha matsyendrasana. Temperance card's fluids are fused in front of the angel's sacral chakra, located three inches below the naval. Like the Temperance card, the sacral chakra is associated with water, emotions, and creativity. Seated spinal twists work the sacral chakra to encourage flexibility and fluidity. This action encourages complexity, which heals and expands the world by benefiting all.

DEVIL = Crow/bakasana. Crows are shapeshifters, transformative creatures reflecting dark, shadowy realms. The Devil sprouts bat wings while balancing on top of his cube. Crow pose is an arm balance, and yogis often employ mind over matter to achieve this difficult posture.

TOWER = Tree/vrksasana. Tree pose requires the yogi to balance on one leg while lifting the arms to the sky, invoking the shape of a tree and the Tower. The yogi becomes stable through the three worlds (lower, middle, and upper). Rooted in the ground, they stretch through the material world and reach toward spiritual ascension.

STAR = Lotus/padmasana. Lotus is the ancient and traditional cross-legged meditative pose of India. Lotus pose is often performed at the beginning and/or end of a yoga practice, while the legs may move into lotus inside other postures. The yogi clears, focuses, and lets the energy of the practice move freely through the body. Lotus echoes the Star card in every way. It is the moment of reaping benefits. Alignment of above and below is reached. Just as yogis bask in mindful clarity, effort, and sweat, so does the Star card filter the sacred water of the universe.

MOON = Half moon/ardha chandrasana. This posture combines the fiery essence of the sun with the cooling essence of the moon, thus echoing the sun and moon depicted inside the Moon card. A yoga practice echoes the ebb and flow of lunar cycles. The yogi's experience on the mat morphs and changes, flying effortlessly one day, feeling weighted down and heavy the next. Yoga, like the moon, reflects the nature of time, the gifts of grounding inside the present moment. Yoga and the Moon card meet us in malleable and ever-changing forms.

THE SUN = Child's pose/balasana. The body assumes a fetal position, thus aligning the posture with the young child illustrated on the Sun card. Child's pose, like the Sun card, is a place of absorption and effortless pleasure. The posture encourages the energy of the sun coursing through the body. It fosters interconnectivity between you and all living things.

JUDGEMENT = Warrior I/virabhadrasana. The yogi reaches toward the sky in a physical imitation of the mythological Hindu warrior Virabhadra, who rose from the earth with two swords, one in each hand. The Judgement card is illustrated with bodies emerging from floating coffins. It is reanimation and rebirth, just like the warrior. The posture and card both require you to stand up, pay attention, and heed the call. It is a willingness to invoke transformation on its highest level.

WORLD = Down dog/adho mukha svanasana. It may feel counterintuitive to align a seemingly basic yoga pose to the World card, the most highly esteemed card of tarot, yet the World card's properties are not reserved for a chosen few or the most enlightened. The World card infuses every moment of our life. The World card, like the down dog, offers the integration of the highest and lowest, expansive and introspective, and every infinite space in between.

Tarot and the Mat

Pull a card before your practice and set an intention with the card. Yogis often take a moment to set an intention or dedicate the yoga practice to a person or a higher ideal. If you already do this, shuffle your cards and leave them near your mat. Set your intention and then choose a card. Conversely, you can choose a card and then set your intention. Leave the card at the top of your mat for the duration of your practice.

Meditate on a card before and after practice. Yoga is a centered and sacred space, so if you bring a card to the mat with you, you can incorporate the card's lessons, meanings, and messages into your practice. You can also project the card with your mind's eye at the front of your yoga mat in a moving meditation.

Open the four suits and directions around your yoga mat with your mind's eye. Just as you open magical spell space with the four suits of tarot, so you can invite the elemental energies and suits to the four sides of your mat before you begin practice. You can do this through your mind's eye as you sit in meditation or you can literally place the four aces in the appropriate directions.

Read a tarot spread before and after practice. I remember back in my college days when I would take advantage of free yoga classes. I would always marvel at how much my studying improved, how my focus turned laser sharp, and how much more retentive my memory was after a yoga class. Perform a tarot reading of your choice before taking a class. Leave the spread out. Revisit your cards and the spread after practice. What new information do you see? What new intuitions do you have?

Yoga Asana Archetype Spread

The questions of this spread are based on basic yoga poses to explore the meaning and metaphor behind them. This spread is helpful whether you are familiar with the practice or not. If you do keep a personal yoga practice, you might want to ponder these questions when performing these asanas.

Cast Your Cards

The cards of this spread are cast in the shape of down dog, an all-over rejuvenating stretch.

Questions

1. Down Dog Pose: What helps me turn inward?

2. Tree Pose: Why is it important to be strong yet flexible?

3. Headstand: What helps me to see the world from a different perspective?

4. Eagle: Can I see what is truly important in life?

5. Cobra: Can I rise above the material world and peer into the unknown?

6. Child's Pose: How do I cultivate a youthful attitude?

7. Death Pose: How can I let go of everything?

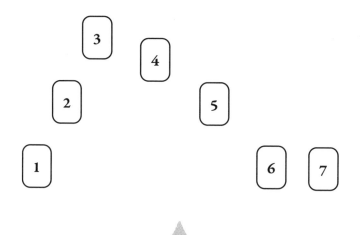

Hints for
Better Dreaming

✦

Keep a dream journal

✦

Tell yourself you will dream
while falling asleep

✦

Jog your memory
upon waking

✦

Dreamwork

Ancient Egyptians and Greeks believed dreams were messages sent by the gods to shape the dreamer's mind. Sigmund Freud told us dreams are caches of unfulfilled wishes and a window to the psyche. Some cultures make no distinction between dreaming and waking life. Scientists sometimes claim dreams are the brain's way of unloading unnecessary information like a computer clearing away data. Artists and mystics mine dreams for ideas and inspiration. Prophetic dreams allow the dreamer to witness future places, events, and happenings.

The subconscious mind becomes observable while sleeping. We are not bound by the laws of physics or time in our sleep, so we weightlessly fly, converse with the dead, and kiss strangers until we wake up sweaty, breathless, and often full of emotion. Dreams help us tackle problems, process anxieties, even rehearse for scenarios we might encounter in waking life.

Improving dream recall is like building the strength and flexibility of your intuitive muscles. The more you focus on the art of dreaming, the more substantive they become. Keep a small journal next to your sleeping area so you can record your dream scenarios upon waking. Begin the process by journaling briefly, noting your thoughts and feelings, before falling asleep.

Dreams tend to evaporate quickly upon waking. Keep your eyes closed and jog your memory upon waking by asking yourself, "Was I just dreaming?" See if some fragment or vision comes back to you. Rather than trying to figure out what your dream means when you are writing it down, focus on recording the details. Interpret the symbols later using the following method:

Deconstruct a symbol from a dream the same way you assess a tarot symbol's meaning.

Select the most notable symbol you had in a recent or recurrent dream.

Symbol:

What symbol means to me:

How this meaning relates to my current life:

EXAMPLE

SYMBOL: Beheaded man

WHAT SYMBOL MEANS TO ME: Beheaded man = Not being connected to the physical body

HOW THIS RELATES TO MY CURRENT LIFE: I am not connected to my physical body when I am in a place of distress. I need to learn how to reconnect during stress and anxiety.

Once you have figured out how the symbol relates to your current life, pull a tarot card for advice on how to integrate this issue.

EXAMPLE: The Six of Swords is drawn, which tells me to cut the emotional cords of old pains so I can stop cutting off my head to spite my body and move in a state of disconnection. I must learn to cut away the bad and embrace the good so I can move forward to better times.

The Dream Oraculum

An oraculum is a divine announcement or prophecy. Consider your dreams as divine messages from the major arcana. Use the oraculum to discover which major arcana sent the dream to you. Once you identify the archetype responsible for your dream, you can gain further information on why it is important and what it means for your waking life. Use the formula below and reduce the numbers until you arrive at their major arcana equivalent.

1. Day of the week you dreamed (using Sunday as day 1).

2. Day of the month you dreamed.

3. The month you dreamed.

4. Your age.

EXAMPLE

Susan dreams that her dog is running away from her. He gallops down the middle of a country road, and once he's over a hill, she cannot catch up to him. She wakes up and performs the oraculum to discover who sent the dream and what it means.

1. 6 (Saturday)

2. 14 (14th of November)

3. 11 (November is the eleventh month)

4. 50 (age)
   ___
   81

8 = Strength

1 = Magician

8 + 1 = 9 = Hermit

ORACULUM READING: HERMIT

INTERPRETATION

Susan is surprised to discover the Hermit sent her this dream. Upon reflection, she understands why. Susan is constantly chasing after things that are out of her reach. The Hermit's message is to slow down and move within. He reminds her the answer is not outside but inside of her. Once she slows down and does some soul searching, her anxiety will diminish and answers will become clear.

Is Tarot Dreaming Us?

Are we dreaming tarot or is the tarot dreaming us? Our relationship with tarot is a two-way street. We turn to tarot for insight, answers, meditation, guidance. Did you know the energy of the cards is watching us? Observing us. Reading us. How often do you pull a card and it's the perfect reflection of your present state—a mirror to your situation? They know, they watch, and they listen.

Have you ever randomly frozen yourself, placed imaginary borders around yourself, and asked, "What tarot card am I embodying right now?" If you haven't, you should. Switch your perspective. What does tarot learn from you? Your actions, your emotions, your work, your love, you daily activity? What would someone or something who is looking at you through the cards see?

Flip a card:

What you want from me is...

How I can best serve you is...

Bedtime Dreamwork Meditation with the Moon Card

Place the Moon card where you can focus on it with a soft gaze. Focus on your breath. Become grounded where you are sitting. Let the edges of the card blur away as you peer inside the card. Once you can see the card's details clearly in your mind's eye, turn out the lights and close your eyes. Examine the darkness behind your eyelids. Place the palms of your hands over your eyes. Move deeper into the darkness. Push forward as if you were swimming down into a pool of water. Pull your hand away from your eyes, place them on your lap, and as the darkness grows lighter, imagine yourself pushing up to the top of a pool of water.

Without opening your eyes, imagine yourself moving through the surface of a pond and greeting the light of the full moon above you. Feel the gentle night air on your cheeks, let the water drip from your body, and listen to the howling of wolves far in the distance. You rise from the water and see a path. It leads from the pond to the top of a high mountain in the distance. You float upon the path, your toes a few feet above the ground, knowing something important waits for you at the mountain-top. You pause as you move closer to the two howling wolves. They quiet as you draw near and you look into their wild eyes without fear. Staring back at you with yellow eyes, they give you a message.

My message from the wolves is...

You move beyond the beasts and make your way up the path past two towers. They loom high above you on either side and you feel the presence of your spirit guides looking down upon you. You continue and begin ascending the mountain until you reach the top. The full moon is fat and bright. Its milky lunar essence spills over you. You look up to the moon and ask for the wisdom and ability to dream in a way that offers you clarity and illumination. The moon smiles back and agrees to your wish. It gives you a message, a message only you can hear.

My message from the moon is...

Shadow Work

Shadow work is essential for those who desire self-actualization. We are multidimensional, holistic creatures who are ever shifting between polarities. We move between sleep and wakefulness, high and low energy, responsibility and pleasure, and, of course, darkness and light. The moon doesn't exist without its dark side, and neither do you.

Shadow work keeps tarot readings on point, especially when you are reading for yourself. Self-reads present a unique challenge. How do we know we are finding the truth of the cards or simply telling ourselves the story of what we want to see? Shadow work is the medicine for self-justification because to do it, you are required to examine things about yourself you don't normally want to look at. It is like a horror movie or gothic fairy tale starring you. Ready to peel away a layer of yourself?

SHADOW SELF IS

◆

Impulse/desire

Strength/weakness

Talents/preferences

Personal belief systems

Infinite creativity

◆

The shadow is like a trash heap or giant basement where you throw everything you'd rather not deal with about yourself. It holds the parts of you you'd like to pretend aren't true or don't want to think about. The shadow is where you place repressed instinct and impulse. This is where everything goes that your mother or caregiver told you you weren't allowed to do. It is where you place all the things "nice people" don't do. The shadow holds murderous, violent inclinations, selfish behavior, deviance, and everything society deems unacceptable. Talk about scary!

Talents, love, and magical qualities inhabit the shadow too. Remember when you loved to sing and that drama teacher told you you couldn't, so you stopped? You threw that lovely voice into the shadow. Talents and curiosities you are afraid to display or explore are stored there. Ever fallen head over heels in love with someone you weren't allowed to love or didn't think you deserved? Their gorgeous face and warm beating heart is tucked away inside your shadow waiting for one more kiss. Qualities, personal attributes, weirdness, anything you fear isn't good enough in comparison to others and want to silence gets crammed in the shadow. Original thinking, creativity, entire ways of being that are true to you can be deeply buried in your shadow. Talk about rich!

You are already shedding light into the shadow by reading this. It's calling on the larger part of your imagination. We justify our behavior and actions all the time. This is why the road to hell is paved with good intentions. *I didn't mean to be cruel to my best friend that time I left her at the mall, but I really wanted to leave. I didn't mean to be rude to my husband, but he didn't understand how I felt. I didn't mean to yell at my daughter, but she interrupted me for the fourteenth time when I was trying to pay the bills.* You can't see these things if you aren't willing to break out of your comfort zone, but once you do, you can take responsibility for your actions. You acknowledge your behavior or desire. Then you are free to make amends. This heals relationships, makes way for growth, and, more than anything, it sets you free.

Five Things Exercise

This exercise takes only a few moments. Write down five things you can't stand about other people. Five qualities that make you go crazy. Five things people do that fill your throat with the bitter bile of anger. It could be five qualities of a single person or from many people. It could be something you observe in friends and family or something you see celebrities or media figures doing. List five qualities that make you hot under the collar.

1.

2.

3.

4.

5.

Now that you've listed five things (and don't worry if you could only come up with three or four, that's okay too), circle the one thing on the list that bothers you the most before reading any further.

Once you've circled it, take a good hard look. THIS is the shadow quality most dominant in your shadow self. This is the quality you have to come to terms with.

The quality I circled is...

Our experience of life is a projection. Remember, the universe is inside of us. What we focus on is what we need to work through. For example, you circled inauthenticity because your pretentious friend exhibits fake behavior that drives you up a wall. If inauthenticity is in your shadow, think about what ways you are being fake in your own life.

You can see in this second example how people move in the opposite direction of their shadow issue. Let's say Susie circled rude behavior. First, she considers how she is rude to others. She would never consciously do such a thing. Instead, she moves in the opposite direction. She puts others' needs ahead of her own because she is afraid to be rude. She puts others first so often, she can barely speak for herself. She has lost her true voice and cannot be authentic unless she integrates this aspect of her shadow.

Integrate the Shadow Reading

Look at the quality you circled in the five things exercise.

CARD 1: How you repress this quality.

CARD 2: How you express this quality.

CARD 3: How you can integrate this quality and move forward.

Romancing the shadow is a way to explore your shadow via our romantic experiences. We involve ourselves with someone or something and our imagination explodes. This magical person seems to hold the key to everything in our lives. The five things exercise reflected how those things we find annoying in others are what exist inside of us. When we romance our shadow, we discover all the things we feel about the person we fall in love with are also qualities existing inside of us.

The greatest love of my life is...

Youth/teen: Write the name of the person, place, or thing you fell in love with or crushed on hard when you were a prepubescent child. It would be a movie star, singer, or classmate. Write their name and three of the qualities that you loved about them. How did they make you feel?

Their name:

1.

2.

3.

Teens/twenties: Write the name of the person, place, or thing you fell in love with or crushed on hard when you were a teen or in your early twenties. Write their name and three of the qualities that you loved about them. How did they make you feel?

Their name:

1.

2.

3.

Present: Write the name of the person, place, or thing you are in love with or crushed on hard right now. Write their name and three of the qualities that you love about them. How do they make you feel?

Their name:

1.

2.

3.

Circle one the most wonderful and exciting qualities of each time period. THESE are all qualities existing inside of you. Perform the following spread to discover how to coax these qualities out of you.

Romancing the Shadow Spread

Write each of the three qualities across a piece of paper and pull a single card for each quality. The card will tell you how to invoke this quality in your life right now.

CARD 1: How to invoke this quality in your present life.

CARD 2: How to invoke this quality in your present life.

CARD 3: How to invoke this quality in your present life.

Diary of Dark Thoughts

You know how it feels better to talk to your besties instead of keeping everything bottled up inside? Nothing helps exorcise inner demons as much as expressing them. A diary of dark thoughts is a book dedicated exclusively to your lowest, meanest, most horrid thoughts and feelings. A diary of dark thoughts is exactly what it sounds like: a repository where you are free to express anything not deemed "acceptable." Once you acknowledge your feelings, chances are they vanish. If not, it might be time to seek professional help.

If you want to start a diary of dark thoughts but aren't sure how to begin, embark on some writing prompts:

>*The darkest thing I think about other people is...*
>
>*The darkest thing I think about myself is...*
>
>*Something I would do if I knew I wouldn't get caught is...*

Once you've completed an entry, pull a tarot card to discover what space will open up inside yourself once you allow this darkness to move through you and disappear. Conversely, if you are still feeling riled up, pull a card asking about how you can exorcise these thoughts from your brain.

A diary of dark thoughts is especially helpful when you are caught up in an obsessive thought cycle, mental loop, head spin, or find yourself caught in a web of passive-aggressive behavior. The trick is to keep writing in a stream-of-consciousness format (without punctuation or spelling worries) until the thoughts have relaxed their grip.

Tarot shadow reversals are not generally comfortable to work with, but they are essential if you are serious about exploring your shadow. Shadow work is about bringing the light of consciousness to the unacknowledged areas in your life. It means taking personal responsibility for actions and behaviors that you would rather push aside and ignore. These are moments you are selfish, cruel, or terrible to another person, place, or thing. None of us want to admit we can be wretched to others, but we all do nasty things and act in horrible ways even if we don't mean to. Sometimes we become the very thing we abhor and then make excuses or brush our behavior aside rather than face what we have done. A shadow reversal is an opportunity to explore how you exhibit the darkest qualities of tarot in your life.

Remember, tarot cards are more than images printed on paper. They are full and rich worlds of experience even though they look like flat images on a card. Archetypal tarot experience is like a wall calendar. Imagine you are looking at the square of Monday, June 22, inside the grid of a monthly calendar. It is a little white box; maybe you wrote some notes or reminders inside of it. Now consider your experience of that day once it is over. Your day was anything but flat! It was colorful, voluminous, and nuanced. It was full of experience, people, color, taste, sound, and all the experiential qualities of life. The same is true of a tarot card.

Keep this quality in mind to shadow-reverse a card. Gaze at the card. Observe its landscape and figures, and note what is happening. Move into the card with your mind's eye and fully embrace the qualities you discover. Once inside the card, become a figure on the card. Look through the eyes of the card. Feel the essence of the archetype as you embody it. Look around your room through the eyes of the card. How do things look different? How do you feel? What do you want to do?

To find the card's shadow reversal, shift the card into its darkest quality. If the card is painted at night, transform it into day. If the card is on a mountain, bring it to a valley. If it is sunny, watch the card become stormy. How does the character you inhabit become opposite of what it was? How does this change how you feel? Now what do you want to do? Observe these qualities and consider how you have done this exact thing in your own life.

Let's shadow-reverse the Empress card. Pull out the Empress card. Enter the card in your mind's eye. You discover she exudes creative energy and life-giving abundance. Bright yellow sunshine shimmers on golden fields of wheat. It is warm and inviting—a wonderland of lush, sensual delight. You move close to her throne to gaze at her luminous skin, dazzling crown, velvet pillows, and gentle eyes. She grants you permission to sit down inside her body and become her.

You gaze through Empress eyes as you observe the landscape and find endless fields of opportunity. The waterfall behind you flows freely with inspiration and ideas. You feel abundance, pleasure, and life-giving love. You use your Empress eyes to gaze around the room you are sitting in. You see opportunity in every corner. Gratitude oozes through your pores, and you hold a deep desire to nurture yourself and others around you.

Now that you have fully embraced the essence of the Empress archetype, it is time to explore her shadow. Clouds roll in to obscure the sunshine. Cold breezes blow across the fields, and a frost wilts the wheat. The waterfall runs dry. The Empress's silken robes become scratchy and uncomfortable. The desire to nurture and love transforms into a need to hate and destroy. Look around your room with these shadow eyes and notice what looks different. When was the last time you felt this urge? When was the last time you tried to destroy something? When did you hurt instead of nurture? When were you cruel and selfish? When did you wound another person or yourself?

Once you have identified the shadow of a card and how you embodied it to another person, place, thing, or yourself, you can take responsibility for it. The power of owning up to your behavior means you are less likely to repeat it in the future now that you have brought the light of your consciousness to it. Let's say the reversed Empress reminded you of when you shut down the creative impulse of a child when they were excited to show you something. You can now have a conversation about that moment. Let's say your partner was feeling emotionally vulnerable but you were so hurt by what they were saying about you that you lashed out, saying the worst thing you could say to them. You now have the opportunity to revisit that moment and bring clarity to it with your partner. It is less likely to happen again with such intensity.

Shuffle and pull a card.

Enter the card in your mind's eye and explore it. Look through the eyes of a character on the card.

Shadow-reverse the card.

Look through the eyes and feel the dark side of the card. When have you embodied this quality?

I embodied this shadow reversal when I...

The action I can take to correct it is...

Shadow reversals are fun when you move into dark cards and shadow-reverse them. Let's say you move into the Nine of Swords. You observe the card with your mind's eye and step through the borders to inhabit the character within. You feel your legs beneath the sheets, feel anxiety at your temples, sense the darkness in the room. Paranoia and strife ripple through your body. You quickly move to shadow-reverse the card and find yourself in a luxurious bed. The dark wall of swords is now priceless gothic art. You find yourself wearing the softest silky nightgown; your head is light with giggles; your eyes dance with pleasure. The room is awash with glowing candles and feather pillows that lull you into a beautiful dream-filled sleep. You feel the sustenance of a good night's slumber filled with pleasureful dreams. The act of imagining this puts you in an emotional state encouraging a beautiful night's sleep tonight. You wake tomorrow only to discover you have embodied the shadow on the Nine of Swords in its highest, brightest possible context.

Adore and Deplore Shadow Reversal Exercise

Select one card you adore and one you deplore.

The card I adore is...

I embody this card when I...

I reflect the destructive nature of this card when I...

The card I deplore is...

I embody this card when I...

I reflect the expansive nature of this card when I...

The crux of shadow work lies inside the Devil card. The Devil is the force of repression created by the ego. The ego is a healthy and natural part of the human psyche. Babies are not born knowing they are separate from the people and things. The ego blossoms with maturity and the understanding that you are separate from other things, as evidenced when a toddler runs into a table or a child falls off a bike or a mother leaves the room. The ego creates the notion of "I."

We need the ego in order to navigate the material world. The ego keeps us safe the same way healthy fear keep us from falling off a cliff. We don't want to destroy the ego or fear. They keep us safe. We don't want ego and fear to control us. Fears and the ego become dangerous when they grow too large and we begin to make decisions and respond out of them. If we can recognize ego and fear when they pop up, they will not hold us hostage.

Identify the ego by answering the following writing prompts:

I like to project that I...

I want people to think of me as...

I feel powerful over others when I...

I get uptight about...

I get angry at myself when I...

I hate when...

I am jealous when I see...

I am terrified when I start to...

The great news about shadow work is when you recognize that:

1. The universe is inside you.

2. Everything in life is a projection.

3. You have the power to respond from your authentic self.

The authentic self is everything inside of you stemming from the High Priestess. She is your blueprint, your essence, and your truth. Without the repression and interference of the devilish ego, the subconscious can respond directly with the highest self. This is when true magic unfolds.

If you ever want to check in to be sure you are responding from the authentic self, check in with your body. Refer to the Three Intelligences of the Body Reading and feel yourself responding from the head, heart, and gut. Once you have done so, you'll know you are coming from the true you.

Light and dark are not equal. We tend to look at the polarities of our life as a balance between high and low or good and bad. Life is, after all, a balancing act. Do not let this idea trick you into thinking light is good and dark is bad. They are not. "Love and light" only offers a piece of a complex puzzle.

NASA tells us 68 percent of the universe is dark energy and 27 percent is dark matter, leaving only 5 percent for normal matter. Einstein tells us "empty space" possesses its own energy. We sit outside and think it is normal to bask in sunlight, but the truth of the universe reveals itself when we sit at a roaring fire while gazing up at the stars. Darkness is the natural state of the universe.

Is there a light and dark side of the moon? Yes, because it is near the sun. Is there a light and dark side of the earth? Yes, because the earth revolves around the sun. Do not be fooled into thinking the light of day is "normal." It is simply a construct that feels familiar and safe to us.

We have thousands of years of survival biology ingrained inside of us. Nighttime was once dangerous, leaving humans vulnerable to theft and attack. We don't need these old fears any longer. Most of us are now lucky enough to live with shelter and electricity. At midnight modern cities sparkle as bright as day.

We also instinctively fear what we do not recognize. Fears keep us safe, but they also cut us off from the pure experience of a thing, especially when working shamanically and walking between worlds. Brushing up against an archetype in its truer form can be terrifying, but that doesn't mean we should turn away from it. Everything new is scary. Our own evolution is scary. This is why we can be our own worst enemy and fight against the very things we desire.

The natural state of the universe is darkness and silence. All possibility exists inside this murky unknown. Rather than fearing the unknown parts of yourself and others, bring the light of your consciousness to it. Embrace it for the possibility that it is. Watch magic unfold in ways you never could have imagined.

Fairy Tales and Tarot

You probably grew up with a slew of favorite fairy tales that captured your imagination. Grimm's fairy tales and tarot share an astounding number of similarities. Understanding the commonality between fairy tales and tarot will help you intuit how both forms of storytelling play an important role in how we view the world and ourselves.

The formula of each device is the same: a fairy tale always begins with extreme darkness and anxiety. Cinderella is abused by her wicked stepmother. Hansel and Gretel are starving in the forest. These poor wretched creatures encounter a form of enchantment: Cinderella meets her fairy godmother. Hansel and Gretel encounter a wicked witch. This enchantment and magic leads to a transformation for the characters: Cinderella meets her prince. Hansel and Gretel outwit the witch and become rich beyond their wildest dreams.

People often come to tarot out of a sense of dread or confusion. "Will my lover return?" "Will the judge rule in my favor?" "If I quit my job, will I find a better one?" Tarot card readers are seldom visited by clients whose lives are moving along beautifully. There is usually a source of pain, confusion, or oppression bringing them to a reader—just like characters at the onset of a fairy tale.

Tarot and/or the tarot reader is the source of magic and/or enchantment. Tarot is a magical device and symbol in its own right. The

FAIRY TALE & TAROT
EQUATION

✦

Darkness/anxiety
+
Enchantment
=
Transformation

✦

energy and magic stems from the reader, but the cards themselves are intensely magical symbols. You have the reading and discover the key to transformation.

My favorite fairy tale is...

Fairy tales and tarot contain unique beginnings and endings. Upon hearing "Once upon a time..." every cell in your body knows you have entered a specific type of story. You unfold, relax, and fall into the lull that only fairy tales will offer you. You can always count on a familiar ending in a fairy tale, as the characters are said to "live happily every after" or with some variant of this theme.

Tarot readings come with their own unique beginnings and endings. They often commence with the lighting of candles and an intimate setting of atmosphere. Prayers and mantras are whispered, questions are asked, the deck is shuffled. The reading becomes a sacred space. Readings end with the final question, one last card, and one never leaves a reading until clarity has been attained. You leave the cards with a specific directive and sense of hope.

I like to begin a tarot reading by…

Fairy tales and tarot exist in faraway landscapes. Fairy tale and tarot each exist in a landscape that is familiar to us yet fantastical. Star Wars exists long ago in a galaxy far, far away. Alice enters Wonderland while Dorothy visits Oz. Tarot's landscapes unfold inside the genre and style of the art and imagination of the deck's creators. Fantastical landscapes are helpful to us because they become the place where possibilities are entertained and tried out before we perform these deeds in the real world.

My favorite imaginary landscape is…

Magic and enchantment run rife in fairy tales and tarot. Fairy tales offer us poisoned apples, pumpkin carriages, and transformative kisses. We find enchanted helpers, animal creatures who speak and care for humans, and fairy godmothers showing up just when we need them. A sense of uncanniness pervades the fairy tale.

Tarot is chock-full of magic wands, powerful swords, even the rising dead. Gods and goddesses preside over archetypal energy, celestial creatures decorate the cards, and animals such as birds, butterflies, and lizards populate tarot landscapes. Energy is exchanged as cards are flipped, and a strong sense of uncanniness unfolds. Synchronicity takes center stage in a tarot reading.

If I could have one magical object, it would be…

Recurring patterns give us extra information. Fairy tales reveal patterns in numbers and rhymes. We find the story of the three Billy Goats Gruff, the three bears, and the famous seven dwarfs. Magical incantations are repeated in triple and always involve a clever rhyming formation.

The same recurring numbers will appear in a tarot reading and give the reader hints at the underlying energy of the issue at hand. A series of aces reveal a beginning, numerous fives reveal challenges, and tens imply endings. Tarotists may be magical practitioners who use the cards for spells and uttering triple rhyming incantations.

My favorite number is…

Good and bad characters populate both worlds. Fairy tales will let you know right away who the "good" and "bad" characters are. We see a wolf, a witch, a troll, or a monster and know we'd better watch out. Tarot contains its own unique "dark" cards, which are the cards people tend to be frightened of or uncomfortable with when they appear. These would include but are not limited to the Three of Swords, Nine of Swords, or the Five of Cups. The advantage of this cut-and-dried approach is that we immediately know what we are up against. We get right down to the nitty-gritty and therefore begin to formulate a plan on how to alleviate the problem or challenge.

My favorite fairy tale villain is…

Universal truths are found in both genres. Fairy tales will usually finish with a universal truth like "there's no place like home" or "love and kindness always win." The universal truth of tarot lies in its archetypes. An archetype is a recurrent symbol or motif that springs from the collective unconscious. Archetypes ground us in our humanity. They give us something to aspire to even if we are lacking these very qualities in our own life or need to bring them out of ourselves.

The lesson I learn repeatedly is…

196

Royalty plays a large role in fairy tale and tarot. They both contain gruff kings, dazzling queens, dashing knights, and delicious princesses (or pages). Royalty is aspiration and it offers like celebrity. They look like us, they feel like us, but they are not us. Royals exist in a parallel world that is like ours but different. They enjoy special glamour and privileges that give everyone something to aspire to and play out our fantasies against.

If I could be king or queen of anything, it would be...

Deadly problems make themselves known immediately. Fairy tales reveal in the first few pages what the protagonist is up against. The Little Match Girl struggles against poverty, Little Red Riding Hood requires safe passage through the woods, Sleeping Beauty comes to terms with her sexuality. Tarot readings almost always involve the biggest problem a person is facing, be it love, money, stability, and life path. People don't visit tarotists when life is fine.

Deadly Problem Spread

This spread asks you to deconstruct your favorite childhood fairy tale or story, deconstruct the symbols inside the story, and then perform a tarot reading.

Your favorite childhood fairy tale/story:

Three symbols from story: Meaning of the symbols:

   1.   =

   2.   =

   3.   =

Circle the most potent symbol that actually existed in your life during childhood.

What this symbol represented in childhood:

How this symbol applies to my current life:

EXAMPLE

Your favorite childhood fairy tale/story: *Wizard of Oz*

Three symbols from story: Meaning of the symbol:

   1. Toto   =   *Companion/safety*

   2. Tornado   =   *Unexpected destruction*

   3. Red slippers   =   *Personal power*

Circle the most potent symbol that actually existed in your life during childhood.

—Circled *tornado = unexpected destruction*

What this symbol represented in childhood:

—*Unexpected destruction came because we constantly moved homes and I never felt safe and secure.*

How this symbol applies to my current life:

—*Losing safety and security are my biggest fears, and I resist change in all forms even when it is a good change.*

Perform a three-card past/present/future spread for how this issue manifests and what you can do to integrate it so it will no longer affect you in a deadly, adverse way.

Chapter Seven

Seven Sacred Cornerstones
of Constant Tarot Magic

A few years ago I was on a bus flying like a bullet from the Catskills to New York City when my phone lit up. It was an old friend. He was reaching out because he'd noticed something different in my life.

"What's your secret?" he texted. "Something's going on with you."

I was particularly glad he had reached out. I was in a moment of flux but hadn't articulated it to anyone until this moment as the bus veered left toward the interstate. Our text exchange would become the basis of the Seven Sacred Cornerstones of Constant Magic. This evolved into a workshop I would go on to teach all around the world.

I explained an exciting discovery. While I loved the sensuality and ritual of casting spells, I also realized the futility of it. My spells are ornate and detailed. The truth was, there were too many things I was interested in doing and achieving. I didn't have the time or the energy to be casting spells all the time. I had figured out a way to streamline the process. Why couldn't I turn my entire life into a spell?

I already employed magical metaphors on a daily basis. I decided that everything I did—every action I took, every intention I set—would become an act of magic. I knew how I was doing it, but I needed to figure

SEVEN STATES OF
CONSTANT MAGIC

✦

Empress = Right Work

High Priestess = Presence

Lovers = Gratitude

✦

✦

Tower = Surrender

Wheel of Fortune = Intention

World = Integration

Devil = Ego

✦

out if it could be applied to a tarot framework. Why can't our entire life be the spell? What would it look and feel like? Would it work?

The answer is yes! The Seven Sacred Cornerstones is a formula based on the Seven of Cups card as drawn by Pamela Colman Smith for the RWS deck. The Seven of Cups card is like a rare talisman holding the symbolic key of magic. Each cup relates to a major arcana card. Each major arcana aligns with a state of magic. Cultivate one of these spaces and you are in a space of constant magic.

Cup One
Statue = Empress = Right Work

Cup one begins at the top left side of the Seven of Cups. The bust inside the cup is crafted in the classical form of Greek beauty. It aligns with the Empress card, which is aspected by Venus and qualities of beauty and love. The Empress is the archetype of mother and the embodiment of pure creativity. Creativity implies work because one must be active to be creative. Creativity is defined as "the use of imagination or original ideas especially as it pertains to artistic work."

The first cornerstone of constant magic is right work. Right work is performing the work you were born to do. This is a utilization of your natural inborn talents, instincts, and passions. The gift of right work is that it is pleasurable. It often commands total concentration, which allows pure consciousness to pour through you as you perform it.

Let's not fool ourselves into thinking performing the work we were meant to do always leaves you bubbling in tasty creative juices. All work has its ups and downs, highs and lows, boring and exciting moments. The key to right work is showing up and doing it.

Right work is not defined by the amount of money or recognition you receive. It has nothing to do with the ego. It has everything to do with being in a state of presence and awareness. Right work is not necessarily work that earns a paycheck. It may be a hobby or a passion. You are lucky if it is your life's work.

To break down the definition of right work, pull out your Empress card. Observe the card as you answer the following:

Are you of service to others? The Empress is often illustrated as being pregnant. Pregnancy is symbolic for any creative act whereby you give birth to a literal child, new idea, or project. The Empress is the archetypal mother. Mothers, in their highest aspect, are of service to the children in their care. They help them grow with encouragement, teaching, and sustenance. When you nurture your inborn talents to others through the work you do, magic ensues.

I am of service to others when I...

Do you express what is in your heart? Empress cards usually include a heart symbol because the Empress symbolizes pure love. Love is the power source for everything in the universe. People usually act out of one of two things, either fear or love. Reflect if you are acting out of fear or out of love when you make a decision or respond to something. Which side of the spectrum is preferable? How does acting from fear compare to acting out of love? Which is the expansive energy and which is contractive?

The energy of love is...

The energy of fear is...

The heart wants what the heart wants; there is no denying its siren song. To live a whole-hearted life, you must be willing to be vulnerable and to break yourself wide open. It isn't always easy and it is rarely comfortable, but when you are brave in your love, true magic unfolds.

The work I love and dream of doing is...

Is your work a spiritual practice? Work becomes a spiritual practice when done mindfully and with intention. It doesn't matter what the actual work looks like on the surface. You could be a ditch digger or a delegate for the United Nations. It is the spiritual goals you set within the context of your work that make all the difference. The landscaper fosters a spiritual connection with nature. The chef transforms their workspace so food becomes a sensual, tantric practice. The student pursues knowledge and excellence behind their papers.

My work becomes a spiritual practice when I...

Are you showing up? The Empress's work (like all the archetypes of tarot) never ceases. Every creative act in the world bears her fingerprint and sparkles with her touch. The key to her magic is that at the end of the day, through thick and thin, no matter what, she appears. She follows through. She puts in the time and the effort.

I show up because if I don't, then...

Cup Two
Veil = High Priestess = Presence

The veiled, glowing figure corresponds to the High Priestess card. Presence is the ability to exist in the moment without attachment to thoughts and emotions. It is the ability to stay alert and responsive without acting out of the past or the future. It is having a clear mind. It is noticing thoughts and distractions but not responding to them or out of them. The second cornerstone of constant magic is presence.

Once you are rooted in a state of presence without distraction, you become the active observer. You speak, act, and move out of personal truth and authenticity. The ego dissolves. The ability to maintain presence may be the most potent of all magic.

Where is your focus? A state of presence means observing yourself and life as it moves around you. What do you spend the majority of your time thinking about? Do your thoughts move to the future, thinking about what you must do and what is to be accomplished? Do you often run past conversations, events, and outcomes in your head? Once you become aware of where your thoughts move, you can notice them and bring your awareness back to the present moment, thereby expanding time.

My thoughts are usually drawn to...

What gifts surround you? A beautiful thing about living in a state of constant presence is that it is like taking a blindfold off. We can only focus on one thing at a time. If we are caught thinking about a past relationship or fantasizing about the future, we may be ignoring a gift staring us right in the face.

*I am looking up from this book at the room around me
and something I have never noticed before is...*

Have you ever taken a vow of silence? A simple exercise to help you reach a sustained sense of presence is to take a vow of silence. Once we stop inserting our opinions, expressing, and making ourselves heard, we observe things we normally would have missed. Take a six- to twelve-hour vow of silence. Choose a convenient time. Let your friends and family know your plan. A vow of silence requires you to abstain from emails and texting.

I feel alert and present when I...

Cup Three
Snake = Lovers = Gratitude

The rising snake connects to the Lovers card. Falling in love is like a narcotic. It brings intense pleasure to life. New love makes colors more vibrant, heightens your senses, and infuses energy into everything. We are never so happy and excited to be alive as when we are newly in love. The Lovers card connects to the third cornerstone of constant magic, which is gratitude.

Gratitude is a portal because it creates space. We are vulnerable when we fall in love. We open up. The space of gratitude is like an open book full of blank pages upon which you can write anything. It is a springboard. Space allows for manifestation.

What do you love? Love is the nature of expansion. What fascinates you? What do you hold dear? What makes you happy it exists?

If I could take two people to a desert island, it would be...

If I could take two things to a desert island, it would be...

If I could take two animals to a desert island, it would be...

Can you appreciate the tough stuff? The trick of gratitude is the ability to have it even when times are tough. This is truly where it pays off. In challenging moments, times of stress, and hardship, making your way closer to gratitude will alter the way you respond to it. Are you able to appreciate the disappointing and distressing things that have happened?

The toughest time of my life was...

I appreciate this time because it taught me...

Do you have a gratitude practice? Start a gratitude practice by selecting someone to be your partner. Every morning (or at your preferred time of day), send this person a quick email listing everything you are grateful for. Your gratitude can be for large or small things; it doesn't matter what you are grateful for as long as it is true. You might be grateful for the comfort of your body, the softness of your pajamas, or the sunlight on your skin.

The importance and challenge of the gratitude practice is to maintain it during challenging times or when you are under duress. It is easy to be grateful when things are going well. It is quite another to be grateful when times are tough or you are suffering. Yet it is in challenging times, when gratitude is found, that your world shifts and you bounce back that much faster.

I am grateful for...

Cup Four
Turret = Tower = Surrender

The Tower card freaks people out. It is the plot twist, the jump scare. It is a challenging yet essential state of intense magic. The Tower actually offers complete and total freedom. The Tower is a total game-changer, an aha moment, the singular moment when everything comes undone. Undoing is not necessarily bad. The release of predetermined outcome, control, and attachments equals surrender. Surrender of control is the fourth cornerstone of constant magic.

Can you release? It isn't easy work, especially when there are so many things to crave, want, desire, and love in life. The only thing we can control is our personal reaction to the events around us. We can't decide ahead of time how things should be. We have no choice but to accept how they are. If we don't, we suffer. We only have control over ourselves. We can't control other people, what they do, or how they feel. We certainly cannot control the events happening around us. When we try to control other people or things and we can't, we get angry. We suffer.

I need to let go of the desire to control...

What are your attachments? Attachments are the things we believe we must have or hold to make us happy. We think we must have certain people, friends, and loved ones treat us in a specific way we dictate. We believe we must have a specific lifestyle and attain a list of accomplishments. We look to everything outside of ourselves and dictate how it must be.

Releasing attachment does not mean we do *not* strive for excellence or love. In fact, it is very much the opposite. It allows you to love more, to achieve more, because once you are attached to nothing, you realize you have nothing to lose.

I am strongly attached to...

Can you surrender? We surrender by allowing old states of being to pass away without grasping them. We all create systems to keep ourselves safe, especially when we are children. The idea of surrender doesn't mean we lie down and let others hurt us. It means we let go of systems and strategies once they are longer useful. For example, a young girl is repeatedly abused by a male relative. She hardens herself when he becomes intimate and learns to leave her body to escape the pain of his actions. This system is often described by survivors of abuse. However, as the girl grows up, she brings this automatic response and defense mechanism into mature, adult relationships. What saved her and preserved her sanity as a child now makes adult romantic relationships impossible to bear. This is an extreme example of something to be surrendered. Letting go of any unneeded behavior will set you free.

What system—what way of being or responding that you still do now—did you learn in childhood or as a teenager? What would happen if you let go of that behavior?

I surrender when I let go of...

Cup Five
Jewels = Wheel of Fortune = Intention

Cup five overflows with glittering jewels and connects us to the Wheel of Fortune's flow of energy and motion. It is flux and flow, highs and lows. The only way not to lose yourself within the wheel's flurry of activity is to stay centered. The gateway to a calm center is through intention. The fifth cornerstone of constant magic is intention.

Intention is like a compass. Setting an intention is like selecting a destination on a map. You point to New Orleans as your objective. There are many ways to reach the Big Easy. You could hitchhike, bus, train, fly, crawl, or dance your way there, but at the end of the day, you know that's where you are going. Intention won't reveal the path; it reveals the destination.

How do you make your intentions clear? Intentions, like tarot questions, do not have to be super specific. They describe a way of being. You can set an intention for your highest good, for the good of all, or for something as simple as inner peace.

My intention in this moment is to...

Can you make actions symbolic? Place an intention behind simple everyday actions to align intention with action. This is the essence of a magical metaphor. Wash away personal negativity as you clean the dishes. Blossom as you sit in the sun. Hop in your car and decide the culmination of your intention is at your destination. The possibilities are endless. The more you apply the richness of intentions behind simple actions, the more magical life becomes.

I can create a symbolic magical action today by...

What do you dream of? Intentions spring from the intermingling of imagination and desire. Everything humans have created first exists in the mind. Describe what your dream life looks like one year from now. What would it look like? What would it feel like?

I see myself...

Cup Six
Wreath = World = Flow

Cup six reveals a victory wreath, thus aligning it with the World card. The World card encourages magic when you are integrating with nature and accessing your five senses: touch, taste, smell, hearing, and sight. The sixth cornerstone of constant magic is flow.

Flow is the optimal state of pleasure in which all of your senses are engaged. Flow produces a sense of aliveness and alertness in the physical body. A state of flow is always available when you activate your inner body. This often happens automatically when you are dancing, moving, hiking, or walking.

How do you move? Where and what is your favorite outdoor activity? Do you like to bike ride or go walking in the woods or even around town? Are you a dancer or someone who feels like walking on the beach is the way to connect with the outdoors? Do you swim, hike, or power run?

My favorite outdoor activity is...

Would you create a new habit? Select a physical activity to perform alone. It could be anything, even a walk, but make sure you can focus on the five senses. How far can you see? What do you smell? What do you hear? What do you taste? What can you touch?

I tried a five-sense activity and it was...

Cup Seven
Lizard = Devil = Ego

The last and final essence of magic comes to us through the lizard, who connects to the Devil card. The Devil is repression and the ego. The ego emerges as we mature. Once we become aware of the ego, we do not destroy it. We learn to recognize it. Dismantling the ego robs it of its power and puts your authentic self in the center of all responses and decision-making. The seventh cornerstone of constant magic is ego.

We begin ego construction as a small child. Babies and toddlers do not notice the difference between themselves and the outside world. It is only when we learn to walk, touch, taste, see, and smell, when we begin bumping into things, that we discover we are "separate" from the outer world. Thus begins the "I" and placing ourselves in the center of our world. Along with the construction of "I," we begin to tell stories about ourselves. These stories are what others say about us and what we believe about ourselves.

Who is your "I"? The ego always comes in the form of "I" or "My." It is the way in which you identify, and it is all the stories you make up about yourself. Who you are transcends the labels you place on yourself. You are so much more than a student, teacher, spouse, and friend. You are the infinite, but the ego wants to pin you down. It will keep you trapped in the most powerful energy even if that is negativity and fear.

I think of myself as a...

What do you fear? Find a piece of paper and write down five dark or fearful recurrent thoughts. These are thoughts that stress you out, are harmful, keep you up at night, make you angry, or make you feel like a victim.

I'm just not good enough to...

I hate when...

I just suck...

Life is unfair when...

Why can't I have...

Now throw these things away, light them on fire, and dispose of them, thereby releasing these thoughts for good. If one should reappear, notice it and continue on your way to a happy and magic-filled life.

Constant magic is an inherently magical state of being. Turn your life into an enchantment, escape the trap of the material word, integrate with nature, practice intention, and embody complete presence. Engage in right work, appreciation, and gratitude. Release control and predetermined outcomes. Above all things, sacrifice and destroy the ego to find the tasty bits of every possible situation.

Chapter Eight

Card Meanings

Major Arcana Keys

KEY 1: ARCHETYPAL UNDERSTANDING

The archetype is the grounding space of the arcana. Archetypes are the original form or concept that appears cross-culturally so everyone understands. This will ground you in the origin and basic meaning of the cards.

KEY 2: OCCULT MEANING

Tarot enjoys an intense spiritual and magical history, and here is where you shall discover the secrets of the cards detailed by occultists of centuries past.

KEY 3: FORTUNETELLING MEANING

Tarot has long been associated with gypsy fortunetelling, carnival tents, and mysterious sequined ladies sequestered in candlelit dark rooms, spinning fortunes to eager ears. Here you will find the traditional divinatory meanings of the cards.

KEY 4: SHADOW SIDE (REVERSAL)

Tarot reversals (a card appearing upside down) are usually the direct opposite of the traditional fortunetelling meaning of the card. The shadow side meaning takes a look at the darker side of the arcana. This means we will look to see how the archetype can be used against oneself, nature, or other people. Read more on the shadow on page 182.

Key 5: Magic

Tarot is nothing if not the ideal object for magical practice. Discover a magical action you can take with your card.

Key 6: Astrological Influence

Each card has been associated with the zodiac. I will be using the Golden Dawn's astrological associations to help those with an eye toward the stars and a love for astrology discover how they might find the archetypes sparkling through in the cosmos.

Key 7: Writing Prompts

Here is where you bring elements of the cards to life. This is the most important part of learning the arcana: how it relates to you!

To perform a classical writing prompt—and this is something I highly encourage—rather than simply jotting down a quick answer, perform the following action. Write in a stream of consciousness without letting your pen/pencil off the paper or fingers off the keypad. This exercise is not meant to be neat and tidy; you can pull out the important parts later if you wish. Keep writing without censoring yourself until you have either filled an entire page or until you have reached a set time limit (three minutes is suggested). Come on, three minutes isn't *really* that much time when you are trying to discover something lodged deeply within your consciousness.

Key 8: Your Meaning

The most important part of your tarot practice: what the card means to **YOU**!

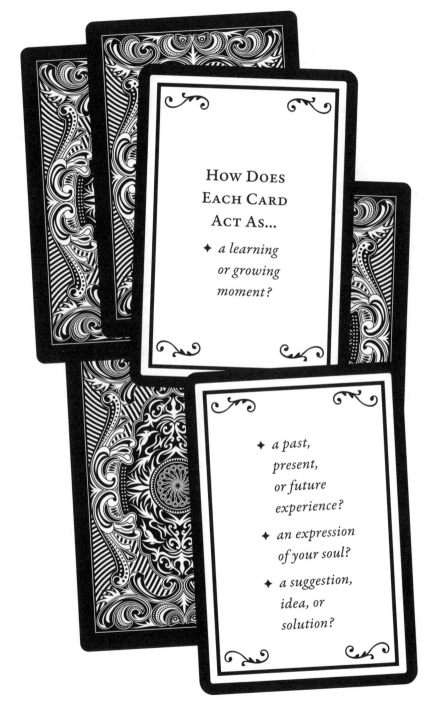

How Does
Each Card
Act As...

✦ *a learning
or growing
moment?*

✦ *a past,
present,
or future
experience?*

✦ *an expression
of your soul?*

✦ *a suggestion,
idea, or
solution?*

0, The Fool

Archetypal Understanding: "Child"

A soul walks down a path, the wind whistling in his ears. An innocent child plays in a field of wildflowers and looks straight into the eyes of

a brown bear without fear. A madman wanders into town. A court jester dances before the king and queen of a medieval court. A hobbled creature sits in an insane asylum mumbling to himself. A man throws away his fortune in the name of a love that will never be his.

The Fool is childlike because he is open to all experiences as they greet him. His previous lessons are carried in his bag without clouding his judgment as he moves forward. His dog reflects the creative principle of the universe. It is companionship and a knowingness that you are never truly alone; you are connected to all things. This knowledge gives you the strength and ability to move forward with ease and face anything that appears on your chosen path. The Fool in search of experience remains open to unexpected possibility.

Occult Meaning

The beginning is the end, the end is the beginning. The Fool is given number zero. Zero connects, like a necklace clasp, to the World card usually portrayed inside an oval-shaped wreath. Describing the Fool on the beginning of his journey, Arthur Waite says that "he will return [to the sun behind him] by another path after many days." For the occultist, the Fool begins on his path down toward the material world from the highest spiritual plane. He hovers like soul consciousness before its human birth. To the yogi, the Fool reflects the bliss body. He is a spirit in search of form and shape.

FORTUNETELLING MEANING

Folly. Foolish behavior. Immaturity. Ridiculous behavior. Silly. Empty-headed.

SHADOW SIDE (REVERSAL)

A refusal to start fresh. An unwillingness to let go of the past. Allowing oneself to be stuck in a rut. Not willing to risk yourself. Cutting off your nose to spite your face. Acting childishly when you know better. Feigning ignorance purposefully to avoid responsibility.

I avoid responsibility when I...

MAGIC

New beginnings, new moons, first day of spring. It is the ability to be surprised and delighted by life. Turning over a new page.

An adventure I've always desired is...

ASTROLOGICAL INFLUENCE

The bright originality of Uranus infuses the card with a fierce independent spirit. Everything is possible.

WRITING PROMPTS

When I am in the mountains, I feel like...

The experience of last year taught me...

I can let go of the past by...

HOW DOES THE FOOL ACT AS...

✦ a learning or growing moment?

✦ a past, present, or future experience?

✦ an expression of your soul?

✦ a suggestion, idea, or solution?

1, The Magician

ARCHETYPAL UNDERSTANDING: "MAGIC"

The Magician casts ceremonial magic over an altar containing all four symbols of tarot. A strange and sexy showman saws his screaming assis-

THE MAGICIAN.

tant in half on the Las Vegas Strip. A mentalist reads the mind of the woman sitting in the third row of his theater. A hired performer pulls rabbits out of hats at a five-year-old's birthday party. Sybil Leek, a famous English witch, performs a ritual at Stonehenge under the August moon. The Magician wows crowds, but he is also known as a cunning showman. He reflects charisma and mastery. The suits of tarot upon his table remind you that you have everything you need at your fingertips, always. His posture is active, reminding you that you are a pure channel of energy.

OCCULT MEANING

The Magician channels energy from above (spiritual and highest potential) with his right hand, which reaches toward the heavens. He directs his attention, his chi, his great will, and uses himself as a lightning rod. He directs energy from the spirit world to the physical plane (our normal everyday life and existence) with his left arm, which points toward the ground. He is the conduit. He is your attention because what you focus on is what you light up in the world. He brings the Fool's energy to the tarot by lighting it up with this powerful action.

FORTUNETELLING MEANING

Charisma. Mastery. Enigma. Charm and power. Show-off. Showmanship. Crafting illusions. Captivating.

SHADOW SIDE (REVERSAL)

He is a monster who uses his charisma and energy to feed his ever-growing ego. A reversed Magician takes the stage and puts talent on display because of a deep need for the approval of others. He never has enough attention to feed the dark hole of insincerity inside. It is lacking the confidence to be authentic and engaging in false behavior.

I misdirected my energy when I...

MAGIC

Magic is infused into the Magician's very name. It is the ability to work with natural visible and invisible forces to create and craft a reality that you have conceived of in your mind's eye. Use the energy of this card to ace an interview or make a lasting impression.

ASTROLOGICAL INFLUENCE

Mercury gifts its ability to take things apart and put them back together. Mercury is displayed in the Magician's ability to re-create himself with finesse, artfulness, and virtuosity on display.

WRITING PROMPTS

I feel alive when I...

My greatest talent is...

I surprised myself when I...

HOW DOES THE MAGICIAN ACT AS...

+ a learning or growing moment?

+ a past, present, or future experience?

+ an expression of your soul?

+ a suggestion, idea, or solution?

2, The High Priestess

Archetypal Understanding: "Soul"

Moonlight radiates though a female creature made of mist and shadow sitting between two pillars. The High Priestess is your authentic self. She

is what makes you *you*. Your hopes, dreams, desires, and inclinations are secreted inside of her. The High Priestess is the deepest part of yourself, your physic blueprint, your inner state. She is often described as virginal, though it should not be taken literally. The virgin metaphor exists because the thoughts, opinions, and ideas of others have zero effect on her. No thing can touch who she is and always will be. She is the silence and wisdom of you.

The High Priestess's veil (also seen behind the Hierophant and Justice) conceals the "real" or interior nature of a person. Her mystery is your forgotten knowledge. She is the truth of your life, the key to your karma. The High Priestess holds the answer to every question. These answers are inside of you.

Occult Meaning

The occultist is interested in how things move from the invisible to the visible world. How does the self manifest on earth? Underneath the magic and energy, how does something come to be? Tarot helps explain the process. The Fool (a piece of consciousness, as in a human, a thought, an impulse) emerges in search of experience. The Magician brings the energy of the Fool to the material world from the spiritual one. It is like calling an angel or spirit down. The High Priestess marks the Fool's emergence in the earthy realm by infusing all intrinsic qualities into it; in this case, it is who you are, unique as a snowflake and here to experience, express, and delight in earthly pleasures.

The High Priestess is aspected by the moon, which is the reflected light of the sun. The sun reflects divinity (the expansive nature of all things). The High Priestess is marked by the moon because lunar energy is the reflected light of the sun. Just as the moon reflects the sun, the High Priestess reflects you as a reflection of divinity here on earth.

The High Priestess's sacred function exists in everything, not just people. She is the unique intelligence embedded in every sentient creature from a sunflower to a kitten. She is what makes a rose different from a daffodil. She is the difference between a bumblebee and a bat. The difference between you and your best friend. This is why she is the deepest, truest essence of who you are. She is what Arthur Waite called "the highest and holiest of the Greater Arcana."

FORTUNETELLING MEANING

Intuition. Silence. Presence. The woman of your dreams. Psychic energy. Third eye. Mysterious portents. Hidden knowledge.

SHADOW SIDE (REVERSAL)

Lying to yourself about who you are. Shame and self-hatred. Ceasing to recognize the divine presence of your existence on earth. Ignoring your gifts and talents. Willingly closing off your third eye. Endless distraction.

Something no one knows about me is...

MAGIC

Moon magic. Divine feminine. Triple goddess. The purest magical energy inside of you. Sacred words. Sacred space. The compact, contract, and agreement between you and yourself.

My deepest secret is...

ASTROLOGICAL INFLUENCE

The moon reflects the ever-mysterious psyche of the High Priestess. Lunar waters pour forth as you unravel into who you were always meant to be.

WRITING PROMPTS

I have always desired...

The one truth I know for certain is...

The book of my life reads like a...because...

HOW DOES THE HIGH PRIESTESS ACT AS...

✦ a learning or growing moment?

✦ a past, present, or future experience?

✦ an expression of your soul?

✦ a suggestion, idea, or solution?

3, The Empress

Archetypal Understanding: "Mother"

Golden sunlight exudes through a female goddess in a field of wheat. A sensual siren reclines on a velvet chaise longue in silken robes. An expectant mother caresses her bulging tummy. A baby snuggles into the soft warmth of her mother's neck. It is the female essence of your earliest childhood memory. Consider "mother earth" or the phrase "mothership." Mother is the concept idea who or what carries us and sustains us in this world.

The Empress expresses all forms of creativity and expansion because the metaphor of birth and motherhood extends further than mother and child. The sensual Empress marks all creative acts you perform from expressing yourself. She is your actions, your imprint, your work. The ultimate creative act is the life you live. The Empress is the outer expression of our inner self.

Occult Meaning

The hologram of your soul appears on earth as the High Priestess. The Empress is how your physical body manifests and becomes real. Waite calls her "the door or gate by which entrance is obtained into this life." The Empress's gateway is your body. It is your eyes as they read and your hands as they hold this book. The Empress is how you express yourself, move, and inhabit the physical, dimensional space of the world.

Fortunetelling Meaning

Fertility. Pregnancy. Motherhood. Nurturing sensuality. Creative and gentle hand. Luxury and beauty. Feminine charm.

Shadow Side (Reversal)

Stifling the creative potential of another person. The urge to destroy. Inserting ideas and opinions where they don't belong. Cruel and distracted. Always busy with something else. Repression of the creative urge inside.

As a child, my caregiver hurt my feelings when they...

Magic

Empress is a blossoming explosion of manifestation. She is the energy of reinvention, sex, love, and beauty. She is the unfolding imagination on display for all to see in sound and color.

If I could create anything, it would be...

Astrological Influence

Venus is the morning star who offers hope to all that gaze at her in pre-dawn darkness. It is love, beauty, and passion giving us a reason to greet the day—the energy of love and attraction infusing with delicious, undeniable charm.

Writing Prompts

I act like my mother (or mother figure) when I...

I love my mother (or mother figure) for...

I feel most creative when I...

How Does the Empress Act As...

+ a learning or growing moment?

+ a past, present, or future experience?

+ an expression of your soul?

+ a suggestion, idea, or solution?

4, The Emperor

Archetypal Understanding: "Father"

The Emperor sits more powerful than a king at the summit of his domain. It is the male counterpart of the Empress. A businessman returns home, tosses his suitcase aside, and hugs his children. The hunter returns from the woods. The groom is mesmerized as his bride moves down the aisle toward him. Virile masculinity pours forth from the Emperor. The Empress is an explosion of creativity, and the Emperor is the organizing principle who is able to put everything in its rightful place so that it may take its shape. The Emperor builds the house that the Empress imagines. This is why the Emperor represents stability and rules, form, and function.

The Emperor is the ability to get things done and to set, create, and implement boundaries. This is why he reflects father figures, familial issues, and authority.

Occult Meaning

The Emperor marks the oppositional force of the Empress. Arthur Waite lays a potent sexual context in the relationship between the Emperor and Empress by saying "he is the virile power to which the Empress responds." She is yin to his yang. The Empress is birth and creativity, and the Emperor is the force giving her talents and expressions boundaries and shapes. In a practical sense, all things that expand must be given parameters. If not, they would go in infinitely. A painter needs the borders of his canvas. A writer needs an ending to her story. The cake cannot be left too long in the oven lest it burn. Thus, the Emperor provides boundaries supporting creation in the material world.

FORTUNETELLING MEANING

Father figure. Domineering. Control. Limits. Heavy hand. Kingdom builder. Action-based results. Effectiveness.

SHADOW SIDE (REVERSAL)

An unwillingness to impose limits on the self. A reckless abandonment of responsibility. Out of control and spinning with misdirected energy. Mental illness and an inability to think or see straight. Obsessive-compulsive disorder. An individual obsessed with power and control who makes boundaries and forces all things to bend to their will.

I overstep my boundaries when I...

MAGIC

The magic of the Emperor lies in the ability to get things done. It is crossing off goals and to-do lists. It is effective and a willingness to control the self. It is kingdom building, maps, and plans. He is habitual behavior that can be adopted or altered to suit your needs.

I am effective when I...

ASTROLOGICAL INFLUENCE

Aries fills the Emperor with the energy of bubbling confidence and the knowledge that anything is possible once you set your mind to it.

WRITING PROMPTS

I act like my father (or father figure) when I...

I love my father (or father figure) for...

I feel most capable when I...

HOW DOES THE EMPEROR ACT AS...

+ a learning or growing moment?

+ a past, present, or future experience?

+ an expression of your soul?

+ a suggestion, idea, or solution?

5, The Hierophant

Archetypal Understanding: "Religious Authority"

Blessings are bestowed in an ancient cathedral. A robed figure preaches fire and brimstone inside the stadium of a megachurch. A televangelist provides an 800 number for donations from a static black-and-white TV. A southern Baptist minister stands before a swaying congregation with the house band playing behind him. A guru sits in lotus in front of his students in northern India. A lama sits in a hall of red-hooded monks high in the Himalayas. A rabbi reads from the book of Torah. A Catholic priest is carted away in handcuffs.

The Hierophant is the symbol who reflects spiritual knowledge in any given society. He is the outer symbol of religion who gives us keys and doorways into spiritual thought. In addition to being the symbolic entity of religion and dogma, he also reflects the teacher and student relationship. He is the element of learning in your life as well as how you pass on what you have learned or how to be true with others.

Occult Meaning

Just as the Emperor and Empress make a couplet, you can pair the High Priestess and the Hierophant as masculine and feminine aspects of the holy. They are both traditionally placed between two pillars. They each have a veil hanging behind them, the marker between the inner self and the outer self. Each relate to mysterious forces invisible to the naked eye.

Arthur Waite tells us the Hierophant is "the ruling power of external religion, as the High Priestess is the prevailing genius of the esoteric (hidden), withdrawn power." Make no mistake: the High Priestess rules the inner realm while the Hierophant bears all outer markers of religion. He is the church, the scripture, dogma, incense, and holy hymnbooks. He is the cathedral pointing to heaven, the foggy monastery high in the

Alps. He is the mala beads, the goddess statues, the books and master classes of spiritual philosophy. The Hierophant requires a congregation, a flock, and followers while the High Priestess is completely self-reliant. She needs only herself.

FORTUNETELLING MEANING

Religious dogma. Ceremony. Conformity to community standards. Priest. Pope. Guru. Cultural expectation. Morals and values. Spiritual rites.

SHADOW SIDE (REVERSAL)

The shadow Hierophant emerges when spiritual philosophy and knowledge is used to control and manipulate individuals and societies. It is spiritual snobbery wielded as power over others. This is done to make oneself feel superior to others, such as when missionaries try to tame "savages." It is when religion is used as an excuse to justify behavior (example: "We killed her in the name of God"). The shadow Hierophant is also the priest, guru, or spiritual teacher who sexually abuses parishioners or steals money and uses it for self-interest.

I once forced my beliefs on another when I...

MAGIC

The magic of the Hierophant comes in the form of ritual and its ability to open up the senses. It is the clothing, candles, and beautiful, sensual items used to create sacred space.

My favorite sacred object is...

ASTROLOGICAL INFLUENCE

Taurus infuses the Hierophant with the sensuous qualities of ritual and sacred art and devoted religious articles. Think of beloved jewelry stroked and used for meditation, the sacred smoke of Indian fires, and the burning of herbs and incense in religious ceremony. All these things are used to activate the senses.

WRITING PROMPTS

My first religious memory is of...

My spiritual upbringing was...

My first spiritual memory is...

HOW DOES THE HIEROPHANT ACT AS...

+ a learning or growing moment?

+ a past, present, or future experience?

+ an expression of your soul?

+ a suggestion, idea, or solution?

6, The Lovers

ARCHETYPAL UNDERSTANDING: "LOVE"

Adam and Eve stand naked amidst the fruit trees and foliage of the Garden of Eden while anointed by an angel and observed by a clever snake. Romeo and Juliet. Eros and Psyche. Samson and Delilah. Tristan and Isolde. Two souls become one in the act of love.

It is the height of attraction. Your cheeks flush fever hot at the thought of the one you love. The touch of their fingertips sends you reeling.

We can take the Lovers at face value and look no further—a pair of lovers, a hookup, a good time. But if we scratch the surface and gaze deeper, we examine love not simply as the binding quality of the universe but also the ability to be intimate with something or someone and hold them close with complete vulnerability. We can consider the sexual implications of this card remembering that sex, like love, can be healing and beautiful or destructive and cruel.

The Lovers card appears to signify love in your life, but it also appears as an invitation to open yourself up to life. There is so much beauty surrounding you.

OCCULT MEANING

The Lovers' hidden meaning is as simple and complex as "human love." Love is the strongest force on the planet, the reason we are here and choose to go on. Erotic and passionate love is how life as we know it continues.

FORTUNETELLING MEANING

True love. Cupid's bow. Romance. Attraction. Two as one. Sweet nothings. Passion. Choice.

Shadow Side (Reversal)

Shadow Lovers appear when the desire to have, hold, and control another is so strong that you suffocate another with love and jealousy. It is putting one's desire above the needs of others. It is smothering affection. It is the attachment of desire to a single person or thing, thinking this is the key to happiness and love, when, in fact, love infuses all things.

I remember being obsessed with...

Magic

The force that creates new life on earth. The deepest urge to create. All acts leading to manifestation and new life. The force from which all magic springs from.

My soulmate is...

Astrological Influence

Gemini brings its twinning energy as lovers reflect twin souls bound in the flames of erotic love.

Writing Prompts

The greatest love lesson I've learned is...

My deepest romantic connection has been with...

When I am naked, I feel...

How do the Lovers Act As...

+ a learning or growing moment?

+ a past, present, or future experience?

+ an expression of your soul?

+ a suggestion, idea, or solution?

7, The Chariot

ARCHETYPAL UNDERSTANDING: "HERO/HEROINE"

The charioteer appears with the clip-clop of horse hooves and crush of wheels. The hero sets off on his journey. A victorious Roman charioteer races through the streets as he returns from battle. Nancy Drew investigates her first mystery. Alice jumps down the rabbit hole into Wonderland. Dorothy packs up Toto and runs away from home. Luke Skywalker leaves his desert planet behind to commence Jedi training.

The Hero is each of us on our life quest. The Fool reflects potential consciousness while the Chariot/Hero reflects the incarnate human setting off on an adventure. Your adventure is determined by your life circumstance, hopes, dreams, and predilections. The Chariot reflects you taking your life by the reins and moving forward in the direction of your choosing. It is having your goal and destination in mind, even if the road is winding and unexpected.

OCCULT MEANING

The Chariot, described by Arthur Waite as "the triumph of the mind," reflects a person's mental ability to steer themselves in the physical world. For the occultist, the invisible is as important, if not more, than the material world. Thus, the Chariot reflects the moment in which the individual uses their personal agency to make their mark in the world. The Chariot is what brings us through adventures in this lifetime. The square, concrete Chariot pictured in the RWS deck cannot actually move because to the occultist it is the spiritual ascension that is important, not the material.

FORTUNETELLING MEANING

Movement. Speed. Gaining ground. Heading in the right direction. Momentum. Traveling in comfort. Triumph.

Shadow Side (Reversal)

The shadow chariot emerges when you go out of your way to impede the forward progress of another person. This includes inserting your opinion when it is not warranted or asked for or insisting you know what is best for another person or thing.

I try to control others when I...

Magic

Chariot magic can be called on when you need a surge of energy for a particular goal or journey. Infuse swiftness and power.

Astrological Influence

Cancer allows the Chariot card to cut to the chase, quite literally.

Writing Prompts

I long for the adventure of...

My life journey has been determined by...

The great adventure that lies ahead is...

The greatest challenge of my life has been...

I look forward to...

How Does the Chariot Act As...

+ a learning or growing moment?

+ a past, present, or future experience?

+ an expression of your soul?

+ a suggestion, idea, or solution?

8, Strength

ARCHETYPAL UNDERSTANDING: "NONVIOLENCE"

A gentle female commands the power of a fierce lion while the magic of infinity circles above her head. The pen is mightier than the sword.

You can catch more flies with honey. Keep your friends close and your enemies closer. Once they are snuggled right up against you, forgive them and set them free, thus setting yourself free.

You set off in the Chariot. You will now discover what you are made of. Strength marks the moment when you must call on your inner reserves of power. The Strength card reflects how you react and respond to external elements of stress, opportunity, and challenge. The icon of Strength in early Italian tarot reflected a man beating off a beast with a club. It reflected man's supposed domination and power over nature. Later on, French decks portrayed a woman gently opening the mouth of a lion. This icon of feminine power stands in direct opposition to using force and will over external factors. Here we see the occult meaning and divinatory meaning mixing. The lion may represent external factors we come into conflict with or the beast may reflect our own base animalistic impulses. Our life and our character is revealed and forced in how we meet and overcome every challenge that rubs up against us.

OCCULT MEANING

For the occultist, Strength is intimately connected, if not interchangeable with, the virtue of Fortitude. While the Chariot is concerned with the journey on the material level, it is through finding and cultivating one's inner strength that the individual is linked to their own divine nature. The moments of stress, duress, and the place where one must reach deeply to overcome adversity are those moments when one realizes they walk hand in hand with something greater than them. It is the link between the self and the self's divine nature and the link between the self and magic and mystery.

FORTUNETELLING MEANING

Power. Valiant winner. Command of others. Force and control but used gently.

SHADOW SIDE (REVERSAL)

Shadow strength emerges when one fights back against anything in reaction. This is the automatic reflection of anger and challenge without the ability to be thoughtful or authentic to the self.

The thing that annoys me most about others is…

MAGIC

Use the Strength card to find vulnerability and gentleness toward yourself or a situation.

I find power in…

ACTIVITY

Write a letter, text, or email of forgiveness to someone you are angry with. The trick to this exercise is to truthfully mean what you say. Forgiveness doesn't work if it is not authentic. You may fall back into anger or resentment, and that is okay. Forgiveness is not always a straight path.

ASTROLOGICAL INFLUENCE

Leo the lion fills this card with leadership qualities and the ability to sparkle with inner vitality.

WRITING PROMPTS

It is important that I forgive…

The strongest thing I have ever done is overcome…

My body feels strong and powerful when I…

How Does Strength Act As...

✦ a learning or growing moment?

✦ a past, present, or future experience?

✦ an expression of your soul?

✦ a suggestion, idea, or solution?

9, The Hermit

ARCHETYPAL UNDERSTANDING: "SAGE"

He stands at the summit of a mountain and shines his inner light for all to see. A red-robed monk retreats to his Himalayan cave where he will spend the next year in solitude. The yogini sits in motionless contemplation in Bali. A monastery is filled with the collective silence of monks who have vowed not to speak. Ben Kenobi emerges into the desert to greet Luke Skywalker.

THE HERMIT.

The Hermit card reflects the archetype of the "wise one" who sequesters himself from society to find his inner wisdom. The High Priestess reflects one's inner essence and the Hierophant reflects the nature of spirituality as expressed by other people. The Hermit is where you venture forth to explore your own relationship with mystery, the divine, and magic. The Hermit is the space only you can occupy. This is where you become the experimenter and arrive at the conclusions only you can. It is inner truth, the sacred space found within the self. Intelligence and self-reflection provide the Hermit with the ability to arrive at solutions and innovations.

The Hermit is also you shining as an example for others through your actions and approach to life and the world. Just as the Hermit stands at the highest point of a mountain shining his light, so do you shine as an example for everyone around you.

OCCULT MEANING

The key to occult understanding lies in the potent symbol of light in the lantern. The Hermit holds his lantern, his light, for all to see. The answer is right in front of you, as plain as the book in your hands. The answers have always been before you. Can you see the truth? Can you leave thoughts, emotions, and ideas around you like scattered leaves and discover the truth standing before you? Waite tells us, "Divine Mysteries secure their own protection from those who are unprepared." The answer is right in front of you. Do you have eyes to see?

FORTUNETELLING MEANING

Solitude. Spiritual understanding. Removing oneself from the fray. Sharing the light of wisdom with others. Withdrawal. Guru inside.

SHADOW SIDE (REVERSAL)

The shadow Hermit emerges when you are afraid to be alone with yourself. It is the obsessive need to be social in order to avoid one's inner issues. It leads to excess in all things, especially food, alcohol, and technology, in an effort to cover up and avoid inner truths.

I need to sit down and deal with...

MAGIC

The magic of the Hermit is special in the way you can call special space and time to the self. Use the Hermit card to cultivate sacred space for the self. It may include a luscious retreat, time spent in nature, or simply the space of an evening to oneself doing activities that feed your soul.

I shine my inner light when...

ASTROLOGICAL INFLUENCE

Virgo's creativity fills this card with the ability to make something from nothing because nothing actually reflects potential.

WRITING PROMPTS

I love spending time alone because...

I feel like I share my light when I...

Life is precious to me because...

ACTIVITY

Take a mini vow of silence. Decide ahead of time to not speak for a minimum of twelve hours in one day.

How Does the Hermit Act As...

✦ a learning or growing moment?

✦ a past, present, or future experience?

✦ an expression of your soul?

✦ a suggestion, idea, or solution?

10, Wheel of Fortune

ARCHETYPAL UNDERSTANDING: "FATE, FORTUNE, DESTINY"

The wheel turns. The Wheel of Fortune spins on the neon-lit ocean boardwalk. Everyone has placed their bets and watches breathlessly to

see where the wheel will stop. Who will be the big winner? Bob Barker's showcase showdown can't begin until contestants spin the big wheel. Fate intervenes: just as an actress is about to run out of money, she books a TV series and garners a huge paycheck.

Spring oozes into summer, which transforms into fall, which freezes into winter, which melts back into spring. Sunrise chases sunset around the earth in an infinite game of tag that won't be won until the sun burns itself out. An infant grows into a muscular teen boy who morphs

WHEEL of FORTUNE.

into midlife and then in old age becomes old, wrinkled, and bald, looking again like his infant self. It is the circle of life.

The symbol is potent and found everywhere from Buddhist mandalas to chakra wheels to your astrology chart. It is the meditative labyrinth, the sacred circles, it is Stonehenge. It is all of us on the planet revolving in a circle around the sun. It is repetition, like the chorus of a song and the gift of beginning again and again. The Wheel of Fortune is the revolving sphere of space and time and our life as it unfolds inside of it. It is cosmic momentum and quantifiable time.

OCCULT MEANING

Waite tells us specifically, "The symbolic picture stands for the perpetual motion of a fluid universe and for the flux of human life." The wheel, at its hidden center, is the internal and external forces of life in motion. It is the blood rushing through our veins, the nature of the solar system, the speed at which the days of our life fly off the calendar. It is internal and external time and how we travel through it.

Fortunetelling Meaning

Winds of change. Forces beyond our control. Luck changing for the better. Success. Fortune. Destiny.

Shadow Side (Reversal)

The shadow wheel emerges anytime you fight against time by not being present in the given moment. You think things will only be better in the future if "such and such" were to occur without realizing you have the ability to be present right now. It is being a slave to your clock and calendar. It is overscheduling and using time as an agent of pressure.

Magic

The magic of the wheel lies in the ability to let go. It is the ability to sit back and watch the nature of the universe play right under your nose. Once you understand its rhythm, like a dancer, you can begin to move along with it and find life unfolding with ease. It is the ability to live seasonally, to roll with the punches without punching back.

Astrological Influence

The prosperity of Jupiter fills this card with richness and delight. It radiates success and glory.

Writing Prompts

I have always believed my destiny is to...

Luck is usually on my side when I...

I embrace the cycles of my life and nature when I...

How Does the Wheel of Fortune Act As...

+ a learning or growing moment?

+ a past, present, or future experience?

+ an expression of your soul?

+ a suggestion, idea, or solution?

11, Justice

ARCHETYPAL UNDERSTANDING: "LAW"

The judge of all matters peers at you with watchful eyes. The judge slams the gavel and declares someone guilty. The prisoner in an orange

jumpsuit is brought to his cell. A woman is strangled by her father for losing her virginity before marriage. A witch is burned at the stake. The divorce is granted. Contracts are settled. The mean girls of the high school cafeteria oust their youngest member; she eats her lunch in the bathroom. The statue of Justice stands carved of marble as she holds the sword of truth and balancing scales. The Wheel of Fortune reflected the laws and motion of the universe. Justice reflects all the laws and motion of literal justice such as the settling of contracts and all legal matters but also the justice of your own actions. You see the way things work in the Wheel of Fortune; the Justice card is about the actions you take. It is how you show up for yourself and others. You reap what you sow.

OCCULT MEANING

The Justice card equates with the natural talents we are born with and the apparent thought that these talents are divinely influenced. Waite claims one's talents and gifts are a mystery that will never be solved: "The operation of this is like the breathing of the spirit where it wills"— in other words, not even we have control over where our talents lie. He claims that talents are like "fairy gifts" but because we are given such gifts, it is in our best interest to let our gifts guide us. In this way we find what we are meant for in this world, and the scales of Justice are balanced. This is why the card echoes the High Priestess in a figure sitting between two pillars with a veil behind them. The Justice card is what you do with what you've been given.

FORTUNETELLING MEANING

Lawsuits won. Scales of Justice. Fairness. All legal issues. Society's rules and regulations. Karma.

SHADOW SIDE (REVERSAL)

Shadow Justice appears when you shirk and wither from responsibility. It is not keeping your word. It is canceling plans and hiding away because you'd rather not face the truth of a situation. It is taking action without thought to the consequences to others around you. It is purposefully burying your talents. It is the feeling of expectation, like the world owes you something when, in fact, the world owes you nothing at all. You are here, and that is everything. The rest is up to you.

MAGIC

The magic of Justice can be called upon in legal matters where you are looking for the highest outcome. Use for real estate, contractual agreements, and all matters with the law.

ASTROLOGICAL INFLUENCE

Libra fills the card with the balancing energy of two scales and the synergy of energy in an effort to be balanced.

WRITING PROMPTS

I have always been good at...

It is important to show up for myself because...

I feel balanced when I...

HOW DOES JUSTICE ACT AS...

✦ a learning or growing moment?

✦ a past, present, or future experience?

✦ an expression of your soul?

✦ a suggestion, idea, or solution?

12, The Hanged Man

ARCHETYPAL UNDERSTANDING: "MYSTIC"

He hangs with pleasure from a T-shaped cross and peers deeply into the nature of your soul. The artist sees a world no one else can see and paints

THE HANGED MAN.

it on his canvas. The writer imagines new worlds and perspectives into existence. The composer arranges the notes so an orchestra can bring an audience to new musical territory. The visionary leads people on a path to freedom.

The Hanged Man is upside down but is anything but still. The gift of the Hanged Man is the ability to look directly through a situation. It is the card of artists and seekers. It is the ability to see things from an entirely different perspective. This is a gift because it is only by tossing aside one's preconceived notions that one can see the world with a fresh pair of eyes. The Hanged Man can indicate worthy sacrifice. It is pausing for a moment, making room for possibility, and at the same time using the space to look deeper at your present situation. One thing is for sure: the Hanged Man appears for you like a signpost in the road and always gives you a heads-up that things are about to become wildly interesting.

OCCULT MEANING

The Hanged Man reflects the moment where the magician sees directly into the source. It is the interconnection of all things in the unifying nature of energy and magic. Nothing ends. Energy never dies; it merely transforms. It describes the relationship between the divine and the universe. Note that the divine and the universe are interconnected yet separate things (As above, so below). Just as the Fool moves out from the sun, so does the universe extend from the divine. The universe is the divine experiencing itself just as you are a universe unto yourself and a piece of the divine experiencing itself. The Hanged Man marks the moment you embody and understand this interconnection. It is the key to everything.

Fortunetelling Meaning

Sacrifice. Pause. Stillness. Trance. Seeing from a new perspective. Emerging consciousness. Inner transformation.

Shadow Side (Reversal)

The shadow Hanged Man appears when you refuse to see anything from another point of view. It is being so attached to one's ideas and opinions that you can't find the room to consider and entertain another's point of view. It is shutting down the ideas of others, and in its worst aspect, it is doing damage to all those around you because you are unaware that what you inflict upon others is what you give to yourself.

Magic

The Hanged Man can be used well for contemplative practice and should be called upon at the beginning of any creative project or when a creative solution is sought. The Hanged Man's eyes will find solutions in the universe around him.

Astrological Influence

Neptune fills the Hanged Man with dreamy qualities.

Writing Prompts

I can clear my head when I...

I experience transcendence when I...

I can see things from a different point of view when I...

How Does the Hanged Man Act As...

+ a learning or growing moment?

+ a past, present, or future experience?

+ an expression of your soul?

+ a suggestion, idea, or solution?

13, Death

Archetypal Understanding: "Death"

The skeleton moves across the field of potential clearing the old so the sun may rise in the distance. A hooded figure emerges from shad-

ows. Death moves forward, scythe in hand, to destroy all things in its wake. The Death card is typically the most feared of the entire deck for those who don't understand tarot. This fear comes from predictive fortunetelling where the flip of the Death card (cue dramatic music) suggests an actual death. Death is unavoidable, as it should be, yet the card rarely regales an actual death—just ask any tarotist who flips many cards a day. Death appears when something is over for good and the ending is within sight. The job is finished.

Occult Meaning

Death carries a unique and rarefied place in occult practice for two special reasons. The occultist uses death as a metaphor for occult under-standing. Occult initiation requires that the initiate metaphorically dies in order to be reborn inside the order, not unlike a spiritual baptism. This is the reason the blindfold is used so when it is removed, the world is seen through a new set of eyes.

Death is also deeply emblematic of occult practice in tarot because it marks the point at which the occultist has completely grasped (as much as they can) the ability for consciousness to manifest on earth, thus understanding the soul's own manifestation on earth. Now this is known, the occultist may work their way back up the Tree of Life on their own terms. This is Christ consciousness. It is giving up the ghost. It is the true resurrection. You rise to meet divinity on its own terms.

FORTUNETELLING MEANING

Change. Entropy. Death, though not literal. Endings leading to new beginnings.

SHADOW SIDE (REVERSAL)

Shadow Death emerges when you refuse to let things go. It is identification of the self to people, places, and things that are no longer important nor relevant. It is all of human attachments and resentments. It is the refusal to let go.

MAGIC

Death magic comes in eloquent endings and getting rid of what your soul is begging for you to discard. It is about moving into the deepest part of who you are, moving into those places you hide from yourself and the rest of the world, and letting go.

ASTROLOGICAL INFLUENCE

Scorpio wields its intense and occult influences over the archetype of Death.

WRITING PROMPTS

I am ready to stop...

I can let go of...

I am ready to accept that...

HOW DOES DEATH ACT AS...

+ a learning or growing moment?

+ a past, present, or future experience?

+ an expression of your soul?

+ a suggestion, idea, or solution?

14, Temperance

ARCHETYPAL UNDERSTANDING: "COMPLEXITY"

A mystical being hovers upon the glimmering pond of biotech diversity, a microcosm of our life on earth. A ballet dancer practices bar drills

at 7 a.m. sharp. The medieval alchemist mixes steaming chemical compounds by candlelight.

You can take the literal meaning of the word "temperance," meaning abstaining from any behavior not in your best interest. It can be the card of balance and making sure you are making room for everything in your life—most importantly for yourself. It is also balancing the spiritual side of ourselves along with the real-world practical side. It is the sacred and mundane, the change of seasons, and how we find ourselves inside of life's ebbs and flows. It is the card of complexity, which is the ability to hold two opposing thoughts at the same time.

OCCULT MEANING

The angel often pictured on the Temperance card echoes our appearance on earth: heavenly creatures here but for a short time. Waite says that "it is called Temperance fantastically, because, when the rule of it obtains in our consciousness, it tempers, combines and harmonizes the psychic and material natures. Under that rule we know in our rational part something of whence we came and where we are going." In a sense, this reflects a spiritual maturity and ability to balance between the seen and unseen (using "temper" as a verb).

FORTUNETELLING MEANING

Honing skills. Energetic mastery. Balance. Natural harmony. Practice makes perfect. Winning combination.

SHADOW SIDE (REVERSAL)

Shadow Temperance emerges when there is no respect for the natural rhythms of life.

MAGIC

If you want to improve your skills, use Temperance to aid you in everything from balancing out your daily life to improving the skill of your choice, from painting to reading to drawing.

ASTROLOGICAL INFLUENCE

Sagittarius infuses Temperance with adventurous and optimistic energy.

WRITING PROMPTS

I become more accepting of others and their opinions when I...

I integrate my own negative energy and transform
*   it into something good when I...*

I can engage in complexity when I practice...

HOW DOES TEMPERANCE ACT AS...

✦ a learning or growing moment?

✦ a past, present, or future experience?

✦ an expression of your soul?

✦ a suggestion, idea, or solution?

15, The Devil

Archetypal Understanding: "Shadow"

A wicked bat-like figure hovers over a pair of chained lovers. The Devil reflects power and control. He is selfish behavior and the inability to reg-

ulate thoughts or actions. He reflects sordid addiction and the thoughts and actions capable of destroying us. The Devil is the container in your subconscious, holding everything you don't want to embrace or admit about yourself.

Occult Meaning

The Devil is the key to transformation. He is known as the "Dweller on the Threshold." He stands at the wall of your ego like a seething video game boss who must be destroyed. Vaporize your Devil like an ancient vampire. Shine light into your shadow by addressing what hides within.

Fortunetelling Meaning

Illusion. Abuse, power, and control. Addictive behavior. Destructive relationships. Self-hatred. Sadomasochism. The inability to say no. Cruelty toward the self and others.

Shadow Side (Reversal)

What is the shadow of your shadow? The key to the shadow is repression and the tension it causes. Therefore, the shadow of the Devil can be imagined as the tiny quivering child inside the seething creature who has created the mask of a monster to protect himself. Vanquish your inner Devil but be kind as you transform the power and energy he wields into a force of generation. Just as we live alongside fear without letting it rule our lives, we can invite the child inside the Devil to come and play. We can free him by removing restrictions.

MAGIC

The Devil grants us permission to move past prior boundaries. His intense power, perhaps only second to the energy of Death, can be used to infuse any area in your life. Temperance teaches us to make use of what we have, not to vanquish it. It is the alchemy of transforming all the power you already hold. Consider the energy you place into a wasteful or self-destructive act. Harness the power of the Devil to channel this energy into something positive.

ASTROLOGICAL INFLUENCE

Capricorn fills the Devil card to the brim with ambitious, goat-like energy.

WRITING PROMPTS

It drives me crazy when other people...
(On the bottom of the page and upside down, write the number one thing that drives you crazy about others; this is exactly the quality of your shadow you need to embrace and integrate.)

Hate is fueled in me when I...

The thing that angers me most about my childhood is...

HOW DOES THE DEVIL ACT AS...

+ a learning or growing moment?

+ a past, present, or future experience?

+ an expression of your soul?

+ a suggestion, idea, or solution?

16, The Tower

ARCHETYPAL UNDERSTANDING: "DESTRUCTION"

Lightning strikes. Brimstone. In the wake of destruction, there is nothing left but to surrender. The art of surrender is one of the finest spiritual qualities leading to evolution and ultimate freedom.

At the point this card appears, there is nothing left to do but go with the circumstances unfolding around you. It is a massive upheaval that you can't fight back against. It can be an aha moment when a life-changing thought, intuition, or flash of insight occurs strong enough to change everything. It can be the phone call, text, or message of news changing your life forever. It is the utter destruction of everything you thought you knew, so strong you must change, adapt, or suffer dire consequences.

OCCULT MEANING

You have defeated the Devil. The Tower reflects the consequences of your old life, behavior, and habits falling into ruin. Your entire life is reinvented as a result of shining light into your darkness. Nothing will ever be the same. It is ultimate freedom. Additionally, Waite tells us the lightning bolt is an occult symbol of "the power which is forever seeking the world." This power is illumination and the revelation of the soul.

FORTUNETELLING MEANING

Destruction. Shock. Chaos. Illusions shattered. Upheaval. Change.

SHADOW SIDE (REVERSAL)

The shadow Tower appears when a person thinks everyone must suffer when they suffer. It is the need to take others with you on an emotional roller coaster. It is the personality who feels if they feel something, then everyone else must feel it too. If they are sad, they are not happy until everyone is sad. At its absolute worst, this is physical and emotional abuse of the self and others.

Astrological Influence

The Tower is aspected by the chaotic god of war energy of planet Mars.

Writing Prompts

I surrender to the fact that...

I accept that...

I release control over...

How Does the Tower Act As...

+ a learning or growing moment?

+ a past, present, or future experience?

+ an expression of your soul?

+ a suggestion, idea, or solution?

17, The Star

ARCHETYPAL UNDERSTANDING: "HEALING"

The wound heals miraculously. The naked subject uncurls under the artist's gaze. When you open yourself up to inspiration—and sometimes opening up is the hardest part—you move forth into something tangible. You embody the Star.

The Star represents the clearing after the storm. It is the peace and calmness and gentle open space appearing after the turmoil of Death, Tower, and the Devil. It is healing and inspiration. New possibility is entertained with delight. It is openness and vulnerability. Above all things it is beauty and clarity.

OCCULT MEANING

Waite calls her "truth unveiled." This is the moment there is communication between the unconscious and superconscious. This metaphor is generally conceived of as artist and muse. The muse is an angelic-like power who visits the artist from above. It is like the light of stars reaching us from the night sky. It is the highest inspiration.

FORTUNETELLING MEANING

Renewal. Inspiration. Fresh start. New hope. Cleansing and clearing. Liberation.

SHADOW SIDE (REVERSAL)

The shadow Star appears when we are so caught up in our own imaginations, we place ourselves over and above all other things. It is ideas of grandeur that supersede daily responsibilities and kind actions and generous behavior. It is thinking one is marked by genius only for them.

MAGIC

Set the Star card on your night table or slip it under your pillow as a reminder that millions of stars in an infinite universe sparkle around you at all times. The universe is conspiring in your favor. Make a wish and know it will come true.

ASTROLOGICAL INFLUENCE

Aquarius fills this card with its healing waters and devout kindness.

WRITING PROMPTS

I am inspired when I...

I feel like I inspire others when I...

I was put here on earth to...

HOW DOES THE STAR ACT AS...

+ a learning or growing moment?

+ a past, present, or future experience?

+ an expression of your soul?

+ a suggestion, idea, or solution?

18, The Moon

Archetypal Understanding: "Mystery"

Mystery captivates us. It is all the unknowable things in our lives, and it is perfectly encapsulated by the Moon card. A werewolf howls at his own

transformation into a hairy beast as the moon emerges from behind a cloud. A winter snowscape sparkles under a lunar sky. We toss and turn on the night of a full moon as emergency rooms and police departments mark an uptick in calls. A couple snuggles closer, watching the moonlight dip and play across each other's face.

The Moon appears when something new and unfamiliar emerges in life. It may appear as a dream, an inkling. It reflects personal unease and mysterious phases of life. They symbolize the unknown. It is the element of twilight and walking between worlds. The moon will often reflect a sudden psychic flash. Because it is aspected by the malleable and changing moon, it reminds us that everything in life is in flux and no matter the issue at hand, it will soon morph into something else.

Occult Meaning

Consider the occultist's journey back up the Tree of Life. She has conquered the Devil, encouraged the Tower to crumble all around her, felt the clarity of the Star, and now the journey into mystery begins. "The path between the towers is the issue into the unknown," says Arthur Waite.

Fortunetelling Meaning

Madness. Dreams. Illusion and deception. Psychic and prophetic power. Emergent truth.

SHADOW SIDE (REVERSAL)

The thin line between reality and the sacred imagination blurs, and a descent into madness occurs. Hysteria. Mental illness.

MAGIC

Gaze at the Moon card. Sip a honey lavender tea. Visualize yourself stepping into the Moon. Greet shadows in the moonlight. Reach into the pool to discover what wants to emerge. The world stirs, trees rustle, and moonlight casts shadows as you greet your heart's desire in the darkness.

ASTROLOGICAL INFLUENCE

The Moon card is aspected by Earth's moon, depicting a magnetic attraction strong enough to control the tides.

WRITING PROMPTS

A dream I will always remember is...

Full moons make me feel...

The strongest psychic moment I've ever had was...

HOW DOES THE MOON ACT AS...

+ a learning or growing moment?

+ a past, present, or future experience?

+ an expression of your soul?

+ a suggestion, idea, or solution?

19, The Sun

ARCHETYPAL UNDERSTANDING: "MANIFESTATION"

The sun is the nuclear fusion responsible for all life as we know it on Earth. It is plasma and gas, bursting with fire and flares. This is the source

of all light and the metaphor for our consciousness. It is our own personal star, the glowing fireball of energy warming our skin, growing our crops and flowers. Our life is dependent on the sun, and while it contains all life-giving properties when it appears in a reading, it also represents the expansion of manifestation. The Sun is evolution. It is your life moving forward, your project coming to fruition. It is bursting out of the boundaries containing you. The gates have opened.

OCCULT MEANING

Revelation of the true nature of the self. The light of truth is radiant. Consciousness is bright and aware because the obscurity of ego and shadow, Devil and Tower, are vanquished. Spiritual ascension. Divine love and understanding on every level. Interconnection of true sight. It is the alchemist's gold.

FORTUNETELLING MEANING

Pregnancy and good health. Expansion and growth. Exuberance and saturation. Energy and attention. Pleasure.

SHADOW SIDE (REVERSAL)

Abnormal darkness. The need to hide away and obscure the truth. Feeling lackluster and hopeless.

MAGIC

Charge your tarot deck and teas by the light of the sun just as you would by the light of the moon. Infuse any object or yourself with solar energy. Cast spells for possibility at sunrise. Cast magic for sleeping and dreams at sunset.

ASTROLOGICAL INFLUENCE

The Sun is influenced, unsurprisingly, by the sun-infusing energy of manifestation and growth through the card. We are each sun-like. We are the center of our own solar system with friends, family, and work orbiting around us.

WRITING PROMPTS

Sunlight makes me feel...

Beach vacations and warm climates are...

I feel healthy when I...

HOW DOES THE SUN ACT AS...

+ a learning or growing moment?

+ a past, present, or future experience?

+ an expression of your soul?

+ a suggestion, idea, or solution?

20, Judgement

Archetypal Understanding: "Transformation"

The earth rumbles beneath your feet. Wild rapturous clouds break open revealing divine light. The train leaves the station, the airplane lifts

off the ground, and there is no return to the way things used to be. It is monumental change and a revelation of what was always meant to be. You are the universe who recognizes the universe within the self. Old habits drop away. The truth is heard and responded to on every level of your body and being. It is the salvation of yourself and an avalanche of evolution.

Occult Meaning

It is the biblical image of judgement, the moment of transformation where everlasting life begins. You see divinity, and divinity sees you seeing it. It is recognition, emergence. The trumpet plays to every part of the soul. You rise.

Fortunetelling Meaning

Wake-up call. Resurrection. Bright new beginnings at hand. Everything changes. No going back. Life will never be the same.

Shadow Side (Reversal)

The inability to rise to the occasion. Delays. Putting one's own needs ahead of others in a way that stunts their growth and emergence. Hearing the call but refusing to respond.

Magic

Use the Judgement card to invoke profound change when casting magic for movement and evolution.

Writing Prompts

An important moment of my life was...

My life changed when I...

Nothing was ever the same after I...

How Does Judgement Act As...

✦ a learning or growing moment?

✦ a past, present, or future experience?

✦ an expression of your soul?

✦ a suggestion, idea, or solution?

21, The World

ARCHETYPAL UNDERSTANDING: "INTEGRATION"

The World Dancer reflects the ultimate integration of all things in one's life as ending and beginning. It is the moment you let go and expe-

rience connection and transcendence in relationships and purpose. All energies create an ecstatic union inside of you. Perfect balance and unbridled joy. Living in the moment. The world is your playground, and no one enjoys it like you do. Complete satisfaction in the self.

You stop asking, craving, and questioning. Longing subsides as you are fulfilled, perfectly content, have achieved your heart's desire, and are at peace with yourself and your restless soul. Moments are experienced with a sense of whole-ness. You stroll through the mist of a Scottish

castle with your best friend, giggling as you step through history. You sneak onboard a Venetian ferry in the choppy Adriatic realizing with pleasure all that has brought you to the present moment.

Consciousness fills your canvas or computer screen. Your actions are filled with meaning and grace. Effortless synchronicity unfolds before you.

OCCULT MEANING

Arthur Waite called the World card "the state of restored world when the law of manifestation shall have been carried to the highest degree of natural perfection." The World card thus represents the achievement of all occult and alchemical work. It is the perfect balance of the elements, intentions, and magic. Occultists aim for the integration of masculine and feminine and find this in the hermaphrodite pictured on this card. It is not an equal half masculine, half feminine but the unique blending, acceptance, and expression of any person's makeup.

Orgasmic consciousness is achieved when the practitioner returns to greet divinity on its own terms. It is your dance with universal consciousness. The universe responds to you seeing it. This is the big bang, the occultist's goal, and the pattern of your life is altered forever.

FORTUNETELLING MEANING

Experiencing your heart's desire. Success. Strongest card of the pack. Travel, excitement, and victory. The grand finale. Complete trust in what is before you.

SHADOW SIDE (REVERSAL)

Allowing the world to overwhelm you with possibility. Blinded by excitement. Repressing the deep truth of who you are. Not allowing yourself to feel pleasure.

MAGIC

The perfect card for any magical goal.

ASTROLOGICAL INFLUENCE

Saturn showers its perfect limit upon the World card.

WRITING PROMPTS

> *I lose all sense of time when I...*
>
> *I feel free when I...*
>
> *My favorite thing in the world is...*

HOW DOES THE WORLD ACT AS...

- ✦ a learning or growing moment?
- ✦ a past, present, or future experience?
- ✦ an expression of your soul?
- ✦ a suggestion, idea, or solution?

Ace of Wands

The Ace of Wands reflects the initial spark of desire—the rush of fire ignited by romantic attraction. It is the energy of passionate obsession, the instant of beguilement and amazement and your heart moving from

zero to sixty miles an hour in the space of a second. The Ace of Wands gets you out of bed in the morning. It fills you with excitement as your eyes flutter open.

The Ace of Wands is the seed, the sprout, and the beginning of the element of fire. It reflects toe-curling longing. Fire marks our blood, passions, hungers. It is the suit of careers, desire, and spirituality. It is pure energy. The energy of fire's flames will nurture and warm when used safely. Fire contains the power to singe or burn when used carelessly or allowed to rage out of control.

It carries the potential to engulf, devour, and incinerate everything if not contained. The Ace of Wands is the internal fire yogis stoke during their physical practice. It is the spirit felt by pulpit preachers spouting fire and brimstone to their spiritually starved congregations. Fire is the combustible, unavoidable element making life worth living. It often gets us all into trouble. It ultimately defines who we are.

MEANING: Spark of passion. Desire. Intention. Inspiration. Male arousal.

SHADOW MEANING: Crushing your desires by never allowing them to see the light of day.

Two of Wands

The Two of Wands reflects electricity stirring the soul to action and contemplation. The Two of Wands reflects the duality of basking in permeating light. The internal fire has been stoked and plans are laid. Interpret the image of the Two of Wands literally: the world is in your hands. Now is the time to plot and plan. The energy of passion doubles and swings in your favor. Make alliances, list goals, create a vision board and write out your plan for action. Outline the novel you've always wanted to write. Make the business plan for your company. This is the card of weighing options carefully. Dual opportunities come your way. Choose between romantic entanglements. Find a partner whose passion equals yours. This is the card of cleverness and daring, not of folly. A well-executed plan combines passion, knowledge, and timing. Hold these elements firmly in your grip as you move forth.

MEANING: Enterprise. Planning. Duality. Meeting your desire at face value. Planning for the immediate future.

SHADOW MEANING: A refusal to take action. Lethargy and boredom.

Three of Wands

Leaping, glowing flames of desire are coaxed into the hypnotic dance of fire. The sorceress casts her spell. Offerings are made. A prayer is whispered. Incantations abound. The send button is hit. Messages and com-

munications fly toward their target, invoking the power of three. Energy is sent flying into the world. Like-minded people gather to aid you in your goal. If the Two of Wands suggests careful planning, the Three of Wands reflects the first stages of the execution of your plan. Plans are in motion. Ripples of cause and effect are visible.

Help arrives in surprising and unanticipated ways: an old friend reappears, a patron appears to fund your creative project, a family member steps in to offer you a loan, or synchronicity appears from out of the blue to help you along. The Golden Dawn named this card "Lord of Established Strength," which suggests protection and power is assured. It is a strong, stable card. As surely as the figure's wand offers support, you can stick to your guns. Your actions reflect strength. The posture of the Three of Wands reflects stamina and fortitude at your disposal.

MEANING: Collaboration. Business partnerships. Moving forward. Trade.

SHADOW MEANING: Refusing to collaborate with others and thinking you can go it alone.

Four of Wands

The Four of Wands reflects a happy home, marriage, and celebration. Shower sparks of midsummer fertility magic, fire festivals, and passion's fourfold stability radiate through the card. The card's appearance marks a return to the natural world and being in touch with the earth when at the height of its radiant power. The passionate stability of fire does not consume but kindles. Fire cultivates pleasure for all who seek its warmth. It signifies revelries, summer festivals, parties, and weddings. At the very long last, you have something to celebrate. The work is done; you've worked hard. Now it is time to rejoice.

Shared joy is richer than happiness experienced alone. The Four of Wands reflects the desire to share happiness and good fortune. The card suggests you inspire others by gifting them with the same treasures and qualities empowering you with joy.

> MEANING: Celebration. Fire festivals. Dancing and laughter. Family and friends. Pleasure.

> SHADOW MEANING: Not allowing yourself to have fun in order to spite the people around you.

Five of Wands

Five young people raise wands against one other. Everyone is out for themselves. Each takes a solid stance, feet flat on the ground. It is the incendiary nature of sparks building toward combustion. This is seen  when crowds are on the verge of violence, when a peaceful protest becomes dangerous, or when skirmishes unexpectedly break out. It is the point in a long-term relationship where the flames of desire are replaced with the intensity of agitation and conflict. The Five of Wands appears when it feels like everyone is out for blood at work or at home.

The lighter side of the Five of Wands reveals an enjoyable challenge, scrimmage, or lively debate. Personal passion changes minds and influences events and others. A secret of this card is revealed by looking into the future. The five figures come together and form the shape of a magical pentagram with their wands. For those who do not wish to engage in fighting and those who shy away from conflict, a moment of truth may be upon you. Will you stand up for what is right? Can you express your opinions and thoughts without railing against those who oppose you? Can you avoid becoming part of the problem?

MEANING: Skirmish. Spoke in the wheel. Up for grabs. Fighting for fun. Drama. Energy. Action. Conflict leading to new ideas.

SHADOW MEANING: Fighting for fighting's sake.

Six of Wands

You have reason to celebrate. A figure carries a staff and rides his horse in a jubilant parade. The crowd waves five wands into the air. Victory parades evoke national, team, and individual success and jubilation. Sporting events culminate in victory marches for win-ning teams in their respective cities. Fire is the vital essence used in celebration the world over. The Six of Wands reflects the image of a victory march. Success is yours. Mission accomplished. Onward movement commences.

It is the card of achievement, but as in all minor arcana six cards, the story is far from complete; there is more to come. It is the space of compassion, kindness, and infinite love. Sixes bear rewards for experience and powering through the challenging times reflected in previous cards. It also reminds you it is only through experience that we discover what we are made of. The number six connects to the Chariot card, who rides above and over all of us in his advance. The appearance of any six asks the reader to consider whether they are giving or receiving.

MEANING: Triumph. Good news. Adulation. Unexpected holiday. Leading by example.

SHADOW MEANING: Being too hard on yourself to enjoy the fruits of your labor.

Seven of Wands

The Seven of Wands is the card of confrontation. The animating nature of fire helps us stand up for what we believe in, even if we feel alone in our battles. Instincts come to our aid when defending passionate and political causes.

Friction heats the situation. We expand like a balloon or puffer fish gaining strength the moment it is needed. We must be wary of fire's bloodlust, even with the best of intentions. If we give into our base instincts, we may win the battle but will have lost the war.

Does the figure on the Seven of Wands ambush the Six of Wands victory parade as it passes below him like Robin Hood? Does he fight off invaders? Is he defending his higher ground from an angry mob like Mary Shelley's Frankenstein? Has he imagined the entire scene? Is he like Don Quixote attacking the windmills of his mind? The minor arcana sevens are highly weighted cards. A situation has developed. The objects and ideals at stake are worth fighting for. We embody the Seven of Wands when we feel threatened and defend our actions or creative work.

MEANING: Defense. Being put on the spot. Higher ground. Putting out fires. A plan is required.

SHADOW MEANING: Purposefully starting fights in order to avoid the work you should be doing.

Eight of Wands

Eight wands fly across the sky. A fertile land lies beneath. A river meanders and a house sits atop a hill. The power of intention is made manifest, visible, and alive in the Eight of Wands. This card echoes the call and response of the universe. An intention is made known through an invocation, prayer, or spell. Others call it synchronicity or coincidence, but the reader knows it is the universe acting in perfect accordance to its laws. It lets us know we chose well. It is the card of karmic action. Intentions sent into the world return to the sender threefold.

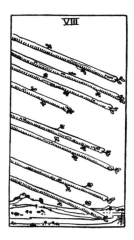

We envision our desire in the mind's eye just as mythological Artemis strings and aims her bow and arrow. The Sagittarius archer, the card's astrological association, links to intuition and wisdom. The wands are mid-flight, their final destination unknown. Eight of Wands echoes the space between wish and culmination. The Eight of Wands often signifies messages of love. Are you vulnerable to love's arrows? Are you the sender or receiver? The phallic nature of a penetrating wand seeking its target is multiplied by eight, the number of synchronicity. It suggests great speed and events unfolding lightning fast. Plans, ideas, and directives are midway, like a lightning bolt midstream, yet the landing place is unseen.

MEANING: Intentions. Action. Messages of love. Speedy results. Unforeseen events. Ramifications.

SHADOW MEANING: Fear of putting yourself out there. Unwilling to risk.

Nine of Wands

The Nine of Wands is a threshold. Thresholds mark the passage between here and there in time, space, and place—a boundary line between the inner and outer, betwixt and between. It is the veil separating worlds,  realities, and possibilities. The number nine is the number of wish fulfillment and concrete results. Eight wands are painted on the scrim like a fence while a figure steps through holding the ninth wand. He glances to his side. What is he looking for?

It is a card of pushing barriers, shattering glass ceilings, and taking energetic reserves and moving into a space of transformation. It reflects moving from a childhood home, going off to college, beginning a new job, becoming a first-time mother. The Nine of Wands is where you push yourself past all comfort zones. The risk pays off. The action contains real and true consequences in your life. It is the bravery to stick up for yourself in the place where you used to cower. It is an exciting creative experience. You see or do something completely new. It is the moment you have received what you have fought long and hard for.

MEANING: Breaking barriers. Unknown territory. Bravery. The will to succeed against all odds.

SHADOW MEANING: Purposefully putting your nose into places it doesn't belong, especially other people's business.

Ten of Wands

Wands are dizzying. Dazzlingly electric, they reflect the essence of erotic love. The dynamic nature of wands will not burn forever. The soul is exhausted as the energy of wands burns out. The individual ravaged and drained by the intensity of wands is displayed in the Ten of Wands.

The Ten of Wands reflects the final stage of energetic reserves. A cycle is completed. The fellow walks away. This reflects taking what remains and departing. He grasps ten wands in his hands and arms, bearing responsibility for his actions. It is cleaning up what one has amassed. His back is bent and his head falls into the wands, signaling a need for rest. A blue sky hangs over a small estate and a neat patch of trees; safe haven awaits. A plowed field, ready for planting and rich with possibility, signals fresh beginnings as the suit renews itself in the ace. The cycle and situation have culminated for now. New prospects soon beckon.

MEANING: The story is concluded. A well-deserved break is required. Time for rest.

SHADOW MEANING: Dragging out a situation that needs to end. Hurting yourself for no reason. A refusal to let go of what no longer serves you. Stop hiding behind pain and angst.

Ace of Cups

The Ace of Cups bursts with emotion, love, and intimacy. The overflowing baptismal water reflects an open heart. Five fountainlike streams spout from within the cup and pour into the pond. The dove, a symbol

of peace, descends with the gift of inspiration. It marks the ability to give and receive. It is the card of rejuvenation; water washes us physically and metaphorically. Energy erupts, reflecting fresh feelings, a waterfall, or even a good cry. The card evokes the auditory sound of bubbling, cascading water. The Ace of Cups is the yogic heart opener of the deck and is connected to the heart chakra, the place we each experience and express love, vulnerability, and peace.

The element of water, reflected by the suit of cups, is the suit of emotions, feelings, and art. The nature of emotions runs a full spectrum from light to dark. Anger and fear linger behind joy and expansion. Not every emotion feels wonderful; some emotions are uncomfortable and strange. A tarot card is like a single snapshot or photograph of you. It only grazes the top of what inhabits the space beneath.

MEANING: Outpouring of emotion. Flow. Heart opener. Expressions of love and gratitude. Opening. Nourishment. Joy.

SHADOW MEANING: Placing attachments on everything you feel emotion toward. Emotions that are bound to expectations.

Two of Cups

The Two of Cups is the soul mate card. The charming Two of Cups echoes the heart's emotional recognition in another. It is a meeting of the like-minded and finding your other half, duality of the soul and discovering the heart's mirrored desire. You meet someone for the first time, yet it feels like you've known each other forever. Conversely, old friends come together, no matter how many months or years have passed, and it feels like you saw each other yesterday. The two of you pick up right where you left off. Sometimes the Two of Cups is you meeting yourself with an open heart.

The Two of Cups can be read as the commitment card. It sometimes speaks of marriage and intimate romantic ceremony. The cups reflect genuine feelings; the home behind the couple is what they seek to build together. Purity of emotion is paramount. It is generous affection towards another.

MEANING: Friendship. Adoration. Reflection. Duality. Mirror. Heartfelt greeting. Deep pleasure. Soul mates.

SHADOW MEANING: Refusing to acknowledge the interconnectivity that infuses us all.

Three of Cups

The Three of Cups carries a simple and straightforward interpretation. The celebration is yours and shared with friends. This card reflects deep bonds of friendship and moving in harmony with others. The Three of

Cups shows us the creative nature of emotion and love in its highest element. Happiness is greatest when shared with others. The threefold law of return states what you put out returns three times in strength. Share with others what you hope to receive. Give to others what you wish you had. The more you give, the more you receive.

The abundant Three of Cups reflects the triplicity of pleasure and flow. Creativity abounds as consorts of the goddess spin, twirl, and dance. The three maidens cheer each other. The lush field bursts with harvest bounty as manifestation multiplies. *Macbeth's* three witches embrace summer's intoxication in a circular dance. The three Graces ritualize summer with their graceful choreography.

The Three of Cups is a reminder to surround yourself with people who lift you up. All life is an energetic exchange. Stop to consider how you spend and conserve personal energetic reserves. Are you surrounded by people who support you or beings who deplete you? Make adjustments accordingly. Merriment, joy, and happiness is yours to enjoy.

MEANING: Deep bonds of friendship. Companionship and camaraderie. Bonding. Support networks. Fun.

SHADOW MEANING: Tearing others down rather than building them up. Jealousy and mistrust.

Four of Cups

The Four of Cups reflects the contemplative mind because the stability of the emotions is expressed via number and suit. Four offers emotional structure. Calm thoughts prevail. A still mind creates space for discovery and possibility. The figure sits beneath a tree. A magical hand holding a cup materializes out of thin air. Buddha, the founder of Buddhism, whose Sanskrit name means "awakened one," is said to have sat beneath the Bodhi (Bo) Tree and gained enlightenment. He achieved enlightenment through the quieting of his mind. To quiet the mind and meditate, the practitioner allows emotions and thoughts to come and go without acting upon them. This is the card of becoming the active observer of your own existence.

The thoughtful Four of Cups is often interpreted as a card of complacency. A simple message moves through the card reminding the viewer to look up. Notice what is right in front of you. An opportunity is at hand, but it may be missed. It is impossible to observe everything happening around you at once. We can only focus on a few things at a time to avoid sensory overload. However, we can choose what we focus on. We can decide what is worth our attention and energy. The Four of Cups offers an opportunity to reexamine potentials surrounding you. Remain open to the unexpected.

MEANING: Boredom. Lost in thought. Emotional stability. Pausing to see what develops. Connection to nature.

SHADOW MEANING: Purposefully ignoring all the gifts and opportunities you've been given so you can sulk.

Five of Cups

The Five of Cups is filled with a dark and deviant presence. Emotional challenges reverberate through the card. The Five of Cups is often considered the card of addiction due to the emotional and chemical basis of depen-

dence. Three cups are turned on their sides, representing loss. They ooze mysterious liquid. Two standing cups remain to the figure's right side. It is unclear what they hold. The figure considers the abyss while draped in melancholic black. His back is turned to the upright cups. Will the figure embrace the cups or will he move toward the bridge stretching across the river? Does salvation lay on the other side? How many of us have worn the cloak of sadness and tears? Will he embrace transformation and choose light instead of dark or will he return to learn this lesson again? If we are wise and learn from our deepest sorrows, they will provide context for happiness. Do we go back for more or do we say enough is enough? Struggle is apparent in all of the minor arcana five cards because the five marks the halfway point. Struggle ensues. Challenge erupts.

Rivers mark distinct boundary lines; they are often the thresholds between lands and countries. Rivers and bridges are metaphorical devices offering the opportunity to "cross over" or traverse a "bridge over troubled water." They provide movement between lands, from the living to the dead, between the conscious and unconscious, or from bad to good and vice versa. Bridges help us cross to a new form of being when moving from the known to the unknown. A bridge, like a door or a gate, offers the possibility of leaving something or someone behind.

MEANING: Loss. Disillusionment. Depression. Sadness. Addictive nature. Melancholy.

SHADOW MEANING: Feeling like your problems are worse than anyone else's. Playing the role of the victim.

Six of Cups

After the darkness and despair of the Five of Cups, hope is reborn inside the Six of Cups. Two childlike figures express gifts of the heart, and the warmth of the soul blossoms like flowers. Cups, once empty, now overflow with beauty. The tangible nature of flowers and foliage suggests the manifestation of desire and results you can count on. The Six of Cups contains the antidote to the bleakness and despair implied in the Five of Cups. Give to others what you wish to receive. Make the first gesture; make your move.

Implied separation and hierarchy traditionally exists between the two figures, just as in all minor arcana six cards. The boyish figure towers over a diminutive girl. Their positioning indicates separation, authority, and the assumption of power. The minor arcana demonstrates a progression of numbers, each growing higher, larger, and closer to its final goal of complete manifestation in the tenth card. The maturity, lessons, and history is now evolving among the higher cards. The unanticipated gift is power and wisdom.

> MEANING: Nostalgia. A walk down memory lane. Rose-colored glasses. Emotional gifts for another. Kindness of the heart.

> SHADOW MEANING: Thinking things will never be as good as they once were. Clinging to past events.

Seven of Cups

The Seven of Cups offers a wide variety of interpretations. The image might call to mind a movie theater where a man stands silhouetted against a projected screen. Filmmaking was still in its infancy when the

RWS deck was created. London's first movie house opened thirteen years before publication of the RWS deck in 1896. It showed grainy, silent black-and-white short films. Given the esoteric title of the card, "Lord of Illusory Success," and Waite's own description as "images of reflection, sentiment and imagination," it is helpful to look at this card as a moving picture. Is it a theatrical projection or is the reader projecting the cups from their imagination? Have they drawn these cups before them like cards in a reading? Does the image spring from the figure or a higher power? Are we focusing on what we want for ourselves or listening to others who think they know better?

Beginning from the top left and moving right:

+ Cup #1: The female head corresponds to the Empress and connects to the planet Venus (recall the sign of Venus on the Empress's garments).

+ Cup #2: The veiled and glowing figure is the High Priestess and connects to the Moon (recall the High Priestess's moon crown).

+ Cup #3: The snake who escapes the cup is the Magician and connects to Mercury (recall the Magician's snake belt, which devours itself around the Magician's waist).

Beginning lower left and moving right:

- ✦ Cup #4: The castle on high rocks reflects the Tower card and connects to Mars (recall how the Tower is placed atop a mountain peak).

- ✦ Cup #5: Glittering jewels reflect the Wheel of Fortune and connect to Jupiter (recall that the Wheel represents fate, fortune, and destiny).

- ✦ Cup #6: The wreath reflects the World card and connects to Saturn (recall the World Dancer's wreath). A skull is engraved on the cup to reflect the yin and yang aspects of life and death.

- ✦ Cup #7: The crouching dragon reflects the Sun card and connects to the sun itself (recall that dragon's breath holds the incendiary power of the sun).

MEANING: Options. Selections. Dreams. Fantasies.

SHADOW MEANING: The inability to make a decision out of fear you will make the wrong choice.

Eight of Cups

The Eight of Cups carries powerful magic and evocative quiet. A figure moves upward. Silent water ripples beneath a sun and moon. A rare solar eclipse as the moon passes before the sun, blotting out light and casting

strange double shadows on the landscape. Did the figure materialize out of a cup? Two stacks of cups lay at the forefront. The figure walks away from them. A close inspection reveals the line of the scrim. The Eight of Cups is a stage card. We are looking at a painted backdrop, not a real figure at all. Is the situation an illusion or does it depict reality?

The card's figure connects to the Hermit card, reflecting the Hermit at the beginning of his journey up the mountain. Walking stick in hand, the Hermit moves toward a lofty summit and away from what has been gained. It is the essence of pilgrimage, the sacred journey of religious devotion. He moves toward spiritual heights, away from worldly goods. It is the high road and the road less traveled and all those phrases imply. What roads have you traveled? What is your current path? Where are you going? Have you plotted your course? What is it you must do this very moment? What can you leave behind?

The figure leaves behind what is no longer needed even if it was something he fought for. Are you satisfied with what you have created? Would you be willing to abandon all? Will you search for something more or stick with the status quo? The element of risk inherent in abandoning all is an essence of bravery. The number eight connects this card to the Strength card. Rumi tells us, "Don't grieve; anything you lose comes round in another form." It is brave to walk away from a situation, person, or thing that you value and be secure in the knowledge that something similar or something better will come into your life. Yet when we are brave and test this principle, we find it to be true. We find love again.

Happiness comes back around. We leave what is comfortable, secure in the knowledge we can do better, strive harder, and create something extraordinary. Our faith and hard work is rewarded. The Eight of Cups implores us to release bonds of fear and desperation to forge new ground.

MEANING: Leaving behind what you no longer need. Abandoning all things for a better and brighter future.

SHADOW MEANING: Constantly running away from what frightens you.

Nine of Cups

The gleeful Nine of Cups says, "Your wish will come true!" Your dream is granted. A genie sits, arms crossed, with a wink and a nod to make your fantasy a reality. Nine cups, the number of wish fulfillment, fan behind

the genie in an arc shape. The cups foreshadow the rainbow shape appearing in the Ten of Cups card as the cycle nears completion. The nine cups sit on a blue curtain that hangs over a table. Could there be additional hidden meaning to a seemingly simplistic card?

The card also reminds the reader to be careful what they wish for. Why should a person exercise care? Wish fulfillment often arrives with unforeseen consequences. The old saying is true, the grass is often greener on the other side. We think something else is better when the real thing stands before us all along.

A final contemplation of this card comes in the form of the ninth position of the Celtic Cross spread, which reflects hopes and fears. How can a hope and fear be two sides of the same coin? If we hope for something, why do we not already have it? The card becomes the marker for the ultimate spiritual and human evolution and a job very well done when we work through fear and deep desires are met.

MEANING: Your wish will come true. Results appear.
Desires are granted.

SHADOW MEANING: The refusal to be happy and content even when you get what you want.

Ten of Cups

The dazzling Ten of Cups is the "happily ever after" card. The cycle of cups reaches its finale. A frolicking family appears beneath an old-fashioned and dazzling rainbow of color. The rainbow evokes feelings of heart and harmony. The dream comes true, and a treasure of fairy gold appears. A quaint homestead stands beside a wandering river. The couple gestures to the sky as if they have summoned or are presenting the rainbow. It is the cherry on the cake of their story.

The Ten of Cups reflects the typical nuclear family. It is the only card in the RWS deck to hold all four positions and stations of the court card family: King/Father, Queen/Mother, Knight/Male Teen, Page/Female Preteen. The four figures represent the Tetragrammaton, or the fourfold name of the Hebrew deity. The female figures, adorned in blue, symbolize the element of water. The male figures, adorned in red, symbolize fire.

Pull out the Two of Cups next to the Ten of Cups to see the narrative culmination. The couple has grown and matured into adults with a family of their own. The same house with red thatched roof stands, and trees have grown right alongside their children.

> MEANING: Happily ever after. Familial contentment. Having what you always wanted. Divine bliss.

> SHADOW MEANING: The reality does not match the illusion. False pretense of happiness. Tearing a family up. Loss of joy. Trouble at home.

Ace of Swords

The Ace of Swords is the essence of the mind. With swift, clever execution representing an excellent idea, intellectual instincts, and mental acuity, the Ace of Swords advises the individual to follow their first instinct. It

suggests a moment of complete clarity. A problem is worked out. It is known to be true. It happens before others weigh in to convince us otherwise or we allow circumstances to influence us. Setting clear intentions each and every day help to place the Ace of Swords firmly in hand. It directs the will and focuses the consciousness. Intentions, inherent or purposeful, inform everything in life.

Swords are a tool at our disposal. Those lucky to possess a sound mind, without chemical imbalance or mental illness, have the ability to choose their thoughts. Choosing thoughts allows destructive emotions or distracting ideas to float away without reaction to them. Attention is like a laser beam: what we focus on receives power. The Ace of Swords reminds us we already have ownership over life's most transformational tool.

To harness the "very great power" of the Ace of Wands, we need only to grasp control of the mind. Controlling the mind means we choose which thoughts we focus on and which thoughts we allow to slip away. This is the work of Zen masters. The opportunity exists every moment, every day, even right now. Gaining control over the mind, we run the computer rather than allowing the computer to run us.

MEANING: A flash of insight. A genius idea. Hole in one. Victory.

SHADOW MEANING: Killing an idea before it comes to light. Something is begging for your consideration.

Two of Swords

The Two of Swords is stillness and calm. It suggests blocking out the world and holding all intrusive things at bay. It is the card of blotting out distractions, chores, annoying parents, houses full of children, responsibilities, and needy coworkers, bosses, or clients.

It reflects a helpful spiritual practice or extreme focus during a problem-solving moment. Alternatively, the Two of Swords can be understood as the card of denial, a refusal to look at obvious facts that are staring you right in the face. Like the Hanged Man, the Two of Swords is a suspended moment in time where events, feelings, and observations are digested.

The duality of the card reflects the ability to hold two opposing thoughts at the same time. It suggests a broad range of thinking and the intellectual advantage of understanding essential truths of human nature. It reflects the empathy of putting yourself in another's place. It suggests the understanding of the existence of a gray area—that no issue is black and white but rather shades between. Rising above the situation gives you a bird's-eye view.

Intuitive reactions to this card vary. Some viewers are unnerved by the image. Others find it peaceful. The former feel the fear of danger or bondage as they observe her blindfold and swords. The latter feel the female takes a protective stance. They see an individual who has voluntarily blindfolded herself to blot out the outer world like a sleeping mask. She focuses on her internal life and meditation like the yogi who quietly centers herself at the beginning of her practice and sets her intention.

MEANING: Reflection. Pause. Interior observation. Not looking at what's in front of you. Pausing to consider how you truly feel.

SHADOW MEANING: Not articulating how you feel due to low self-esteem. It is an inability to express the self because you can't find your inner truth about the matter at hand.

Three of Swords

The Three of Swords is a simple yet powerful card that expresses the symmetry of heartbreak. It is a visually stunning image that is often used as a tattoo. A blood-red heart floats in the air. Three swords pierce the heart

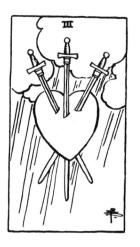

with exactitude and precision. Cumulus storm clouds surround the heart. Rain falls in thick sheets. The Three of Swords is one of the scariest cards of the deck. The Three of Swords can tear the heart to shreds, and it usually does.

In relation to our personal lives, it suggests discovery or participation in a duplicitous love triangle. The betrayal of friendship tears at the heart. Family members attack our jugular vein. Gleaming swords plunge into a scarlet heart with perfect symmetry. The surgical perfection of the damage suggests the heartbreak is intentional, therefore making it all the more painful. It is the betrayal card, especially in terms of a love triangle. The beauty of this card resides in the wound letting in the light. It is the ability to feel pain and discomfort, which is marked by holistic deep love and compassion on the other side.

MEANING: Heartbreak. Distress. Betrayal. Cruelty on all sides. Emotional and mental pain. Piercing agony. Heart opener.

SHADOW MEANING: A heart that is so tough and reflective, it refuses to be vulnerable.

Four of Swords

The Four of Swords represents rest, repose, and the calm inner sanctum of the mind. The space of this card offers restoration and sanctuary for the weary soul. The card's advice says relax; don't worry. The fervent heart can take a break. Sleep. Things will look and feel better tomorrow. The balance and stability acts in direct opposition to the Nine of Swords. It is carefully arranged and orderly thoughts.

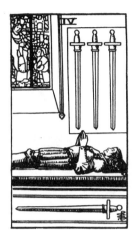

Silence prevails in a peaceful tomb residing in a stone-gray chapel. A single sword is carved into the coffin. Three swords hang above the figure who rests in effigy. A colorful stained glass window lets in the light. The Four of Swords is an effigy, or funerary sculpture, of a fallen knight. He rests inside a tomb or in the corner of a sacred cathedral. This placement suggests a sleep as deep as death—a sleep so rich and full, as Shakespeare's Hamlet says, "To die—to sleep—no more; and by a sleep to say we end the heartache, and the thousand natural shocks that flesh is heir to. 'Tis a consummation devoutly to be wish'd." The heartache referred to can be seen in direct correlation of the pain of the preceding Three of Swords. The storm clouds have passed, the feelings felt; time now for sweet restoration. The card evokes the yogic savasana, or corpse pose, a restorative position. Corpse pose is as important as the extremely physically challenging poses because balance and regeneration are as important as flexibility and strength.

MEANING: Stability of the thoughts. Rest. Sleep. Restore. Peace. Calm. Quiet mind.

SHADOW MEANING: Hiding in bed or behind technology in order to keep responsibilities at bay.

Five of Swords

The Five of Swords is cruelty between people. A terrible fight has broken out. A clear winner, loser, and mediator are seen. The consequences are real, events are set in motion, sentiments have been made. They can't

be taken back. Perhaps you were too truthful or just plain cruel. Maybe you were the victim of aggression. A nasty text was sent to the wrong person, and now you are busted. The group nature of this card infers bullying in groups or people ganging up on one another. The man collecting the swords holds a devilish advantage. He takes pleasure in what has been taken by force and caused pain to another. He delights in another's pain.

The Five of Swords reminds you of the power of your words and the impact you can have on others. It is as if the three heart-piercing swords have become human in the Five of Swords card. The suggested metaphor becomes literal. The smallest figure in the background foreshadows the despair of the Nine of Swords. The water's surface and clouds reflect an agitated energy. The karmic implications of the card remind the reader that participating in aggressive acts will inevitably result in you standing in each of the character's shoes. Why cycle through any of these stages? Take the high road, release the ego, and dissolve any energy leading to such disagreements.

MEANING: Cruelty. Inflicting pain. Cheating. Not playing
    fair. Bullies. A game with no winners. Over-the-top
    drama.

SHADOW MEANING: Self-mutilation.

Six of Swords

The Six of Swords is the card of literal or figurative journeys. Passage, crossing, and movement radiate as two figures are ferried across the water. Their faces are hidden. Six swords are stuck at the front of the boat. A distant shore is seen. The appearance of this card often implies better times lie ahead. The rippled water on the right of the boat and the smooth water on the left reflect the transition from trouble to ease. The imagined depth of the water and river can be viewed as the emotional depth of the relationship. The card reflects a literal move, such as the purchase of a new home or relocation to a new city, state, or country. It can reflect moving forward and making progress with a child. The appearance of the card also suggests traveling and vacations.

A mythic sense envelops the card. It echoes moving into a new plane of existence or to the underworld, netherworld, or otherworld. Charon, the Greek ferryman spirit who transports dead souls over the River Styx to the realm of Hades, haunts the image of this card. According to the myth, dead souls paid Charon a single coin for their passage. Funeral rites included placing a coin in the mouth of the corpse during burial. Corpses without money or plagued by improper burial rites were doomed to wander the riverbed. The implied message reminds the reader to prepare for movement into the unknown. Do not dwell in a single place for too long. The Six of Swords is a deep, eloquent card no matter if the implied trip is metaphorical, joyful, or painful.

> MEANING: Better times lie ahead. Journey. Evocative relationships. Passage. Movement.

> SHADOW MEANING: Refusing to depart from a negative situation. Not accepting the help of others although you require it. Insisting on staying in one place.

Seven of Swords

The Seven of Swords reflects trickery or betrayal. What are you trying to get away with? Cutting corners at work or school? Harboring a secret life of crime? Snooping behind someone's back? A man wearing a crimson  fez carries five swords in his hand. Festive tents with open flaps fly cheerful flags behind him. A gathering of individuals or soldiers crowd a campfire in distant silhouette. The man looks behind him as he tiptoes away.

The figure moves on his own volition. His movement suggests you move without the validation or opinion of others. You are finished checking in or seeking approval. You may feel timid and full of the instinct to hide your actions. Wait to tell others until your deed is done. This card suggests you move quietly, without fuss, broadcast, or fanfare. Does everything you do require an announcement or update? Seek your own approval. Forget the rest.

The mystical nature of the number seven reveals a magical and original thought process. You see something that others do not. You bear a distinct edge. You speed past any contender. It is time to collect what is important to you and go forward while watching your step. Leave no trace behind.

MEANING: Hatching a plan. Editing. Quietly moving under the radar.

SHADOW MEANING: Deceiving others but also fooling yourself. Lies and schemes. Deception with dire consequences for yourself and others.

Eight of Swords

The Eight of Swords feels frightening to many. A woman is blindfolded, marking an intense interior life and a shamanistic experience. She is bound at the seashore, marking the convergence of elemental threshold space. Her pointed feet hover above sand and water; she is disconnected from the earth and all worldly concerns. An oval prison of swords surrounds her. A turreted castle looms from distant cliffs as if the past slips away in the ocean mist. The woman appears to be held hostage. You could be imprisoned by a domineering relationship, family member, or even be a slave to your own tumultuous inner life. It suggests an oppressive religious or moral code, where you feel as if you are unable to express your individuality. Perhaps a situation feels restrictive: the bills are piling up, you are faced with overwhelming confusion, or you feel like you have no good choices. Like the Three of Swords, the illustration leaves little to the imagination. A female figure is held captive in bondage and blindfolded. The figure is held in dire straits—or is she?

An esoteric reading of this card, like the Two of Swords, suggests the blindfold signifies transformation and initiation. This is a voluntary act. She is like a caterpillar in a cocoon transforming into a butterfly. The swords are not a prison but mark the boundaries of sacred ritualist space. The woman sees with a new set of eyes when her blindfold is removed. A sexual interpretation of this card (aligning with the Devil card) marks a proclivity for S&M, bondage, power, and control. What do you gain when you relinquish all control?

The eight swords in this card are magical in nature like the Seven of Swords whose blades will not actually slice or the Two of Swords that are light as a feather. These eight swords stick up from the sand with little support. Magical realism inside any tarot deck can be used as a reminder of enchantment, glamour, and unseen forces at play in your life. Nothing is actually as it seems. All of life is an interpretation, a story, like the tarot. One card carries infinite meanings. One day in your life has a thousand possibilities. A single experience has multiple interpretations.

> MEANING: Restriction. Imprisonment. Darkness. The past fades away. Initiation. Cocoon.

> SHADOW MEANING: Placing bounds on others. Cruelty. Restrictions on other people. Taking the breath out of a room.

Nine of Swords

The Nine of Swords is a card of intense despair or the dark night of the soul. It reflects perpetual slavery to the thoughts running rampant circles in the head. You feel powerless to stop. Falling deeper into darkness, wide awake at 3:30 a.m. with an alarm set for 6:30 a.m., you beat yourself up, chide yourself, second-guess yourself, hyper-focus on passive-aggressive situations, and lose sleep. This card signifies insomnia, nightmares, and depression. It also reflects an individual who is holding themselves to impossible standards. When the Nine of Swords appears in a reading, it reminds us to treat ourselves with kindness and compassion instead of judgment and criticism.

A nightmare of epic proportion envelops the imperiled woman, who sits up in bed. We've all been there. Her head rests in her hands. What is so terrible you don't want to look it in the eye? Nine stacked swords rise above her in darkness. Do you have an escape route? Her hair is as white as a sheet. A colorful quilt covers her legs. Swords are the "scariest" suit of the deck because they reflect the mind. They reflect internal dialogue. We often speak to ourselves in ways we would never speak to another.

MEANING: Horror. Distress. Mental agony. Passive-aggressive behavior. Temporary blindness.

SHADOW MEANING: Using the past and present to torment the self. Refusing to look for an answer when the answer is right in front of your face.

Ten of Swords

Swords represent the mind. The Ten of Swords appears when the mind is made up, having finished calculating the situation and becoming unchangeable. In many ways, this card also reflects things we cannot

change about other people. It stands for the actions, opinions, and morals of others. The suit of swords is a reminder of the power of the individual mind; we are free every second to choose our thoughts. We can change how we approach the task at hand or the way we react to unalterable events even if the events or other people can't be altered. The ten swords additionally suggest acupuncture, concentrated chakra work, spinal issues, and themes of physical support.

A golden dawn pushes up against an inky night sky and gray clouds. A man lies on the ground near the threshold of a beach with a mountain range in the far distance. Ten silver swords pierce his spine, neck, and face. Blood streams from his head. His right hand makes a strange, secret gesture with his fingers and thumb. The bloody nature of the Ten of Swords often inspires fear in the viewer; however, the card is not as dark as one might imagine. Tens suggest the ending of cycles and stories. A hushed theater a moment before the curtain falls. The last act. The situation at hand is over whether it reflects pleasure or pain.

The figure makes a hand gesture matching the Hierophant's sign of benediction or blessing. The hand blessing appears in Christ depictions in early Byzantine art. The benediction is formed with the right hand and with the last two fingers curled down. Gemini also rules the hands. A subversive reading of this image suggests that the speared figure is the Hierophant. This reading implies that the old religions are dead and irrelevant. How will you reinvent yourself?

MEANING: Finale. Ending. Dead. Done. Over.

SHADOW MEANING: The metaphorical picking of a scab until there is nothing left.

Ace of Pentacles

The Ace of Pentacles sits in an open palm. It is a gift, money, or inheritance. The Ace of Pentacles reflects the miracle of physical manifestation in the material realm. The garden is the perfected world of cosmic

harmony and design. It carries the life-giving power of the sun. The card is a reminder of all the natural power already in your possession. It is the generative power providing energy toward growth. It is seasonal cycles. The Ace of Pentacles is the daisy growing through concrete. What will you grow in the garden of your life?

Pentacles are pieces of the material world like cells or molecules. The pentacle is the circle, the same shape of everything the material world consists of. It is a suitable symbol to reflect those things we can see, feel, and touch. The pentacle is the shape of the sun, the center of our solar system. It reflects the shape of each planet and moon revolving inside the solar system. The pentacle is the shape of the earth. It is the shape of human eyes. It is the shape of coins, human currency, and the original suit in older tarot decks. It is the shape of human molecules. This reminds us when we study something small, we are also examining something quite large. Pentacles are the building blocks of life and all things in the material world.

A gate is a threshold leading out of the garden. The Ace of Pentacles marks the passage from one plane of reality into another. The safety of the garden is left behind in lieu of adventure and the thrill of the open road. The girl becomes a woman. It is the true gate of manifestation. All things are possible. What begins as a thought becomes real in the material world. An idea comes to fruition, a path is revealed, a possibility is encouraged.

MEANING: Inheritance. Money. Opportunity. Beginnings. Origin. Potent.

SHADOW MEANING: Refusing to use the funds at your disposal due to pride or prejudice.

Two of Pentacles

The light-footed Two of Pentacles is the card of making a choice and weighing options. It is an active and physical card. Rolling waves behind the figure echo the up-and-down nature of options, choices, and out-

comes. The Two of Pentacles can be understood as a lesser Temperance card and has the uncanny ability to appear in spreads and situations where important choices are being made. This includes serious matters of the heart, home, and finance.

Aside from choice, the Two of Pentacles is also about delicate balance. Pentacles represent our material stuff: our shoes, cars, even the dust bunnies under your bed qualify as pentacles. Pentacles are things we can touch, feel, and taste. Your pet, favorite comforter, and the sandwich you had for lunch—all pentacles. Pentacles represent our bodies—our muscles, flab, bones, and blood. Pentacles also represent the green stuff—our money. It could be juggling two lovers or balancing your finances in tumultuous times. The Two of Pentacles is about the managing of your stuff, so remember, the more stuff you have, the bigger the balancing act.

MEANING: Choice. Play. Fun. Opportunity. Weighing two delightful options.

SHADOW MEANING: Dancing around the heart of the matter because you fear your choices.

Three of Pentacles

The enterprising Three of Pentacles is the card of collaboration. People come together united by a common vision or goal. It reflects building, manifesting, and invoking creativity in the material world with outside help or expertise. One may embark on gar-den, home, or professional projects or renovations. Help is assembled for a creative project. A photographer assembles an assisting team. A couple seeks financial advice and guidance. Business collaborations are formed. The card implies growth in all areas.

The Three of Pentacles leaps out viscerally. One can hear the echoes of the chamber, sense the cool stone of the chapel, and detect the faint smell of incense when gazing deeply into the card. The figures are theatrically adorned in colorful costumes, especially the hooded figure. Pamela Colman Smith crafted a deceptively simple image laced with rich historic symbolism and secret clues.

MEANING: Choice. Collaboration. Creative projects. Building begins.

SHADOW MEANING: Tearing apart the things you have created to spite yourself or other people. Taking away what is useful to others.

Four of Pentacles

The Four of Pentacles reflects stability in the material world. It is the card of having a solid foundation of resources. A gentleman clings greedily to pentacles that seemingly protect him. He wears a crown and clothing sig-

nifying a high station in life. A cosmopolitan city behind him reflects his wealth of resources. It matters little if he has worked for his money or inherited it. The point of this card is that it is time for him to let go.

One cannot build a future while clinging to the past. You have worked diligently. You have all you need at your fingertips and stand on solid ground. The Four of Pentacles appears to remind you that it is important to let go. The act of release opens new potentials and possibilities for a new windfall.

The Four of Pentacles can also be read as one who feels cast off or excluded from regular society. The separation between the figure and the city becomes literal in this reading. The material nature of pentacles is the cause of separation. One may use money issues (either too much or too little) as a way to set oneself apart from others. The sense of separation may manifest as an obsessive-compulsive manipulation of objects and things. The advice in any case remains the same: it is time to loosen your firm grip.

MEANING: Foundation. Stability. Security. Growth. Achievement. Miser.

SHADOW MEANING: Holding on to everything so tightly that you cause it to fall away.

Five of Pentacles

The Five of Pentacles reflects a moment when insurmountable challenges lie ahead. All appears lost. It is a moment of angst and anguish not faced by the solo traveler but by a pair. A challenge is faced together. This card often reflects the ups and downs of long-lasting relationships, marriages, friendships, and the tumultuous nature of parenting. The moonlit snowscape of Puccini's *La Boheme* is evoked as white snowflakes fall to the ground in somber beauty.

The beauty and hope thriving within the Five of Pentacles card comes via the bright light shimmering through the stained glass window above the couple. Salvation is possible should they choose to seek it. If the Five of Pentacles appears for you and you happen to be going through a tough time, let it stand as a reminder that things will get better. You will make it through stronger, tougher, and wiser.

The Five of Pentacles recalls the ups and downs of our relationships. All couples have their biorhythms. When the Five of Pentacles appears, it suggests things are tough, but you can weather the storm. These struggles are precisely the moments that define you as a couple. With the bitter comes the sweet. What doesn't kill you makes you stronger.

> MEANING: Tough times. Financial hardship. Mismanagement of assets. Highs and lows of relationships.

> SHADOW MEANING: Holding on to resentment and anger. Refusing forgiveness keeps you prisoner to the cycles of the past.

Six of Pentacles

All the sixes in tarot rest in the center of the Tree of Life. This center is called Beauty, and it aligns with our heart. Pentacles concern themselves with the material world: physical things, money, our flesh, homes, cars,

flowers—everything we can touch, feel, and see. So, the Six of Pentacles is the beauty of the physical world. It is the energy of giving and receiving.

Gaze at the Six of Pentacles. Which figure or object are you on the card right now? Are you giving or receiving right now? Are you usually spending or receiving? If you are donating—to charity, for instance—do you do so out of genuine concern or because it makes you feel superior? If you find yourself on the receiving end, how does it feel looking for the next handout? What might you do to help yourself up off the ground?

How do we infuse and value what we pay for? We magnify what we focus on. When we spend money on something, it is another way of directing our attention. What do you spend most of your income on? My guess is housing and food. Are you getting your money's worth? This is not about prestige, name brands, and who can afford a multimillion-dollar McMansion. This is about quality. You probably spend a good deal on your rent/mortgage. Is your home an oasis, a retreat? Do you spend a ton of money on food? If so, is it fresh, nourishing food? Point is, when you are putting your money and attention on something, make it the clearest, kindest expression of who you are. You honor yourself with your financial choices.

This is also the card of charging and being paid what you are worth. It is not undervaluing yourself. Is it easy to ask for what you want and deserve?

MEANING: Beauty. Giving. Receiving. Acts of charity. Getting paid what you are worth. Spending habits.

SHADOW MEANING: Using money to define who you are and wield imaginary power over others.

Seven of Pentacles

Seven pentacles have grown to fruition. A gardener pauses to lean on his tool, lost in thought as he looks at his crop. A tendril reaches forth. He reflects on his work. This card is all about the results you've received and pausing to consider your next step.

Now is the time to take stock and evaluate the path you've chosen and the seeds you've planted. Reexamine motives and perceived outcomes. The Seven of Pentacles reflects the moment your results are seen. This card successfully poses the question, "Where do I go from here?" Romantic advances are accepted. Is the person what you expected? A promotion is received, but what comes next? Can you do something better, quicker, or in a more efficient way? More will evolve. Will you coax it to receive the ideal outcome? What slight adjustments can be made now to bring it home with rapturous success?

MEANING: Results. Pause to reconsider plans. Assessment.

SHADOW MEANING: Stalling by pretending to work.

Eight of Pentacles

The Eight of Pentacles is the card of master craftsmanship and productivity. A young fellow with curly hair works on a bench. He holds a mallet in his right hand, a carving implement in his left, and wears an apron.

Examples of his handiwork line the wooden wall next to him. A city may be seen in the distance as the artist forges his own unique creative space.

Is there anything better than doing what you love? Being lost in the act of creation? That is what the Eight of Pentacles is all about. Ignore the fact that the figure on the card looks like Willie from *Eight Is Enough*. Speaking of eights, eights in tarot symbolize splendor, and pentacles always mean a bit of money could be made. The pentacles lead up the wall or tree like a ladder. He is working on a pentacle, whose five points represent earth, air, fire, water, and spirit. The apron he is wearing is symbolic of Freemasonry. When the Eight of Pentacles appears, it means that it is time to get busy. The Eight of Pentacles can also be a confirmation that the work you are dedicating yourself to is perfect. You are beautiful in the act of creation.

This card is pleasure in work. It is sharing your work proudly with others. It is being lost in the moment of creation. It is also the card of the artisan and reflects specific talent and dedication. It is gorgeous artistry and the talents that are unique to you. It is you showing up for the work you were put here to do.

MEANING: Craftsmanship. Dedication. Hard work.
Pleasure in handiwork. Diligence.

SHADOW MEANING: Using work as an escape from
emotional issues and outward responsibilities.

Nine of Pentacles

The sumptuous Nine of Pentacles is the card of luxury, wealth, and riches. It is the desire to surround oneself with beauty, not as a status symbol but for the pleasure of refinement and appreciation of craftsmanship.

The European vineyard implies inheritance. Traditionally, European vineyards, like castles and large estates, are passed down through generations.

The manor house in the background of the card represents your House of Spirits. A House of Spirits is your ancestral heritage. It is the metaphorical "house" you descend from. "Spirits" are all those who came before you: mother, grandmother, and so on. Understanding one's place in the vine of personal ancestry offers comfort. We can reexamine our life as part of an intricate fabric of human existence whether we know our families or not. It links us to a mysterious past and an unknown future.

Pentacles, like the cells of our body, can be understood as containing our inherited DNA. A House of Spirits comes with gifts and curses. Are we ready to change the pattern? Is your behavior authentic to you or is it learned? What born talents do you possess? How do you use them? What behaviors and traits run strong in your family? What would you like to keep or cast away? The space of the Nine of Pentacles provides a warm and pleasurable place for the contemplation of such things.

MEANING: Pleasure in one's own company. Family tree. Luxury. Eloquence. Slowing down. Beautiful things. Accomplishment.

SHADOW MEANING: Hiding away inside the world you have created no matter how beautiful or luxurious it is. You can't hide from who you truly are.

Ten of Pentacles

This is material culmination and is the most densely populated card of the deck. A child, couple, and hermit-like grandfather figure linger at the threshold of a medieval city. The innocence of youth, the maturity of adulthood, and the wisdom of old age is reflected. The grandfather and child each lay a hand on the family's pets. This action echoes the circle of life and families reunited. It is generational love, inheritance, and companionship.

Your situation reaches its conclusion, and the results defy your imagination. You possess everything one could want. The Tower card is referenced as it hangs on a tapestry to the left of the card. It reminds you of what was endured to reach this satisfying moment. The Justice scales hang above the grandfather's head, letting us know events and actions are balanced. You know who you are and have found your people. You understand yourself in the grand scheme of things. What you have built has staying power.

Ten pentacles decorate the card in the shape of the Tree of Life. The tenth circle of the tree represents the physical world. The entire Tree of Life is now activated. It reflects riches, pleasure, and manifestation. All possibilities lay before you.

MEANING: Wealth. Legacy, family, and home. Generations. Knowledge and possessions passed down. Endings but also new beginnings. A portal opens.

SHADOW MEANING: Refusing to share with your family. Actively working to keep people apart. Miserable interpersonal relationships.

COURT CARDS

✦

King = Father

Queen = Mother

Knight = Son

Page = Daughter

✦

COURT CARDS ARE

✦

Aspects of you

Friends/family/people

Roles/behaviors

Attitudes

✦

COURT CARD ENERGY

✦

King = Mature male

Queen = Mature female

Knight = Teen

Page = Youth

✦

Court Cards

Court cards can feel like a problematic and challenging piece of tarot to understand. It is easy to confuse a king with the Emperor or a queen with the Empress. It all looked like card soup to me when I first started reading. Rest assured, the court cards are easy to interpret.

1. Court cards represent aspects of you and the different roles you cycle through in any given day.

2. Court cards represent people, the players all around you. They are your friends, family, and coworkers. The courts are the people you date and marry, they are your children, the strangers you pass on the street, and the people you watch in movies and on TV.

3. Court cards reflect pieces of advice and attitudes and ways of being that will help you accomplish any task at hand.

Observe the court by pulling the court cards from your deck. You'll find four pages, four knights (often pictured riding on a horse), four queens, and four kings. Place each card in a row according to their suit. Start with page and follow with knight, queen, and king.

The first thing I notice about the court cards is...

Pull the pages a few inches to the left and in a single vertical line. What do the pages in your deck have in common? What differences do you notice between each page?

The pages all have this in common...

The pages are the youngest members of the court card family, reflecting the energy of a young child before puberty. This childlike vitality is full of wonder, curiosity, and learning. Remember playing in your childhood bedroom? Remember the vibrant colors and textures of your cherished toys? The pages pour their energy into what captivates their attention; they live in the moment. Time stretches out before them like an endless summer.

My favorite place to play as a child was...

My favorite childhood games were...

My favorite childhood books and stories were...

When I was a child, I was fascinated with...

Pull the knights toward your pages and keep them in a single vertical line. Examine their posture and clothing for similarities and differences. What do your knights have in common? What differences do you notice between each knight?

The knights all have this in common...

The knight reflects teen energy. This is the hormonal overload and movement of the young adult years. A knight is usually on a horse. The horse energy aligns with teen energy and the unbridled freedom, excitement, and passion of the age. Can you recall how deeply passionate you felt as a teen?

As a teenager I was...

I learned to drive when...

My biggest teenage love/crush was...

As a teen, all I wanted to do was...

In high school I really cared about...

Pull the queens an inch or two toward the knights and keep them in a single vertical line. What elements do your queens share? What makes them different? Carefully examine their environments for clues to their similar or different personalities.

The queens all have this in common...

The queens represent mature female energy. This is the soft yet firm energy of a mother figure and holds nurturing and empathetic qualities. Consider your own mother and the other mothers you have known in your life. This is one who is grown, able, and fully realized. She is sure of who she is. She exudes the qualities of her suit.

My mother/caregiver was...

Mature females are powerful when they...

I am of service to others when I...

Now look at your kings and align them with the rest of the court cards in a vertical line. Note the visuals on your kings that are similar and different. What does their facial expression tell you about their personality?

The kings all have this in common...

The kings reflect a mature masculine energy. The king is a man fully realized, adult, and capable. Consider your father or other fathers you have known in your life. The king is a man who has arrived at full maturation.

My father/caregiver was...

Mature males are powerful when they...

I extend control when I...

Gender helps us utilize the masculine and feminine energy inside the court cards, regardless of our personal identification. Tarot makes use of archetypes, and archetypal understanding helps us move deeper into the cards. This is not meant to be sexist and can feel stereotypical; however, this helps us grasp the card's meaning until we move deeper and find its complexity.

This book does not suggest that all males are commanding and all females are soft and yielding. Use the generalized archetype to understand that masculine cards tend toward forcefulness and expansion while feminine cards carry a nurturing and fecund energy.

Make two columns separating the males from the females.

+ Pages and queens reflect embracing, intuitive, perceptive, thoughtful, creative female qualities.

+ Knights and kings reflect forceful, certain, goal-oriented, outward, commanding male qualities.

A day in the life is how we each cycle through aspects of court card personalities through our day. I am expressing Queen of Swords qualities (articulation) as I write these words. You express Page of Pentacles energy (curious and bookish) as you read my words. You and I will both embody the Queen of Pentacles when we make dinner tonight. We cycle through the personalities and expressions of all the court cards all day long.

Example: Let's imagine you are a dancer living in Los Angeles.

10:00 A.M. MUSIC VIDEO AUDITION = KING ENERGY

You walk into the audition and strut your stuff. You own the room and the dance floor. Kings reflect absolute mastery. You dance your face off brilliantly and run out the door because you are headed to your favorite class next.

12:00 P.M. DANCE CLASS = PAGE ENERGY

You can't wait to get in there. You step up into line with the other dancers. The moment you become the student of anything and anyone, you have entered page territory and energy.

2 P.M. BABYSITTING JOB = QUEEN ENERGY

Time to get to work watching two adorable tykes. You pick them up from school, bring them to their mansion, and prepare almond butter and organic strawberry sandwiches while practicing their ABCs. Assuming a role of authority while nurturing and teaching is queen energy.

8 P.M. CELEBRATION = KNIGHT ENERGY

You've been cast as a backup dancer for J.Lo's new tour! Time to celebrate with your friends. You order a round of bubbly, toast each other, and end the night with delicious debauchery that can't be described here—ha! When you get crazy, you are invoking the knight's wild energy.

Discovering the court personalities through the lens of high school is helpful because we have all gone through this unique experience. Thinking of the court cards as your best friend, first boyfriend/girlfriend/crush, mother, or father is a way to personalize the cards. Understanding the personalities of each court card is like meeting a new group of friends. You'll ingrain the meanings of the court cards and never be confused as to what they represent. Engage with the court cards on a personal level to master them.

Examine the cards through the personalities of the people who fill your life. As you read the meaning of each card, make a running list of who each card reminds you of. They can remind you of friends and family or characters in literature, film, or media. Pull out each court card as you read their descriptions. If you have more than one deck, pull multiple versions of each court card to compare, contrast, and note how the deck creators conceived of each archetype.

PAGES: YOUR NEAREST AND DEAREST FRIENDS

Get to know the pages by reflecting on your closest female friendships. Who was your best friend? Your confidant? What were they like and what traits did they hold?

KNIGHTS: LET'S HEAR IT FOR THE BOYS

Get to know the knights as those guys you were friends with or the boys you dated. First love is profound, full of emotion, and can fizzle out as soon as it begins. It is as erratic as knight energy! The golden boys of high school and college will remain forever locked in memory. They will help you understand the concept of a knight card.

QUEENS: THE MOMS WE KNOW AND LOVE

The mothers and grandmothers populating our lives.

THE KINGS: THE DADS OF THE DECK

The fathers and grandfathers populating our lives.

Page of Pentacles

The Princess/Earth Girl

You know that friend who is obsessed with collecting things? Her room is full of stuffed animals, her makeup counter a sea of beauty and

hair products. She harbors borderline handbag and shoe obsessions. Shopping with her is a flurry-filled fun day where you wind up spending way more than you ever meant to.

Pentacles reflect earthly possessions, the physical body, and money, so this page is always playing with her things. Pentacles also add a certain groundedness. She is buried in books, vinyl records, even tarot decks. Whatever she is obsessed with is what she wants to collect. She is the friend most likely to surprise you with gifts, bags full of brownies, and the stuff

you love. She is soft and sensual, adoring the look, feel, and touch of the material world.

The Page of Pentacles makes a fabulous friend because her advice is practical and down to earth. She can talk you off of any ledge. She'll run you a bubble bath and bring you a gin and tonic to soothe your heart and soul. She picks out the perfect presents for everyone. She looks at you lovingly and says, "Let's go shopping!"

The person who most reminds me of the Page of Pentacles is...

I am like the Page of Pentacles when I...

Looking at the Page of Pentacles card, I notice...

Page of Cups

THE ARTSY/WATER GIRL

You know that deep and expressive friend—the one who is always creating something? She's the writer buried in her notebooks, pounding away at her laptop. In her studio she's covered head to toe in bright paint, brush in hand. She scribbles poetry after midnight and recites Shakespeare during long walks in the woods. This Page of Cups is the artsy girl. She is always feeling her feelings and expressing herself.

The Page of Cups wants to feel everything life has in store for her. Her personality is fluid and prone to ups and downs. She represses nothing. She snuggles up to you during rom-coms and delights in bringing you to museums and any cultural institutions.

The Page of Cups gives great advice because she sees and speaks through the heart. She is a deeply compassionate and insightful friend. Sleepovers often end in hair-raising events as she is prone to psychic flashes and paranormal activity. Ghosts and spirits are drawn to her dreamy, empathic nature. She is deeply in touch with her psychic abilities, can explain your dreams, and is an amazing tarot card reader. She often gazes at you from under her long, feathery eye lashes and reminds you "You were meant for something better…"

The person who most reminds me of the Page of Cups is…

I am like the Page of Cups when I…

Looking at the Page of Cups, I notice…

Page of Wands

THE GOOD TIME GIRL/FIRE GIRL

You know her: she walks into a room and everyone stands up and takes notice. She commands attention without doing anything. She's lit

from within and sparkling with X factor. The Page of Wands is a spitfire, the giggliest of all your friends. Full of energy, she's a cheerleader, dancer, and athlete. Her passion and enthusiasm are apparent in her community service work and care of others. Her boundless energy and enthusiasm are infectious.

If it always looks like she's up to something, it's because she is. She's the friend you are most likely to get into trouble with. After all, fire attracts fire. She encourages you to live on the wild side and try things you never imagined

yourself doing because wands are the risk-taking suit. You can find her running from the police on any given weekend. She doesn't stop to think; she just shoots like a fiery comet across the night sky.

The Page of Wands is a fantastic friend because she always reminds you how much fun life is. Her presence always cheers you up. She's always offering her hand and inviting you to come along for the joyride. She's always grinning at you from behind a steering wheel and saying, "Let's go for it!"

The person who most reminds me of the Page of Wands is...

I am like the Page of Wands when I...

Looking at the Page of Wands, I notice...

Page of Swords

The Smart Girl/Air Girl

Make way for the valedictorian because the Page of Swords is the straight A student we all wish we were. Wildly smart because she is in love with thinking, she holds herself to high standards because it feels good, not because anyone is pressuring her to. She takes her responsibilities seriously and is found on debate teams and editing the school papers. She loves nothing more than a good mystery.

The Page of Wands retains a laser-sharp focus. Nothing distracts her once her sights are set on something. It can be confusing to you when all you want is to have a little fun. This same quality makes her an amazing friend because her X-ray vision cuts to the core or heart of the matter at hand. She always has the right words that you need to hear. You may not always follow her excellent and well-thought-out advice, but you always respect it. She never makes you feel bad when she looks at you laughingly and says, "I told you so!"

The person who most reminds me of the Page of Swords is...

I am like the Page of Swords when I...

Looking at the Page of Swords, I notice...

Knight of Pentacles

RICH BOY/GROUNDED GUY

The Knight of Pentacles embodies handsome beefcake dreaminess. He's the stuff of '80s teen dreams. He is often from a wealthy family because pentacles reflect money and often massive riches. He traditionally holds the pentacle in his hand as he considers what to do with the money he has earned or inherited. He drives a flashy, expensive car, wears a slick wardrobe because he loves his things to look good, and yes, he's got that amazing cherrywood smoke and brandy smell.

The Knight of Pentacles cares about his hot bod because pentacles reflect the body. He loves to pass time working out, running, lifting, and practicing martial arts. He's found on wrestling, football, and baseball teams. He's the guy in school most likely to become prom king. Everyone secretly hopes he might ask them to be his date, but because pentacles are solid and grounded, he usually sticks to his relationships rather than playing the field with multiple partners. This exclusivity just makes everyone go crazy and want him more.

The Knight of Pentacles type is the perfect first serious relationship, an ideal first everything (wink, wink) because when he's with you, he truly cares about you. You aren't just another notch in his belt. He's carnal and sensual, with an eye for all good things in life. Wrapped in his strong arms, his lips trace your neck as he whispers, "I want to feel you..."

The person who most reminds me of the Knight of Pentacles is...

I am like the Knight of Pentacles when I...

Looking at the Knight of Pentacles, I notice...

Knight of Cups

Poet Boy/Dreamy Dude

The Knight of Cups is the artist, acoustic musician, and sensitive boy. He's deep, thoughtful, and creative. This knight oozes whatever emotion he's feeling, and he's not afraid to show it. When your eyes are locked in his gaze, it feels as if he looks through the center of your soul, around the planet, and then back again. He is interested in your thoughts and feelings and wants to know you—the real you, the one you hide away from everyone. It feels luxuriously safe to be around him, let your hair down, and laugh your face off.

Cups carry the expressiveness and fluidity of water. It is an emotionality unfolding and inviting you in. You curl safely inside this dreamy, comforting space. The Knight of Cups is a slave to his emotional response, so he has a tendency to fall in love with more than one person at a time. He doesn't do it to be devious; it is simply his nature, and if you understand this rather than taking it personally, you'll be free to enjoy his gifts and delights.

The Knight of Cups sheds tears freely in your arms and laughs maniacally while tickling you. He decides universal beauty resides on your cheekbones as he holds your face in his warm hands. He tells you salvation is found in your eyes and perfection is attained as he strokes your lips with his fingertip. Your eyes grow wide and your heart melts in a pool around you as he leans in to whisper, "I understand you..."

The person who most reminds me of the Knight of Cups is...

I am like the Knight of Cups when I...

Looking at the Knight of Cups, I notice...

Knight of Wands

LOVER BOY/ELECTRIC SPARK

Watch out for this flame. The Knight of Wands is the star of anything he does. He's the hero quarterback, star of the school play, valedictorian

of the class, and the dude who lights everyone's heart on fire. He plays the field in sports and in relationships, knowing he's a spark plug. He loves watching you ignite into flame as you draw close to his fiery embers.

He dates dozens yet settles with none. He runs hot and cold, asking someone else to the formal but pulling you close under the disco ball so you can feel every muscle beneath his cheap polyester suit. The two of you tussle in cornfields. He sneaks into your sleepovers. He repays your love and devotion by systematically seducing each and every one of your girlfriends.

You know you shouldn't, but he attracts you like a forbidden slice of red velvet cake. It's impossible to resist his scorching sexiness; you fall apart when he whispers into your ear, "You're so hot..."

The person who most reminds me of the Knight of Wands is...

I am like the Knight of Wands when I...

Looking at the Knight of Wands, I notice...

Knight of Swords

Bad Boy/Gone with the Wind

The Knight of Swords is devastating in every way because he is so intense. He's caught up thinking and calculating, and when his thoughts turn to you, you can barely escape with your clothes intact. The suit of swords contains the decisiveness and cunningness of the element of air. Standing before the Knight of Swords is like standing close to a thunderstorm: you feel the barometer drop and the wind shift and momentarily lose your bearings, but that's okay. It's not love if you aren't losing your balance.

Swords are edgy, sharp, and dangerous by nature. The Knight of Swords is rebellious. He's anti everything. He's often from the wrong side of the tracks and rides a motorcycle, the perfect speedy vehicle. The Knight of Swords carries the fastest energy of the deck. When he appears, a message is coming as quick as the wind.

The Knight of Swords is the ideal vampire boy: fast and dangerous, with immortality on his side. He's seductive, wicked, and all consuming. He pins you under the stairwell after school, planting hot kisses on your good girl cheeks. He leads you toward empty classrooms and slides his palms under your uniform while you pray a nun doesn't walk in to discover you.

When he whisks you away, you are in for the ride of your life, so be sure to hold on tight. Feeling his cool hands sliding across your smooth skin, his dark-as-midnight eyes glisten intensely as he whispers, "I want to surprise you..."

The person who most reminds me of the Knight of Swords is...

I am like the Knight of Swords when I...

Looking at the Knight of Swords, I notice...

Queen of Pentacles

THE HOMEMAKER

The Queen of Pentacles is that mom who makes everyone feel at home. Yes, it's the house you wish you grew up in, the one whose door is always open to you. This queen makes everything feel soft and taste delicious. Warm cookies are waiting on the table when you return from school, and she's always hiding something delicious up her sleeve.

The Queen of Pentacles and her earthly connection make her a handsy and loving human. She gives the biggest hugs, smothers you with kisses, and no one can comfort you like she does; when you are feverish and drenched in sweat, she's right there. Her connection to the natural world makes her an avid gardener. Flowers and vegetables leap toward her cultivating hands. She is like a master sculptor, leaving her imprint on everything she comes into contact with. You feel safe and loved when she pulls you close and whispers, "Nurture yourself and love your body."

The person who most reminds me of the Queen of Pentacles is...

I am like the Queen of Pentacles when I...

Looking at the Queen of Pentacles, I notice...

Queen of Cups

THE THERAPIST

The Queen of Cups is the mom everyone runs to for advice. She has a talent for listening and creating space without judgment. You wake up terrified from a nightmare and the Queen of Cups is there to soothe your frayed nerves and sing you back to sleep. She anticipates your needs before you do. She has a homeopathic remedy and essential oil on hand for any mood or emotion you may experience. She casts her crystal eyes in your direction and you know you could never lie to her. It's pointless. She already knows every secret tucked away inside you. She is a creature who is more than the sum of her parts, and she glides with a foot in each world.

The Queen of Cups is the dreamy, soft New Age mom who enjoys attending workshops and yoga retreats. Her home is cozy; she's apt to sage cleanse on a daily basis. You hear a light tinkling of chimes every time she draws near. She paints, writes, and has a passion for theater and the arts, contributing to them often with her otherworldly talent and creativity. You feel valued and important because she'll drop everything when you need her and focus on you. She takes you under her arm and whispers, "Always follow your heart..."

The person who most reminds me of the Queen of Cups is...

I am like the Queen of Cups when I...

Looking at the Queen of Cups, I notice...

Queen of Wands

THE FIRECRACKER

The Queen of Wands is a sexy, mesmerizing mom with flashy clothing, flawless makeup, and innate sexuality. She thrives on excitement and drama and is as happy throwing a party as she is going to one. Her love life is confounding because she flirts with everything and everyone. She is genuinely in love with life.

She's the mom girls run to when they get into trouble and the mom all the boys drool over. Always straight talking and never one to shy from any subject or conversation, she encourages you to go on the pill, encouraging safe sex above all things. She blows you kisses as you run out the door and reminds you, "Follow your passion and have fun!"

The person who most reminds me of the Queen of Wands is...

I am like the Queen of Wands when I...

Looking at the Queen of Wands, I notice...

Queen of Swords

THE BUSINESSWOMAN

The Queen of Swords is the super successful power mom. She's smart, articulate, and challenges you to do your best in school and life. She's there to help you with homework; she'll help you sort any issue with logic and objectivity. She carves time out of her busy schedule when you need her, and when under her tutelage all of life's responsibilities fall away as the two of you align your energy.

She's a mom likely to fill your schedule with activities and clubs, always keeping an eye on future professional advantages to be gained. Should you find yourself in trouble, she's there in a flash, defending your position and successfully arguing your case until you are released from accusations. Her image and inspiration flash across your mind when you stand up for yourself, argue your position, or debate the finer qualities of the things you believe in. She is the one who leans confidently close and whispers, "Never forget how damn smart you are."

> *The person who most reminds me of the Queen of Swords is...*
>
> *I am like the Queen of Swords when I...*
>
> *Looking at the Queen of Swords, I notice...*

King of Pentacles

THE CEO

The King of Pentacles is the ultimate provider. He is happiest when he is churning out money because pentacles connect to the security and

safety of earth. His ego is connected to his financial status because he believes that financial security affords people freedom. He's the dad who's had your college fund going since the moment you were conceived. He teaches you how money will earn dividends as well as how to budget, save, and donate. He's delighted with himself when he spoils you silly with gifts.

The King of Pentacles looks devastatingly handsome in his tailored tweed suits. He'll treat you to lunch when you visit him at the office. He loves to take you on vacation to wild and scenic places such as mountains because he finds the world enchanting. He is, after all, a man of the earth, and as such he has tremendous respect for the natural world. This also feeds his intense passion for real estate management and investment. It is not enough for the King of Pentacles to see the blinking numbers of his bank account flashing across a computer screen. He wants to see, feel, and touch his empire. Nothing is more enjoyable to him than wandering through his vineyards and squeezing his grapes for ripeness, taking his exotic sports cars out for a spin, or appraising his latest estate acquisition. Your heart melts when he draws you close and whispers, "Always protect yourself..."

The person who most reminds me of the King of Pentacles is...

I am like the King of Pentacles when I...

Looking at the King of Pentacles, I notice...

King of Cups

THE COMPOSER

The King of Cups is the visionary and the artsy, dreamy dad. He opens your heart and the world because he constantly surprises you with new ways to look at the dream of reality as it unfolds around you. He provides you with books, treats you to popcorn at movies you'd never think to see, and has a wild cast of eccentric characters he claims as friends. He walks with you on the beach and teaches you to listen to conversations between the surf and sea foam.

This consummate philosopher keeps you up late into the night turning over ideas about the wonders and intricacies of the universe. He'll guide you through any of the world's museums. He fosters and answers any and all of your curiosities. He's your date to the ballet, the opera, and the symphony. He slips poetry in your pocket when you aren't looking.

You are the apple of this emotional man's eye, his very own dream come true. He encourages you to be true to yourself, encourages your originality, and supports any passion. He draws you close with a gentle smile and whispers, "Create something beautiful."

The person who most reminds me of the King of Cups is...

I am like the King of Cups when I...

Looking at the King of Cups, I notice...

King of Wands

ROCK STAR

The King of Wands is the most intense dad of the bunch. He's full of adventure and impulse, and his life-long goal is to share his passions and

ignite the sparks of transformation through the world. He stirs the pot, follows his own rules, and will never bend to another's will. This means he's also the dad most likely to embarrass you by making a spectacle of himself. He jumps up, claps, and yells during your school performance while everyone else sits politely. His excitement always gets the best of him, but you can hardly blame him, even when he mortifies you.

He's serious fun to be around because he's always on the hunt for adventure and cooking up trouble. The element of fire energizes him with a wild charisma. He is principled and spiritual, so he is just as likely to be a guru or human rights advocate as he is to be a rock star or showman. He leans in close and eggs you on when he whispers, "Go ahead and DO IT!"

The person who most reminds me of the King of Wands is...

I am like the King of Wands when I...

Looking at the King of Wands, I notice...

King of Swords

INTELLECTUAL

This is the super smart, domineering, and brainy dad. He's taught you to refine your divine intellect since you were a child. He's always encour-aging you to voice your opinion and empowers you by challenging you to do your best. This dad can get caught up in having things in line with his type A personality. His words feel sharp and dangerous when he lashes out with his razor tongue. He tends to be strict but is full of a kindness that he expresses through his words. He expects you to do your best at school and homework.

The King of Swords prizes conversation above all. He encourages the family to dine together sans technology and wants to hear from everyone at the table. He adores debate and intellectual sparring. This wordy dad is as likely to be a lawyer as he is to excel in the field of science. He loves to lecture, professionally and privately, and is often an author on his subject of expertise. His eyes twinkle when a mystery pres-ents itself, and he pulls you close and whispers, "Figure it out..."

> *The person who most reminds me of the King of Swords is...*
>
> *I am like the King of Swords when I...*
>
> *Looking at the King of Swords, I notice...*

A Parting Wish

Look how far you've come! Spooky. Gothic. Sexy. Supernatural. Not quite human. I'm putting on my leather boots, black liner, loads of lashes, and prowling with you. Let's keep pulling cards—for darkness, for you, for your supernatural self. Don't wait for someone to tell you your destiny; create your own.

Let's read tarot in a museum. Speak starlight with van Gogh. Dialogue into darkness with Rembrandt. Activate abstraction with Pollock.

Let's hop on our brooms and fly to a cathedral. What does the pew say? Does the buttress whisper? Stained glass glows only for you; what does it want you to see? Pull a card. Light a candle. Embody a saint. Pray as if your life depended on it.

Let's take our tarot to a graveyard. Speak with the dead. Trade secrets with a gargoyle. Create a deck of cards from grave rubbings. Bury ourselves in dirt. Haunt every house.

Deal your cards but read them in reverse. Rearrange your past. Read tarot naked. Move beneath throbbing strobe lights. Invoke the goddess with your hips. Become the bass line.

The world is whispering. Don't stop divining at cards—ask the wind for an answer. Let birds be your guides. Invoke sacred space everywhere.

Embrace your destiny. Be your best psychic. Weave your own fortune.

My parting wish for you is simple: no matter how you embody the cards and how they embody you, be the magic you are!

Notes

Tarot Basics Cheat Sheet

ELEMENTS: The four elemental suits connected to every aspect of life and the universe.

FIRE/WANDS = ACTION/PASSION: Passion, drive, and excitement. Erotic sexuality. Personal callings and chosen careers. Spirituality, drive, and our ultimate destiny. The fire propelling the energy of life.

AIR/SWORDS = THOUGHTS/COMMUNICATION: Thoughts, ideas, and mental activity. The stories we tell ourselves, the narratives we create, and all forms of communication: written, verbal, and inferred.

WATER/CUPS = FEELINGS/EMOTIONS: Art, ideas, and emotions. The kingdom of water rules our feelings. Emotions move and change as quickly as water. It is the transformative world of pain, joy, sorrow, love, and every emotion in between.

EARTH/PENTACLES = MATERIALS/THINGS: The landscape of elemental earth. Imagine the feeling of earth at your fingertips: crumbly dirt, smooth rock, freshly plowed fields, and vibrant mountains, trees, animals, and people. Pentacles are all the items inside the material world, everything we can see, touch, smell, and taste. This world reflects all things (persons, places, things), including money, goods, and resources.

Symbolic Meaning of Numbers

One = Beginning

Two = Partnership

Three = Creativity

Four = Structure

Five = Challenge

Six = Heart expansion

Seven = Mystery

Eight = Infinite perfection

Nine = Wish fulfillment

Ten = Ending

Tarot Structure

MAJOR ARCANA

✦ 0 through 21 (Fool through World)

✦ Big moments, major life events, and cross-cultural concepts: Innocent, Trickster, Sage, Lovers, Death, Transformation, Mystery, etc.

0. FOOL: New cycles, beginnings, risk, adventure

1. MAGICIAN: Action, awareness, power, charisma

2. HIGH PRIESTESS: Intuition, inner knowledge, potential, authenticity

3. EMPRESS: Motherhood, nurturing, creativity, abundance

4. EMPEROR: Structure, rules, form, shape, limits

5. HIEROPHANT: Teacher/mentor, dogma, belief, sacred space

6. LOVERS: Love, passion, Eros, sexuality, choice

7. CHARIOT: Victory, progress, will, mastery, movement

8. STRENGTH: Compassion, courage, self-control, fortitude

9. HERMIT: Introspection, spirituality, retreat, solitude

10. WHEEL OF FORTUNE: Destiny, fate, fortune, turning point

11. JUSTICE: Work, law, karma, decisions, responsibility

12. HANGED MAN: Stasis, philosophy, surrender, mystic experience

13. DEATH: Endings, resurrection, transition, evolution

14. TEMPERANCE: Balance, duality, complexity, alchemy

15. DEVIL: Addiction, control issues, deviance, greed, gluttony, slavery

16. TOWER: Destruction, release, catharsis, aha moment

17. STAR: Inspiration, hope, delight, clearing, artist/muse

18. MOON: Mystery, dreams, psychic, strangeness, subconscious

19. SUN: Expansion, growth, clarity, vitality

20. JUDGEMENT: No going back, evolution, rebirth, awakening, highest calls

21. WORLD: Travel, completion, integration, highest self

MINOR ARCANA

+ Everyday lessons, experiences, and events

+ Four elemental worlds

COURT CARDS

+ Aspects of your personality, attitudes to adopt, and other people in your life

PAGE = Childlike awareness and curiosity

KNIGHT = Expansive teen energy

QUEEN = Mature female compassion and nurturing

KING = Mature masculine control and structure

How to Read Tarot

+ What catches your attention?

+ Tell the story of what you see on the card.

+ Choose a single symbol and interpret as an answer.

+ What does a symbol mean to you?

+ Read like you are telling a story to a child.

+ Go with your first instinct.

Tarot Spreads

1. Think of a question.

2. Shuffle the deck any way you like.

3. Place the deck facedown.

4. Select cards off the top of deck.

One-Card Spread (perfect daily spread)

1. What do I need to know?

Three Card Spread

1. Past   2. Present   3. Future

Should/Shouldn't Do Spread (triangle shape)

1. My Situation

2. Shouldn't Do   3. Should Do

Remember To...

+ center yourself

+ call to your highest guidance/self

+ ask for the information you need to be shown

Characteristics of Powerful Questions

+ take personal responsibility

+ state the desired outcome

+ begin with "how" or "what"

Notes

Master List of Questions

I created a master list of questions when I wrote the book *365 Tarot Spreads*. I wanted to make sure I covered every conceivable question a person could ask. I present to you these questions so you never, ever run out of things to ask, question yourself about, or journal.

Use these questions as resources and options in your readings or for personal writing prompts. Most importantly, never stop asking.

GENERAL

How can I get to where I want to be?

What are my options?

What am I willing to change?

What did I accomplish?

What could I have done better?

What do I think about this?

How will I feel if I don't do this?

What assumptions am I making?

What do I have to do to overcome this obstacle?

What should I embrace?

What could I embrace?

What do I want to experience?

How do I want to grow?

What do I want to contribute to the planet?

What brings meaning to my experience?

How do I best spend/invest/leverage my time?

How can I brighten someone's experience today?

What choices can I make differently?

Where am I wrong?

What can I give today?

Why am I here?

What is my mission in life?

What could I have done better today?

What can I do better tomorrow?

What is the most important thing I can accomplish tomorrow?

What new thing can I try tomorrow?

Who are the most important people in my life
    and what am I doing for them?

What do you represent? What do you want to represent?

How can I love myself?

What is my ideal state?

What would it mean to be my highest self?

What does my best life feel like?

What opportunities should I look for?

What stops me from pursuing my goals/dreams?

How do I create new opportunities for myself?

Am I putting any part of my life on hold?

What is my highest priority right now?

What do I need to achieve my ideal career?

What do I need to achieve my ideal diet?

What do I need to achieve my ideal home?

What do I need to achieve an ideal physical regimen?

What do I fear most?

What helps me live with my fears in a manageable way?

Why might I settle for less than I am worth?

What limiting belief do I hold onto?

How can I cultivate good habits?

What empowering belief do I need to incorporate?

What can I do today to make my life more meaningful?

Do I appreciate myself?

Do I appreciate my significance?

When I look at myself, do I see divinity?

What questions should I be asking myself?

What worries me?

Where should I break the rules?

Is this what I truly want to be doing?

What is the greatest lesson from my worst problem?

What do I hold on to that I must remove?

In the haste of daily life, what am I not seeing?

Why do I matter?

What is one fear holding me back?

What was the lesson when you did something you weren't proud of?

What is the number one change I need to make in my life
   in the next twelve months?

Am I procrastinating something right now? If so, what?

How am I my own worst enemy?

What do I wish I didn't know?

What have I given up on?

What big lesson could others learn from my life?

What mistake do I learn over and over again?

What do I intend to accomplish before I die?

What do I do when I think other people don't like me?

SOULFUL

How do I best become still?

How can I best respond to internal whispers?

How do I remind myself I'm blessed?

How do I achieve freedom from worry?

How do I foster more connection with the world around me?

What drains my happiness?

What is my greatest distraction?

What should I pay attention to?

CAREER/WORK

How can I work less and achieve more?

What do I love to practice?

Other than money, what have I gained from my current job?

What is my purpose?

What will I regret not doing?

What will the short-term results be?

What will the long-term results be?

MONEY

What do I do with the majority of my money?

How can I increase my finances?

How can I help others with my money?

What is the best way I can work with the energy of money?

LOVE

How can I align with my ideal partner?

Where can I find my ideal partner?

How do I get to know my ideal partner?

What sort of person do I enjoy spending time with?

What is the primary importance of a romantic relationship?

What is a deal breaker for me in a relationship?

How do I fall in love as passionately with my work as I would with a lover?

What should I do when I love someone who doesn't love me back?

PHYSICAL

What is my body telling me?

What is worse than death?

How can I improve my health?

PERSONAL TRUTH *(important to know because these cement negative behavior in place)*

What I really don't want to know is...

What I ignore is...

What I tell myself that is not true is...

PHILOSOPHICAL

Is it possible to ignore time?

What is the essence of my work?

How can I feel like the ocean?

How can I observe more deeply?

Why is depth important?

How can I become more sensitive?

What qualities make a good work of art?

What am I trying to communicate?

What states of being are interesting?

What moves you?

Do I feel loved?

What is love?

What is distance between people?

What is my personal archetype?

Why are personal characteristics important?

What do I understand about life?

How do I remain myself?

What do I think about desire?

What do I understand about myself?

What is an original mind?

How do I expand personal barriers?

What kind of people's lives do I consider poor?

With the exception of beauty, does nature possess something that transcends beauty?

Why does the opinion of others matter?

Why do people care about power and influence?

Why do I feel inferior?

What is the quality of good work?

What is the essence of everything?

Why should I question my life?

What is the most important thing about life?

How do I free my mind?

What is the root of jealousy?

Spiritual

Why is there poverty and suffering in the world?

What is the relationship between science and religion?

How does one attain true peace?

What is wisdom?

Glossary

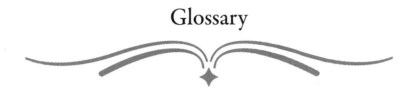

ACE: The first card of a suit reflecting the number one.

AFFIRMATION: A statement of thinking or intention designed to be repeated and used to encourage positivity and/or power, such as "Every day, in every way, I get better and better." When applied to tarot, may include a card reference: "The Star guides us toward inspiration."

ALCHEMY: An ancient philosophy and historic tradition, partly the basis of modern chemistry and medicine, using the transmutation of elements. Many tarot decks incorporate alchemical concepts and symbolism.

ARCANA: The Latin word for secrets or mysteries.

ARCHETYPE: A fundamental pattern of thought or an original universal concept shared cross-culturally, such as Mother, Quest, Hero, Good vs. Evil, etc. These archetypes are all illustrated in tarot, particularly within the major arcana.

ART DECKS: Tarot decks carrying particular artistic styles and art. Using visual expression, art decks offer new emotional and intuitive insights.

ASANA: A yogic shape or physical posture.

BLISS BODY: The deepest core of our being, the self, which transcends mental, physical, and emotional expressions and behaviors.

CARD OF THE DAY: A practice by which a daily random card is drawn from the deck and interpreted. It is often revisited at the end of the day.

CARTOMANCER: A person who performs readings and divinations from tarot, playing, or oracle cards.

CARTOMANCY: The practice of making a divination by any form of cards, including tarot.

CLIENT: Usually refers to a paying querent/sitter having a professional reading.

CODIFIED: To arrange in a systematic code, plan, or formula.

CONSECRATION: An action, opening, or blessing performed to establish a relationship and bond with a new deck of tarot cards.

CONSISTENCY: In a reading, consistency means to choose a system in advance and stick to it for the duration of the reading. This includes the spread, use of reversals and adhering to a chosen ritual (if one is chosen).

CORRESPONDENCE: Linking similarities between objects or concepts based on their attributes or qualities. In tarot this is often done between systems, such as astrology.

COURT CARDS: The sixteen cards in a tarot deck assigned to each suit's court figures, usually king, queen, knight, and page.

DECK COLLECTING: Collecting numerous tarot decks for personal use or ownership.

DIVINATION: The practice of gaining insight and knowledge via esoteric method, including cartomancy, astrology, ritual, scrying, etc.

DOGMA: A set of principles set forth as absolute truth by a supposed authority. Dogma often applies to religious systems and spirituality.

DROPPED CARD: A card (or cards) that falls out of a deck during shuffling and may be taken to have specific meaning in interpretation outside of the spread. Also called a jumper card.

EGO: The idea or image of yourself providing you with a sense of identity based on what you imagine is true and on what other people have told you about yourself.

ELEMENTS: The four classic elements of earth, air, fire, and water corresponding to the suits of pentacles (earth), swords (air), wands (fire), and cups (water).

EPHEMERAL: Lasting for a brief period of time. Early tarots, created for the masses, were block printed on thin slips of paper and thus easily lost and destroyed, therefore they were ephemeral.

ESOTERIC ARTS: Qabalah, tarot, astrology, magic, numerology, pathworking, shamanic journeying, etc.

ESOTERICISM: Hidden or secret teachings usually relating to the relationship between human beings and the universe.

ESOTERICIST: An individual who works specifically with hidden knowledge, secret teachings, or mystical philosophies.

FREE ASSOCIATION: Tarot images become a point of departure in which the symbols on the card make way for a free association of new ideas and fresh meanings.

FULL MOON CLEANSE: Energetic cleansing of a tarot deck achieved by placing cards in a pool of moonlight for the duration of an evening.

GOLDEN DAWN: An English secret magical society founded in London in 1888. The Golden Dawn developed a Western magical initiatory system. They taught tarot as a base unifying tool and concept, which included astrology, divination, astral projection, Qabalah, and alchemy.

GRIMOIRE: Often used in reference to witchcraft, a grimoire is a handwritten book of personally recorded spells and magic including the use/creation of spells, talismans, charms, divinations, etc. A tarot grimoire is a personal tarot magic notebook.

GUIDED VISUALIZATION/MEDITATION: Following a sequence of instructions to journey into the sacred imagination. Often used to enter into the archetype of a tarot card.

HERALDIC DEVICES: Coats of arms and symbols conveying genealogy rank and power and often inserted into early tarot decks commissioned as art objects by powerful families.

HISTORICAL DECKS: Reproductions, reconstructions, or reinterpretations of the great tarot decks of the past.

ILLUSTRATED MINORS: A deck in which the minor arcana is fully illustrated with scenes depicting the card's meaning, as opposed to a "majors only" deck in which the minors are represented with only symbols of their suit.

INITIATION RITUAL: A rite of passage into a group or society. It often infers a rebirth and is seen in organized religion via baptisms, confirmations, or bat mitzvahs, and in the profane world via graduation ceremonies or rites inside secret societies and fraternal organizations when a member is accepted into the fold.

INTERPRETATION: The process of explaining the meaning of the cards laid out in a spread.

INTUITION BUILDING: Activities and exercises performed purposefully to strengthen the intuition as one would strengthen any muscle in the body.

INTUITION: Any means of gaining knowledge without direct and conscious reasoning.

JOURNAL: A record of readings, keywords, spreads, notes, etc., made by a reader.

KEYWORD: A phrase or word associated with each card to assist interpretation in a reading.

LAYOUT: A specific arrangement of cards. See *spread.*

LWB: The little white booklet that often accompanies a deck giving suggested interpretations of each card, explanation of particular symbolism and sample spreads.

MAJORS/MAJOR ARCANA/TRUMPS: The 22 cards of the major arcana depicting 22 archetypes: from Fool (0) to World (21). The majors are essential for any deck to be defined as a tarot deck.

METAPHOR: A symbolic representation of something else to convey a complex idea or meaning. Tarot is used as a metaphorical not literal device for example, the Two of Cups does not mean you will actually juggle two balls but consider two opposing choices.

MINORS/MINOR ARCANA: The ace to ten of each of the four suits.

MYSTIC: An individual who seeks to transcend ordinary human knowledge via direct communication with the divine, intuition, spiritual ecstasy or nature.

NUMEROLOGY: The study and association of occult significance of numbers.

PATTERN: Numerical of symbolic elements in a reading revealing special significance. For instance, multiple tens suggest endings or multiple storm cloud symbols suggest disruption.

PSYCHIC: A person who receives information from means that cannot be explained by rational, logical means. A psychic may perform divination using tarot cards, but not all tarot readers claim to be psychic.

QUERENT: An old-fashioned term used for a person receiving a reading. Can also be called a seeker, enquirer, or sitter.

READER: The person who reads and interprets the cards.

REVERSALS: The interpretation of any shuffled card that appears upside down in a spread or reading.

RITUAL: Any form of repeated activity usually conducted prior or following a reading. A ritual can include lighting a candle, spoken words, or simply tapping the deck on the table. More elaborate rituals can be conducted when using the cards for magic.

RWS: An abbreviation of the Rider-Waite-Smith tarot deck published by the Rider Company, created by Arthur Waite, and illustrated by Pamela Colman Smith. Also called the Rider Deck or the Rider-Waite Deck. Rider-Waite-Smith is used to acknowledge artist Pamela Colman Smith, whose name was originally left out of the title.

SHADOW WORK: Exercises to unearth the unconscious parts of the mind and repressed aspects of the personality.

SHUFFLE: Any means of mixing the cards prior to a reading.

SOMATIC: Relating to the body and separate from the mind.

SPELL: A set of words and actions to bring about magical results.

SPREAD: Any method of laying out the cards for a reading. A spread is usually indicated by having set positions with individual meanings, such as "future," "challenges," "family." The positions in a spread provide additional context for the interpretation of the cards. See also *layout*.

STYLE: The manner in which a reading and interpretation is derived and delivered. Each reader develops their own particular style unique to them. Styles are unlimited and broadly include fortune-telling, psychological, Jungian, psychic, intuitive, counseling, etc.

SUIT: A tarot deck is arranged in four suits: pentacles, swords, cups, wands.

SYMBOL/SYMBOLISM: An object or happening that is used to represent something other than what it basically or literally is. For example: a metal crown, symbolic of royalty and power, or a collapsing tower, symbolic of sudden institutional change.

SYNCHRONICITY: A term created by Carl Jung to reflect meaningful coincidence appearing on one's life path.

TREE OF LIFE: The central illustration of Qabalah, most usually expressed as ten concentric circles or a matrix of ten circles connected by twenty-two paths, symbolic of the Hebrew letters.

VISUALIZATION: The practice of using imagination to experience a card or enter into the scene of a card and explore it interactively.